DYING TO GET
Raw Food
By: © 2003 Shelly K

TABLE OF CONTENTS

Copyright © 2003 by Shelly Keck-Borsits

Disclaimer: This publication contains the opinions and ideas of the author. It is intended to provide helpful and informative material on the subject matter covered.   It is sold with the understanding that the author is not engaged in rendering professional services in this book. If the reader requires personal advice or assistance, a competent professional should be consulted.

The author disclaims any responsibility for any liability, loss, or risk, personal or otherwise, which is incurred as a consequence, directly or indirectly, of the use and application of any of the contents of this book.

The author disclaims any responsibility for any liability, loss, or risk, personal or otherwise, which is incurred as a consequence, directly or indirectly, of the use and application of any of the contents of this book.

Second Edition

Design: Cover Design. Shelly Keck-Borsits
International Standard Book Number: 1591096383
Publisher: Shelly Keck-Borsits
Author: Shelly Keck-Borsits
Editor: Lisa OBorne - visit Lisa at http://www.at1withnature.com

Dying To Get Well
http://www.dyingtogetwell.com

Raw & Juicy: The Healing Power of Raw Food
http://www.rawandjuicy.com

Raw Food Message Boards & Chat Room
http://www.rawandjuicy.com/messageboard.html

Chapter 1: My Story

My nightmare began at the end of 1996. My life from the end of 1996 until just recently, December of 2002 has been one that I would not wish on my worst enemy. My health prior to the end of 1996 was good. No serious illness, no weight problem, nothing except perhaps a yearly cold or flu. I was a 25-year-old who was over the 'partying' state, ate well, exercised daily, and for the most part was health conscience. I was doing yoga daily and had been for approximately two years. Everything was going well, I had great health, a wonderful boyfriend, now husband, and life was good.   But how quickly and drastically everything would change.

I believe the first thing to happen was the daily presence of excruciating migraines and severe muscle tightness in my shoulders and neck. You know the feeling you get if you are watching a scary movie and something-unexpected pops out at you and for that brief second you inhale and every muscle in your body tenses? That is how my muscles felt. Only it wasn't just for a brief moment, I was living in that state constantly. My body was just locked in this 'tense' state. My muscles would not relax no matter what I did. My muscles on the top of my shoulders and in my neck became as hard as rocks. These muscle problems, coupled with the migraines left me down and out. I had never had a migraine prior to this in my life. I had experienced headaches, but never a migraine. What I was experiencing were full-blown migraines that did not let up day or night. The migraines and muscle tension came on and it didn't leave. They didn't leave when I went to bed, when I would take aspirin, when I would try to lie down and rest -- never.   The pain was never-ending and excruciatingly painful. It stayed with me so intensely I thought I would die.

These migraines and muscle pains were then accompanied by a pain at the base of my skull that felt as if someone had put a knife in my brain stem. I thought for sure that something must be wrong in my neck. I thought perhaps that was why I had such a relentless migraine, that there was just something wrong with my neck. I felt agonizing pain from the shoulders up. After the pain did not go away for days, I became concerned and made an appointment with my doctor.

I had just been into see my doctor a couple of weeks prior to this 'sickness', for an appointment to get on birth control. It was my first time on birth control so I had a lot of questions. She told me of this wonderful new birth control injection. My doctor at that time, a female, said I would love it because it actually takes your periods away. **What?** I can take a shot and not get my period? **HOW WONDERFUL!** She literally raved about it. She told me that the only thing I had to worry about was perhaps gaining 5 lbs. and not getting my menses. She told me how women loved it because they could go swimming, have sex, etc., and do all the things they can't do when they have their periods. She pushed its convenience by asking me how good I was about remembering things. She told me if I didn't want to have to worry about 'remembering' to take a pill everyday, then the shots would be the perfect solution for me. That was it. No pamphlets, no bad side affects mentioned other than the ceasing of menses and perhaps a five pound weight gain -- that was it. Trusting my doctor's glowing recommendation, I opted for the birth control in the form of injections that would last for three months at a time. Little did I know that would be the worst mistake I would ever make.

In my appointment to her with my raging migraine and neck and muscle pain I asked her straight out if the birth control injection could be what was making me sick? She told me no. I should have trusted my instinct, but I didn't. Shoulda, woulda, coulda … hindsight is 20/20, as they say. She said the symptoms I was having were not at all related to the birth control injection. Years later I found out the symptoms I reported to her are listed as side affects of the birth control injections. Okay, I know some of you may be saying... "If you thought the shot could be making you so sick, why didn't you just stop taking it?" Like I just said, hindsight is 20/20. I had 100% confidence in the words of the licensed professional that was treating me. She said with absolute certainty that the shot didn't make me sick and I believed and trusted her.

In that appointment she wrote an order for me to go to the hospital for x-rays of my neck. X-rays came back okay. I was into see her again as the pain just worsened and was relentless. I was in so much pain I couldn't even cry because crying made the pain worse as it caused more tension. I wanted to die. I couldn't sleep because the pain was so bad. It was day and night, night and day. From the shoulders up I felt as if I were dying. I was in such tremendous pain it got to the point where I believed something had to be seriously wrong. I started fearing the worst. I believed I had to have a tumor or something at the base of my skull. My fears were amplified by her telling me she wanted me to go see a neurologist about an hour away from my hometown. Her office made the appointment for me.

The neurologist did some tests on me and asked me some questions and then told me I was suffering from stress.   I told him about the fact that I was on birth control injections and asked if they could be causing the pain. He too told me no, it wasn't the shots, it was just stress. Stress? What? I had a great boyfriend, great friends, was working for myself -- everything was great. I told him that I didn't have any stress.   He told me it was like my muscles from the neck up were in a state of 'shock' and he just needed to relax them. He told me he needed to give me a shot into each shoulder muscle and in a day or two I would be feeling better. I didn't; my pain only worsened.

My story only goes downhill from there. It was a living nightmare for years. Endless doctor's appointments with several specialists from neurologists to a heart doctor, tons of prescription drugs, endless pain and no answers. As this all was going on, I continued going every three months for my birth control shot. With this **unknown** illness the last thing I needed to worry about was having a baby in a sick body.

I started to lose hair, lots of hair. I had already started wondering if I was dying of cancer. The hair loss and the relentless pain at the base of my skull made me think I had a brain tumor that nobody could find. The only thing that perplexed me was, if I was dying of cancer, why was I getting so fat? My weight started ballooning out of control. And, as it did, I started eating even less and tried exercising even more, which was close to impossible because the pain was unbearable. I forced myself through my yoga and Richard Simmons workout tapes with tears streaming down my face. But all to no avail. No matter what I did the weight kept piling on me.

The weight gain however was the very least of my concerns. I was so violently ill 24 hours a day, 7 days a week that I couldn't sleep. I became an insomniac. I was getting no sleep at night and I was in horrific pain during the days. Most of my days I was suffering from what appeared to be flu like symptoms: Vomiting, diarrhea, muscle pain, fatigue, etc.

I would vomit with such force that I felt like my insides were being ripped apart. The initial headache and pain at the base of my skull, for which I went to see the doctor, was also still with me every minute of every day.   I became plagued with sinus infections and yeast infections. I would go to the doctor with a sinus infection, be put on medication and end up with a yeast infection. These two went hand in hand for years.

My muscles, especially from the shoulders up, were so sore my husband couldn't even touch me. My leg muscles were so weak that I couldn't stand long enough to do dishes; I had to sit on a stool to do them. And even with the stool as support, I would still be in then tears literally the entire time because I was just in constant pain. My neck was so weak I could hardly hold it up. For about two years of my life I kept a towel wrapped around my neck when inside the house because it was as if I had lost all control of the muscles in my neck and I couldn't hold my own head up. What was wrong with me? Nobody knew.

My sex life was becoming non-existent. I simply didn't want it. I attributed my huge loss of libido to my chronic headaches, pain and fatigue. When we **would** have sex I would be in great pain. My lubrication was gone and I would bleed from any penetration. I felt as if I was trapped in the body of an 80 year old, and not a healthy 80 year old, but that of an 80 year old that was dying from some rare disease.

Doctors didn't know 'what' was wrong with me, but not a one of them thought twice about writing prescriptions for me. Try this, try that, take this, and take that. And I never thought twice about taking the drugs they were so readily giving me. I continued to take the drugs that they continued to dish out because I was so desperate for relief. Millions of other people do this too. We are desperate for an end to our pain and we put all of our faith in the trained medical professionals.

Unfortunately none of the drugs were ending my pain; in fact, most of them were only making me worse.   For a long period of time I stopped going to the doctors because every time I would take the medications they were prescribing I would end up feeling worse instead of better.

Leaving the house, even to run daily errands, became almost impossible. I started suffering severe panic attacks. At the time I didn't even know that's what they were. I just knew that I went from being someone that had no problem speaking in front of people or striking up conversations with strangers, to someone that couldn't deal with even looking the checkout girl at the grocery store in the face. I felt all eyes were on me. To go into public, or even just to get in my car and drive, I felt was the end of the world. I felt as if I was dying. I couldn't catch my breath, my face would feel as if it were on fire, and I could tell it was beet red. On top of all of this pain and the panic attacks I was trying to pretend in front of friends and family I was not having any pain and that I was okay. I would take Excedrin Migraine during the day to dull the pain, and Tylenol P.M. at night to try and get even just one hour of sleep.

I had three separate doctors -- one general practitioner/osteopath, one general practitioner/ob-gyn, and one neurologist -- tell me that the birth control shots wouldn't cause me to be sick, and I had no reason not to believe them. They couldn't have been more wrong. After about a year on the shots however I stopped taking them. Not because I was worried they were making me sick, but because I believed I was dying. There was no use in taking it at that point either because my sex life had virtually become non-existent.

For years my health continued to decline. I was at one osteopath for months sitting in traction and having manipulations to end my muscle pain and the pain at the base of my skull. Thousands of dollars later, and no insurance, I just stopped going because nothing he did helped me. I saw a heart specialist who told me stop drinking caffeine, which I told him I had done for about the past year, yet no change.   He told me his wife had an unexplained irregular heartbeat too and not to worry, it wouldn't kill me. I saw eye doctors for my vision because it was inexplicably blurry. I wore glasses but it wasn't that type of vision problem. No matter what prescription they gave me everything was fuzzy -- very blurry with no defined edges on things. They too told me they could find nothing wrong with me. I would have spells where I would lose feeling in my face, my arms and sometimes my legs. My mother was scared I had Bells Palsy. One day it was so severe she rushed me into the doctor believing I had suffered a stroke. After sitting in the doctor's office for about 10 minutes the symptoms started to subside and feeling returned to my face and my arm. That went on for months, yet the doctor had no explanation why it was happening.

Eventually, I ended up having an unnecessary sinus surgery. The ENT (ear, nose and throat specialist) told me I had polyps and that they were probably the cause of all my migraines. He told me if I had surgery I could end all the sinus pain and pressure and migraines. Sinus surgery was almost the end of me. In the surgery itself, the doctor ripped my nose so I had to stay under longer than planned. Coming out of the surgery, guess who had a reaction to the anesthesia? Yep, you guessed it, yours truly. I was violently ill.   I got so sick after that surgery that I should have ended up in the hospital, but by then I was so terrified of doctors I begged my husband not to take me. The night home from the surgery I shook so violently that my husband had to sit on top of me for hours to control the shaking. He called the doctor who performed the surgery at his home and told him that I was shaking and running a high fever. The doctor told him that I was having a reaction to the anesthesia and that I would be fine. That was the first time I ever saw my husband truly scared. By the look on his face I thought I would die that night. At that point, I actually wanted to die. I feel so ashamed saying that because I know how precious life is, but I know others out there may be in that same dark place that I once was. I want those people to know they can get their old, healthy life back! I want them to know that there is an end to their pain.

I made it through the night but the pain did not go away. I was supposed to be getting better after the sinus surgery, but I wasn't. I could hardly move. I felt so weak. The migraines were more violent than ever. The doctor said I was having a reaction to the Vicodin they put me on and to get off of it. As the days went buy I was not getting better, the pain was still there. The pain at the base of my skull, the pain and pressure in my head, the sore neck and shoulder muscles were all still with me. The doctor told me it would take a month to recover. A month came and went and I had no improvement. The ENT then told me he wanted me to go see a neurologist friend of his. I did.

The neurologist had me keep a sleep diary, which was easy to keep because I wasn't sleeping so there was nothing to write. He put me on pills to try and make me sleep, which incidentally didn't make me sleep, but wired me up even more than I was when I wasn't on them. They also made me sick so I stopped taking them. And I stopped seeing him. I was fed-up. Sound familiar?

I went back to the general practitioner/osteopath that I had seen for months for all of my pain 'from the shoulders up' is how I referred to it.   I needed answers. Over the past five years I had had brain scans, x-rays, MRI's, blood tests. Everything and anything that could be run was run, yet it all came back negative. The doctor came into the room and I told him everything. I just unloaded. How the initial pain, the pain that I had been complaining about for years, the pain at the base of my skull, the migraines, the muscle pain, etc. was still with me and it had gotten so bad that I couldn't even bend over and tie my shoes for fear that I would pass out. I felt as if I was being strangled all the time. He opened his charts, and while flipping through them he said, "You know, you have been coming in here since January of 1997 with these same symptoms. Can you think of any event, a fall, a car crash, a blow to the head, anything like that that happened around that time?" I thought hard about anything that could have happened, but I came up with nothing.

He pressed on different points of my body, of which all of them hurt -- I will give him that -- and he said that these were the points that hurt on people who have fibromyalgia. He told my husband and I that he thought I had fibromyalgia. He said there were no tests that you could run to 'prove' the diagnosis, but that the pain I was experiencing was a typical fibromyalgia symptom. He went on to tell me that he wanted me to go to the internet and do some research on fibromyalgia.   He also told me, "They don't know exactly why but anti-depressants seem to alleviate some of the pain fibromyalgia patients have." At that moment I just wanted out of that office so I agreed to look up fibromyalgia on the internet and agreed to take the anti-depressant he wrote me a prescription for and we left.

As soon as my husband and I got into the car I immediately broke down into tears. **"I am NOT crazy!"** I cried. **"I am not DEPRESSED! I don't need anti-depressants! I'm in pain, not crazy or depressed! I don't care what is wrong with me NOW; I want to know WHAT caused me to become sick in the first place."** I was terrified of the diagnosis of fibromyalgia. I knew someone with fibromyalgia and she was always in pain. She wore sunglasses all the time because she was sensitive to light, and she walked hunched over with a cane yet she was only in her late 30's. She told me that she was in constant pain and that it was something she would have to live with all her life because there was no cure for it.

I repeated to my husband, "I don't want to take anti-depressants." He convinced me though to let him stop at the pharmacy so he could go in and have the prescription filled, that way if I changed my mind I would have them. I agreed to let him stop.

When I got home, I called one of my girlfriends who was working in the medical profession. I told her that the doctor told me he believed I had fibromyalgia. I told her that he wanted to put me on an anti-depressant to help with the pain. I asked her if she had ever heard of anything like that. She agreed with the doctor and told me that she too heard that people with fibromyalgia are put on anti-depressant medication to help lessen their pain. After quite a long conversation she convinced me to try it, encouraging me that it was safe. My husband too said,"Just try it; the doctor wouldn't give it to you if it could harm you." Against my better judgment, against my instincts, I started taking the anti-depressant that the doctor prescribed for me.

Well, you know what they say, **trust your instincts!** If you have an instinct or a gut feeling about something, learn to trust it. Don't always rely on what other people tell you, even if those other people have degrees hanging on their walls. If you come away with nothing else from my book at least go away with that, when your mind and body is telling you something learn to LISTEN!

Nothing happened until about a week after being on the anti-depressants. I was sitting in the truck with my husband and he was talking to me and all I remember was that I felt drugged. I didn't care what he was saying to me. I didn't care how I answered him. I was tired; I just wanted to nap. For a few days I felt actually pretty good. I thought it was the anti-depressant helping me and at first thought: HOORAY! I'm cured! But soon I learned the truth. I was not feeling good because of the anti-depressant, I was feeling better because it knocked me out and I finally got some sleep. I literally had not slept a sound night in years. So at that point the much-needed sleep I got was beneficial.

I hated how I felt on the anti-depressant. It made me a zombie. That's all I can say. The pain was still there; I just didn't care that I was in pain. Unless you have been put on this medication, that probably doesn't make any sense to you. I can't even explain it, it was like just sitting there, not caring about anything. People would talk to me and I would just be like, "um … huh, whatever". I was in a daze. And, I was on the lowest dosage possible.

I started wondering if I really did have fibromyalgia. The doctor told me to start researching it on the internet, and like the good patient that I was, I did. I was reading stories and articles here and there and while there were similarities it just didn't sound like that was what was wrong with me.

Then, in my search for information on fibromyalgia, I came across an article that sounded as if I had written it!! But the story I was reading wasn't written by someone with fibromyalgia, it was someone who became ill after having taking birth control injections. The same birth control injections I had taken. I couldn't believe my eyes. I was reading this woman's story and just crying. Everything she said I could relate to!

Immediately it was like everything just started to fall right into place. God really does work in mysterious ways.   All of a sudden something the doctor had said to me in my last appointment just popped into my head. I could see his face and him looking through my charts and I could hear his voice say...

"You know you have been coming in here since January of 1997 with these same symptoms. Can you think of any event, a fall, a car crash, blow to the head, anything like that that happened around that time?"

Oh my God! The birth control injections! When did I start taking those birth control injections?   Immediately I called the doctor's office that gave me the birth control injections.   I found out that I had my first injection of the birth control in November of 1996. That was just a few weeks before I first started seeing the third doctor, the general practitioner/osteopath that eventually told me he believed I had fibromyalgia.

I didn't know what to do with this information. I felt sick that I had remained on those birth control injections for a year just further poisoning myself. I shut off the computer and tried to calm down. It was a lot to take in. A few days later I started researching again and I found a few more stories about bad experiences with these same birth control injections. They too sounded as if I had written them myself. It was if someone had had a hidden camera in my home and had been watching my life and was telling my story.

I put up a web page with my story and asked other women to contact me if they had similar experiences. I was not at all prepared for the flood of emails I would soon start to receive. I put my web page up with the hopes that I could find women or a doctor that could tell me how to reverse what had been done to my body by these birth control injections. Instead of finding a cure however, I just found one devastating story after another. I was sickened by the large number of women who were so greatly affected by these injections that were still on the market.

Women started asking me if I could create web pages for their stories. I did. The demand for free web pages for their stories was so overwhelming I had to request that they add their stories to my guestbook so that they could enter their stories themselves. It was unbelievable; I was receiving emails from women all over the world thanking me for telling my story because they too were suffering in many of the same ways that I was.

Knowing I found the underlying cause to my pain I sent a fax to the doctor who told me he believed I had fibromyalgia. The fax told the doctor about the information I found out about the birth control injections and how I suspected that they were the root cause of my illness. Also in that fax I asked him to request all of my medical records from all of the other doctors I had seen over the past few years. I gave him all the contact information for the different doctors. A few days after faxing that letter I made an appointment to get off the anti-depressant (I had been on it for about a month), and to talk to the doctor about my fax since I did not hear from him or his office after sending it to him.

My husband went into the doctor's office with me. I told the doctor I wanted off the anti-depressant because it made me feel like a zombie. I asked if he got my medical records in from the other doctors, he responded that he did get a couple of them in. He would not discuss them with me however.

I asked him if he could have me take a hormone level test. He told me that that was useless. Yes, that is the exact word he used -- *useless*. He explained that women's hormone levels are impossible to chart because there is such a fluctuation in them. I felt myself getting upset. I could tell by the look on my husband's face that he was too. The doctor kept returning the conversation back to the subject of fibromyalgia.

The anger that was rising in my body gave me some courage and I just came right out and asked, "What about the birth control injections? I have quite a few stories, just like mine, all of them sick after the injections and healthy before them." He answered in a defensive tone, "I don't believe it was the injections, so much as the amount you were given". I was completely speechless. I don't even know if either my husband or I said another word. I just remember walking out of his office.

I can't remember if it was the next day or a few days later I called that doctor's office and demanded all of my medical records. They said they could send me their records on me but that they could not send me any of the other doctor's records.

When I got my records from his office a few days later I was disgusted to read in my records that he had made a notation in my records stating...

**8-15-97 neck pain; h/a's problem started couple mos ago. h/a's improving
since off Depo Provera.**

This is the doctor that treated me for months, to no avail by the way, with spinal manipulations, traction, and massage beds. Worse yet I had no insurance at that time and had to pay the 8,000.00+ in doctor's bills out of my pocket. He treated me for months and took my money, yet he never once mentioned to me that he noted that my headaches were getting better after I stopped taking the birth control injections.

Right there in black and white he made a notation about my headaches improving since being off the birth control injections. I couldn't believe it! He knew I was on those shots since I first saw him in January of 1997, yet when I asked him in January if the shots could be responsible for all of my mysterious pain he told me no. Yet months later he makes a note in his records that I am improving now that I am off the shots. WHAT? He never discussed that with me. After my initial questioning of the birth control shots in January of 1997 I never mentioned the shots to this doctor again until 2001. But in August of 1997 he made his own notation about the shots in my records so apparently he himself was questioning the fact that these shots made me sick.

I didn't even bother requesting any more records from any more doctors. What good would it do me? I was poisoned and nobody knew how to cure me.

The crisis of searching for the cause of my illness had finally ended, but my fighting had just begun. In my fight I learned that the birth control injections were not only the **worst** thing that had ever happened to me in life, but also ironically one of the best things that could have ever happened to me as well.

I have always believed that everything that happens to us in life, be it good or bad, happens to us for a very specific reason. I believe I needed to experience the pain, disease, and the recovery firsthand so that I could not only heal myself, but so that I could share the information of what I have learned about healing disease naturally with others who are suffering. I believe it is my duty to help others who have given up hope in the medical community and worse yet, given up hope on the thoughts of ever being pain free. I am living proof that there is a light at the end of that very long, dark tunnel. I have recovered from a living hell. I am not trying to be overdramatic. That is exactly what it was, a living hell. I'm sure there are millions of people in the world who are suffering even far worse than I did. I want to let those people know that I have done it! I have cured what was said to be incurable. I have cured myself from torturous, daily pain that no prescription drug could ever take away! But I am not alone. In my research for this book I have read about people all over the world who have used the same natural methods I have used to cure my disease, to cure their diseases -- fibromyalgia, diabetes, arthritis, lupus, AIDS, heart disease, Bright's disease, tuberculosis, different types of cancer, and a long list of others. There is a safe cure to illness and disease. There is a natural cure to illness and disease. I am not lying, these other people who have also cured their so-called "incurable" diseases are not lying, disease **can** be cured naturally, when you know how.

I am going to show you the exact steps I took to reverse my disease so you can take these steps too. You too can change the quality of your health by following these steps I have laid out for you. It is my sincere hope that this information will help you to not only better understand your body and its ability to heal itself naturally, but to also help lead you into a new, strong, fit, and DISEASE-FREE, healthy body! Once you experience this healing for yourself there is no doubt in my mind that you too will become a teacher and go on to share this same information with others near you who are so needlessly ill.

My very best wishes to all of you!

Shelly

Chapter 2: The Truth About Symptoms

The information I am about to share with you in this chapter, the **truth** about symptoms, was completely new to me. I had never had one of my parents or doctors tell me that my cold, flu, or fever was often times just my body's way of cleaning house. It was just always instilled in me that 'symptoms' are bad, dangerous, even deadly, and should be treated with drugs. Most people have this same upbringing.

Unfortunately we live in a society that teaches us from the time we are babies to drug away our symptoms. This is the 'norm' for us. Your parents took you to the doctor as a child every time you became ill, you got a pill and that was that.
From that very early age the majority of people are taught, myself included, that we should be AFRAID of symptoms. Fevers should be given aspirin. A runny nose or sore throat should be suppressed with cold medication, be it prescription or over-the-counter. Diarrhea needs to be brought to an end with some spoonfuls of Pepto-Bismol. When we are constipated we are told to take Milk of Magnesia or some other unnatural laxative. When a headache strikes, nip it in the bud with Excedrin, aspirin, or Tylenol. And round and round we go on the drugging merry-go-round!

Most people are unaware that symptoms can actually be a good thing. It is not common knowledge, though it should be, that if the body were allowed to run its course, it would heal itself. We are a society that 'drugs' our symptoms, and in doing so, we are preventing true healing from taking place.

SYMPTOMS OFTEN ARISE BECAUSE OUR BODIES ARE TRYING TO HEAL THEMSELVES

What I didn't know, but what I eventually learned on my road to recovery, was that the majority of the time that we have **'symptoms'**, such as headache, fever, chills, bloating, indigestion, runny nose, cough, sore throat, sinus infections, yeast infections, swollen tonsils, etc., etc., it is our bodies way of saying, "You have toxins inside that need to be detoxified." Your body is constantly trying to keep itself well.

Dr. Fuhrman, MD, author of Fasting and Eating for Health states, "Many people are unaware that symptoms such as a runny nose or fever are the treatment the body has prescribed to remedy the condition. Increased mucus production is the body's means of washing away infected cells and removing virus particles from the body. Fever aids in the body's immune defenses, activating the white blood cells and inducing interferon secretion from the brain.

Interferon is a powerful substance that stirs the fighting arm of the immune system into action. Typical cold symptoms that people attempt to suppress with drugs are nothing more than attempts of the body to restore homeostasis and remove the disease itself. By drugging away their symptoms, people keep themselves sick longer and can even turn a minor disease into a major one."

He also stated, "Your system has means to protect itself from irritants. Is this a sign of illness or of health? Coughing is a sign of health; the body produces a cough as an effort to keep the lungs clear. A healthy body offers a vigorous response when we try to poison it. The body may cough, sneeze, develop a fever or rash, and even produce mucus or diarrhea in its attempt to rid the system of unwanted waste."

In the book, The Mucusless Diet Healing System, Professor Ehret, a man responsible for curing thousands of patients from numerous so-called incurable diseases stated the following about symptoms...

"A COLD
Is a beneficial effort to eliminate waste from the cavities of the head, the throat and the bronchial tubes.

PNEUMONIA
The cold goes deeper and will eliminate and clean the mucus from the most spongy and vital organ, the lung. A hemorrhage occurs to clean more radically. The entire system is aroused, causing higher temperature by friction of the waste in circulation. That proves alarming, and the doctor suppresses by drugs and food, actually blocking nature's process of healing - cleansing. If the patient does not die, the elimination becomes chronic and is called consumption.

CONSUMPTION.
The consumptive patient eliminates continually his mucus caused from erroneously increased, mucus-forming foods, thru the lungs instead of thru the natural ways. This organ itself decays more and more, producing germs, and it is then called tuberculosis.

The vital organ (lung) - the pump - works insufficiently on circulation, the entire cell system decays more and more, and decomposes before the patient dies.

TOOTHACHE
Its pain is a warning signal of nature: "stop eating; I must repair; there is waste and pus; you have eaten too much lime-poor food, meat."

RHEUMATISM AND GOUT
Mucus and uric acid particularly accumulated in the joints, since here is the less dependable part of the tissues for the passage of the circulation, heavily loaded with waste and uric acid in the one-sided meat eater's body.
The stomach is the central organ of disease matter supply. There is a limit to the ability of this organ to digest and to empty itself after the meal. Every food (even the best kinds) is mixed with this acid mucus, continually remaining in the average person's stomach. The wonder is how long the human being can stand such conditions.

GOITER
Is a deposit by nature of tremendous waste to keep it from entering the circulation.

A BOIL
Is in principle the same, only the elimination is outside.

STAMMERING
Special accumulation of mucus in the throat, interfering with the functioning of the vocal chords. I cured several cases.

LIVER AND KIDNEY DISEASES
These organs are of a very spongy construction, and their function is that of a kind of physiological sieve. They are, therefore, easily constipated by sticky mucus.

SEX DISEASES
These have for their origin nothing more than mucus elimination thru these organs, and are easily healed. The use of drugs alone produces characteristic symptoms of syphilis. The more drugs that have been used, especially mercury, the more carefully the treatment must be conducted.

EAR AND EYE DISEASES
Even short or long sight is congestion in the eyes and trouble with hearing congestion of those organs. I healed a few kinds of blindness and deafness by the same principles.

MENTAL DISEASES
Besides a congested system, I found that any one mentally diseases has congestion, especially of the brain. One man on the verge of insanity was cured by a four weeks' fast."

In the book, The Miracle of Fasting by Paul Bragg, N.D., he bluntly stated that it is ourselves that are to blame for our aches and pains. He makes it clear that symptoms are nothing other than Mother Nature's way of telling us we need to make a change. In that same book he stated, "Poisons start to collect in various parts of the body causing you illness, aches and pains. These are Mother Nature's flashing warning signals that you are not living the healthy lifestyle that She and God intended for your body! Perhaps you blame everything and everybody for your problems, instead of analyzing your lifestyle habits for the real causes!"

In Dr. Robert Sniadach's Essential Natural Hygiene course he states, "The symptoms for which the drugs or medicines are administered are actually evidence of the healing process. When drugs are ingested or injected, the body must leave off, partially or wholly, the cleansing/healing efforts and attend to the greater threat, which the drugs represent. When healing efforts are discontinued the symptoms disappear. Physicians interpret the disappearance of symptoms as a "cure" or a healed condition. Thus they mistake drug or poison effects for healing effects. In reality the body has more problems than before. Now it has, in addition to its prior problems, the problem of expelling a destructive poison (Rx *drugs/medicine*), too."

OUR BODIES INNATE ABILITY TO HEAL ITSELF

Suffering from food poisoning is a perfect example of the body's awesome healing ability. Within hours or sometimes within just minutes of eating rotten, spoiled or poisonous food your body starts immediately trying to expel the toxins via causing vomiting, diarrhea or both. If someone ingests something poisonous, say for example a household-cleaning product; the instructions on the back often say to induce vomiting immediately. Clearly in those two cases vomiting and diarrhea are lifesavers. So why at other times when we are vomiting, having diarrhea, or experiencing other 'symptoms' do we believe these bodily functions are bad for us? The answer is simple. Our treatment of drugging symptoms is a learned behavior. This learned behavior is a behavior that needs to be **unlearned** if you want to get well.

We are trained from childhood that taking drugs, as long as they are prescribed by a doctor or can be purchased over-the-counter, is not only SAFE, but also a quick and easy solution to ending discomfort and pain. Sure the drugs may be a quick solution, but they are not a safe solution! Drugs never cure they only suppress. And, **all** drugs are toxic.

We simply do not know the truth because the truth was never taught to us. If you are reading this book it is because you want to be well again. I am living proof that you can cure yourself naturally even when doctors tell you that your pain is incurable. One thing I had to do, and probably one thing you will have to do, is **unlearn** everything you have previously been taught about symptoms and disease.

A DRUGGED SOCIETY

You can't watch television or listen to the radio without seeing or hearing advertisements for all types of prescription drugs and over the counter medications claiming to be able to end your suffering. Forget being able to flip through a magazine without seeing one of the many pharmaceutical companies promoting their newest 'miracle' cure. As a society we are addicted to drugs. Whether the drugs are illegal, over-the-counter, or prescribed they are all toxic.

Our nation's children and teenagers are needlessly being put on drugs for ADD, acne, depression, etc. to 'control' their symptoms. These drugs only cause further damage they don't cure the problem. Do you really want to just 'drug' your child? Don't you want a cure for your child instead of just suppression to his or her problem? Are you really willing to trust the doctor and believe that the drugs your child is on are safe? No drug is completely safe -- they are all toxic. Talk to just one parent whose child has had a severe reaction to one of these drugs, or worse yet who has had a child die as a result of one of these drugs, and I guarantee you that it will at least make you question whether what you are doing is right or wrong. We have to realize that most symptoms our bodies have are nothing other than signs that your body is trying to rid itself of toxins.

YES! YOU CAN LIVE WITHOUT PRESCRIPTION DRUGS!

You may feel you need your drugs because your pain is intolerable without them. You may feel you need to stay on prescription drugs because the doctors tell you they are a must for your condition. Whatever reason you are on prescription drugs or over-the-counter medications, please know that you can be weaned off these medications. You can go on to live a life that is not only drug-free but also pain-free. The doctors that I write about in my book, from past to present, have successfully reversed many types of diseases with the same natural methods I used. That is because there is no "cure" there is only the body's natural ability to heal itself. All of these cases that I have read about and will comment on have all required that the patient be weaned off all of their Rx drugs in order for their disease to be reversed. You cannot ingest toxins into the body and be healthy. By putting toxins into the body you are forcing your body to be at constant work eliminating those toxins. By putting this extra workload on your body it will not be able to efficiently conduct the daily work it needs to do in order to keep your body disease free.

You may be on 20 or more different medications and the thought of going off of them may seem impossible or terribly frightening to you I know. I completely understand how you feel. But please, I encourage you to finish out the book and apply the information I give you. If you do, it will change your life.

URGENT NOTE: You can never just stop taking medications on your own. You must always have a doctor help wean you off your medications. More than likely the doctor you are going to is one that says you must be on these medications and won't be willing to help wean you off them. Don't worry if that is the case, on my message boards at the web site http://www.rawandjuicy.com/messageboard.html I have a resource area where you can search for a natural Hygienist to help professionally wean you off of your current medications.

WHY SHOULD YOU LISTEN TO ME?

Why should you listen to me? I'm not a doctor. I have no degree. I have no medical training whatsoever. I haven't even attended college. So why listen? The reason you should listen to me is because I am someone who was once sick, and is now well. I am not someone who has never been sick trying to tell you how to get well. I am someone with EXPERIENCE. I have been where most of you are, and I turned things around when all doctors and all of their drugs failed me. I obtained for myself the very **one** thing that all who are suffering from illness and disease so desperately desire -- a cure.

In my next chapter I will give you the information I learned about how and why we become diseased. The cause of disease isn't a mystery, as some doctors would have you believe. The cause of your disease, no matter what name it is given, is also the cause of almost every other disease. The information may be shocking, even sound downright absurd to you, I know. I too read the same information and initially thought, "There is no way all disease can be caused by the same thing, no way!" I've been where you are, and then I learned the truth. Now, I'm no longer living in pain. You don't have to either. You too can learn the truth.

Chapter 3. The Cause of Disease REVEALED!

WHAT IS CAUSING ALL OF MY PAIN?

In my struggle for good health I learned that all of my symptoms were merely my body's way of fighting off toxins and disease. But what caused the disease that caused the symptoms in the first place? When you are sick and suffering you instinctively wonder, "What is the underlying cause?" Since we don't know the answer, we turn to our doctors in the allopathic community. After all, they are the trained professionals right?

We ask our doctors "what is causing all this pain?" Doctors either give an immediate response by simply 'listening' to your symptoms, or requiring you to have some additional testing, and then they tell you either one of two things:

1) I don't know (conventional medicine doesn't know) what is wrong with you but we can give you some medication and/or surgery to help you deal with the pain.

Or

2) Your pain is caused by something we call, 'FILL-IN-THE-BLANK-WITH-DISEASE/DISORDER-NAME-HERE'.

If your doctor does give you a diagnosis that 'names' your disease you naturally feel some relief just because you then at least KNOW what you are up against. That was my biggest battle in my 5+ years of being sick. I didn't know what was causing my pain. It was impossible to fight what I didn't know.

No doctor or specialist knew how to cure me. Eventually I was given the wastebasket diagnosis of fibromyalgia. I call it the "wastebasket diagnosis," as even many MD's will admit, because fibromyalgia is what they say you have when they don't know what else to do with you. They give this chronic and excruciating pain -- pain that comes from nothing other than a body being completely enervated -- a name and tell us - your incurable. Don't get me wrong! The pain is real. I don't want a bunch of nasty hate mail from fibromyalgia patients. I too was suffering from this pain and it is truly unbearable. The point I am trying to make here is that we should not get wrapped up in the 'NAME' that has been given to our pain or disease. Easier said than done, I know. But let me explain **why** I am telling you this...

Fasting Your Way To Health, a book by Lee Bueno Aquer, was the first book I read on 'drugless healing.' Fast Your Way To Health is a book about a woman who was given a death sentence by her doctors and she refused their medications and turned to fasting and God instead. She cured herself of vascular rheumatoid arthritis, which she was told was incurable. The second book I read on the subject of drugless healing was **The Miracle of Fasting** written by Paul Bragg, N.D., and his daughter Patricia Bragg. Paul Bragg cured himself from tuberculosis. Throughout Paul Bragg's life he went on to help literally thousands of others reverse their so-called incurable diseases. I was extremely intrigued by the fact that both Lee Bueno Aquer and Paul Bragg, even though they had completely different diseases, were completely healed by virtually the same methods. This intrigue had me devouring any and every book, web page and article I could find on the subject of drugless healing. If they could reverse their doctor diagnosed incurable diseases, why couldn't I?

I continued to read book after book and web site after web site on natural healing and fasting. I read one miraculous story after another of people being cured naturally from everything from Bright's disease to Breast Cancer. How on earth had I not heard of these astounding stories before? Why are all these celebrities out doing these benefits to raise money for "A CURE", when the "cure" is right here in black in white? Our bodies can repair themselves if we set forth for them the proper conditions to do so.

Why aren't the doctors giving me, giving US, this information? I felt totally betrayed. To me it just seemed too impossible to believe. I had tried everything and nothing had worked. How could something so simplistic help me get well when the medical community, with all of their scientific knowledge could not help me get well? Had I not healed myself via these same methods I am going to share with you in this book, I would probably not have believed it myself.

I did more than just continue to study and research this drugless healing possibility. I also started to experiment with it personally. I started taking the advice the books were giving out. To my sheer amazement, it was helping. I was finally for once getting real results.

With the prescription drugs I would have 1 of 3 reactions:

1	I would have an adverse reaction to the drug and would have to switch to another drug or just stop taking it.

1	I would get some brief relief while on the medication but as soon as I would stop taking it, the pain or the infection would come back.

1	I would take one medication for one thing, and it would cause something else to be wrong with me. I would take antibiotics for my chronic sinus infections, and the antibiotics would cause me to get yeast infections. It was a never-ending circle.

But with the drugless healing methods I was trying, I was getting rid of the pain for good, not just suppressing it. As the days went by I began feeling a little bit better every day. Soon I was watching health problems that had plagued my body for years just vanish.

I had been on everything from Ambien for my insomnia, Celebrex for my severe muscle inflammation and joint pain, Excedrin Migraine for my daily migraines, antibiotics for my sinus infections, etc., but no drug ever cured me. I eventually came to learn why that was so. All drugs are toxic. Drugs cannot cure. There are NO cures, only the bodies own ability to repair itself.

As I continued to research and experiment, I was totally dumbfounded when I encountered statement after statement saying... "Every disease is caused by the same thing." Sure, everybody said it in his own way of course, but the gist was always the same ... **There is ONE cause to every disease**!

THE CAUSE OF DISEASE REVEALED!

We are sick and diseased because we are suffering from **autointoxication**. Autointoxication is described in the dictionary as self-poisoning caused by endogenous microorganisms, metabolic wastes, or other toxins produced within the body. By dictionary definition that is only partly correct.

We are diseased because we are suffering from both endogenous (from within the body) and exogenous (from what we take into the body from the outside) toxemia, or poisoning. [*In my next chapter I will give you specific ways you may be poisoning your system.*]

That's it. That's the answer. The one cause to all disease is autointoxication, or self-poisoning!

I know you were looking for something perhaps a little more complicated, or a little more profound, but that's it. It really is that simple. I can tell you from what I experienced for myself that is a true statement. But you won't have to just take my word for it. I will provide you with information and resources where you can see the stories of many others that prove this statement is true too. These people have also reversed their illnesses and diseases that the medical community told them were incurable.

I realize that my book may be the first book you have ever purchased on the subject of 'drugless healing'. So, for those of you who have not already heard it said that there is but **one cause of disease**, let me share with you just a couple of quotes I've gathered on this topic from some of the books I have read on my road to recovery. Some agree that autointoxication is the cause of all disease and some just say that it is the common cause of most diseases.

Professor Arnold Ehret, author of The Mucusless Diet Healing System and Rational Fasting stated, **"Every disease, no matter what name it is known by Medical Science, is CONSTIPATION, a clogging up of the entire pipe system of the human body. Any special symptom is therefore merely an extraordinary local constipation by more accumulated mucus at this particular place. Special accumulation points are the tongue, the stomach and particularly the entire digestive tract. This last is the real and deeper cause of bowel constipation. The average person has as much as ten pounds of uneliminated feces in the bowels continually,** poisoning the blood stream and the entire system. Think of it! Every sick person has a more or less mucus-clogged system, such mucus being derived from undigested and uneliminated, unnatural food substances, accumulated from childhood on."

Paul Bragg, ND reiterated this same theory in his book The Miracle of Fasting when he stated **"I have come to regard autointoxication (self-poisoning) as the worst enemy in the fight for Agelessness and Longevity."** Bragg also boldly said, **"Autointoxication itself is your health's greatest enemy."**

John Tilden M.D (1851-1940) had stated **"Every so called disease is built within the mind and body by enervating habits."**

Dr. Fuhrman states in the book Fasting and Eating For Health, **"Toxicosis is a common cause of disease. In order to understand the nature of the disease process one must first define toxicosis. Toxicosis means nothing more than the retention of elements within our system that are foreign to normal cellular function. It could also refer to the retention of an increased quantity of a substance that would be normal in small amounts but irritating or toxic in higher quantities."**

Dr. Lorraine Day, who cured herself from a very advanced stage of breast cancer states on her web site http://www.drday.com, **"It is what you put in your mouth that determines whether you're sick or well."** She repeats this information in the two VHS tapes I've watched her in titled, You Can't Improve on God, and Cancer Doesn't Scare Me Anymore.

In the book Juice Fasting and Detoxification, by Steve Meyerowitz he states, **"A sick person's system is filled with poisons from the diet, pollutants, lead, arsenic, medication, nicotine, cellular and metabolic waste products from wrongly combined foods, addiction to sweets, coffee, cigarettes and excessive eating -- not to mention inadequate nutrition. You may get headaches upon waking, encrustation around the eyes, body odor, coated tongue, stuffy nose. The body discharges poisons in any way it can. A cold is merely a relief valve to relieve the lungs, blood, liver, and lymphatic system of congestion. Stress combines with diet to compound the effects of this overload by impeding the**

normal flow of impulses. The nervous system can then no longer properly conduct the flow of vital energy to the various glands and organs. Lack of clarity, confusion, frustration and instability result. If ignored, these poisons become entrenched in the body and in time develop into chronic pathologies."

10,000 DISEASES, OR JUST ONE?

Medical Science has given name to 10,000 diseases/disorders. Some of you may find it hard to believe there is just one cause to all of these 10,000 different named disorders/diseases. That's fine, I was skeptical too. Maybe there are even a few diseases that cannot possibly be linked to auto-intoxication. I truthfully don't know. I can tell you this however, in my research for this book, I've seen diabetes, pneumonia, Bright's disease, cardiovascular diseases, many types of cancer, lupus, fibromyalgia, sinusitis, arthritis, migraines, acne, psoriasis, obesity, and schizophrenia, *just to name a few*, linked to autointoxication. If your skepticism comes solely from the fact that you don't believe 1 thing can cause 10,000 different disorders/diseases, then let me share some information that may help you gain a different perspective on the situation.

Most of you know that there are thousands of different diseases and disorders. It seems that almost every day some new mysterious disease is being uncovered. There are approximately 10,000 given names for our pain. What you have to ask yourself is simply, "**How do they come up with these names for diseases?** Let me answer that question for you by applying the theory that all disease is caused by auto-intoxication (self-poisoning).

In an acute disease (short-term and corrective), the body may choose an avenue such as the lungs, nose, and sinuses through which to eliminate. For example, a sinus infection is given its name because you have an 'infection' in your sinus cavity. In chronic disease (long-term and degenerative), your body has really become enervated. Your body can't just fight off the toxins anymore through causing your body to have a 'cold', a fever, a sinus infection, etc. You are taking in more toxins than your body can get rid of and it starts storing these toxins in a number of different places in your body. Your body may store these toxins in different places than my body will. Some of the places the toxins start to store themselves in are your joints, your arteries, and your fatty tissues. The toxins may even start building their own 'houses' to store themselves in inside your body. This results in things like tumors, and/or cysts forming in your body.

In either case, acute or chronic disease, it is almost always WHERE the toxins store themselves in your body that determines the **name** the disease will be given by our experts in medical science and conventional medicine. So, while there are currently over 10,000 **names** for our pain, there really only needs to be one -- **AUTOINTOXICATION**.

DISEASE ITSELF IS THE CURE!

For billions of individuals worldwide the word 'disease' strikes immediate fear and conjures up ideas of an agonizing death! Conventional medicine teaches that disease is to be drugged, cut out, and FEARED. People have a true fear of the unknown. Only a very small percentage of people will ever take the time in their lives to do the research and find out 'what' really causes disease. If you were taught, from the time you were young, that disease is a safety mechanism brought about by your own body to protect itself from toxic substances would you be so fearful of the word? Of course not. We fear the unknown and conventional medicine breeds that fear.

Disease does indeed need to be paid great attention, however it does not need to be feared, just understood. To help you better understand the cause of disease I want to share with you Dr. Herbert Shelton's work Life's Engineering. The information in Shelton's "Life's Engineering" is a must read. Please do not haphazardously skim through the next few pages. Read it, absorb it, and understand it. Why do abscesses, gallstones, and tumors form? The formation of these growths that cause us great concern are in reality curative and protective measures of our brilliantly alert and knowledgeable bodies.

LIFE'S ENGINEERING
Dr. Herbert M. Shelton

The greatest engineering feat of which we know anything is the building of a complex animal organism from a microscopic ovum. Think, for instance, of the marvels of the human body with its pulleys and levers to perform mechanical work, its channels for distribution of food and drainage of sewage and its means of regulating its temperature and adapting its actions and functions to its varied environments and needs. Its nervous system and the eyes, ears, etc. are constant sources of wonder. We regard the radio as a wonderful invention, as indeed it is, but we are all equipped with more wonderful "sending" and "receiving" sets than any radio manufacturer will ever produce. All human inventions have their proto-types in the animal body.

In studying the wonders of the body, its structures, functions, development, growth and its varied powers and capacities, it is well to keep in mind that the building and preservation of all these things is from within. The power, force or intelligence that evolves the adult body from the fertilized ovum is in the body, is part of it and is in constant and unceasing control of all its activities. Whether it is an intelligent power or a blind energy, it works determinably toward the latest results in complexity of structure and function. In development and maintenance, and in health and disease, the movements of life appear to be guided by intelligence more often than the conscious intelligence of man. Indeed, unless we grant that something can come out of nothing, that intelligence can come out of that which has no intelligence, we must believe that the conscious intelligence of man is a subordinate part of that broader intelligence that evolves his body and which inheres in it.

If we view a few of the engineering feats performed by the body in cases of injury and disease, we are forcibly struck with the truth of Sylvester Graham's remark: "In all these operations the organic instincts act determinably, and, as it were, rationally, with reference to a final cause of good, viz., the removal of the offending cause."

To begin with, let us consider the natural healing of a wound, scratch or broken skin. We have become so accustomed to this familiar phenomenon that we have come to regard it as an almost mechanical process. But a close examination of the process shows us the presence of that same marvelous intelligence that built the body from a tiny microscopic speck of protoplasm to its present state.

Whenever the skin is broken or cut there is an exudation of blood that coagulates and forms an airtight scab. This scab serves as a protection to the wound and remains for a shorter or longer time as is needed.

Underneath this scab a wonderful thing occurs. Blood is rushed to the injured part in large quantities. The tissues, nerve and muscle cells, etc., on each side of the wound start multiplying rapidly and build a "cell-bridge" across the gap until the severed edges of the wound are reunited. But this is no mere haphazard process. Everywhere is apparent the presence of directing law and order. The newly formed cells of the blood vessels united with their brothers on the other side so that, in an orderly and evenly manner, the channels of circulation are re-established. In this same lawful and orderly manner the connective tissues reunite. Skillfully, and just as a lineman repairs a telegraph system, do the nerve cells repair their broken line? Muscles and other tissues are repaired in a similar manner. And what is a wonderfully marvelous fact to observe, no mistakes are made in this connective tissue, but each tissue connects with its kind.

After the wound is healed, when a new skin has been formed so that there is no longer any need for the protecting scab, nature proceeds to undermine and get rid of it. As long as the scab was useful it was firmly attached to the skin so that it was not easy to pull it off, but when there was no longer need for it, it was undermined so that it fell off of its own weight.

What more evidence than this does one require to know that the same intelligent power that built our bodies is also the power that heals it? What better evidence do we want that the healing process is accomplished in the same orderly manner and by means of the same functions with which the body is built, maintained and modified to meet its present needs.

We get a still more wonderful view of how nature performs her work if we observe the healing of a fractured or broken bone. If an arm or leg be broken, this same marvelous intelligence that has brought us from ovum to adulthood immediately sets about to repair the damage done. A liquid substance is secreted and deposited over the entire surface of the bone in each direction from the point of fracture. This section quickly hardens into a bone-like substance and is firmly attached to the two sections of the bone. Until nature can repair the damage, this "bone ring" forms the chief support whereby the limb can be used. By the same process of cell multiplication that we saw in the healing of the wound, the ends of the bone are reunited. The circulatory channels are re-established through the part. It is then that the "bone ring" support is softened and absorbed, except about an eighth to a quarter of an inch about the point of fracture.

If you strike your finger with a hammer, a very painful bruise is the result. There is an effusion of blood under the surface, with inflammation and discoloration. The tissues are mangled, the cells are broken and many of them are killed. But does the thumb always remain so? No. As time passes, new tissues are formed to replace the dead ones and the dead blood and tissue cells are carried away by the bloodstream. The inflammation subsides, the pain ceases and the bruise is healed and soon forgotten. Thus again is manifested the marvelous intelligence of the power that superintends the workshop which we call our body. Once again we watch its work and see its marvelous efficiency as a workman.

A similar manifestation of the body's self-healing, self-adjusting and self-repairing powers is seen in the common accident whereby a sliver becomes embedded in the flesh. If it is not removed immediately, nature or vital force, does a skillful little piece of engineering and removes it for us. Pain and inflammation are soon followed by the formation of pus, which breaks down the tissues towards the surface of the body. Gradually increasing in amount, the pus finally breaks through the overlying skin and runs out, carrying the sliver along as a souvenir.

A remarkable engineering feat is presented to us in abscess formations. Ordinarily the abscess is limited by the thick protective wall of granulation tissue that prevents the abscess from spreading and prevents rapid escape of the pus into the circulation.

In appendicitis the loops of the bowels around the appendix form friendly adhesions. They adhere together and form a strong wall against further spread of the trouble. Within this enclosure this abscesses form. The line of least resistance normally is into the bowels so that practically every case, if not interfered with by meddlesome doctors, will rupture into the bowels and the pus will pass out with the stools.

Where the ice bag is employed for one or two days prior to the usual appendix operations, there is a noticeable lack of effort on the part of nature to wall off the appendix from the rest of the abdominal cavity. However, where the ice bag has not been employed, a distinct walling off of the acutely inflamed and gangrenous appendix from the general peritoneal cavity is found. So greatly does the ice bag interfere with the curative and protective operations of nature that once of the leading abdominal surgeons of this country declares: "I have entirely discarded the use of the ice bag, and in cases brought to me in which it has been used, I always announce beforehand that I expect to find a gangrenous appendix and am seldom surprised. Clearly the ice bag should never be used in cases of actual or suspected appendicitis. "Nature can do her own work in her own way, and all our so-called aiding of nature amounts to is nothing more than meddlesome and pernicious interference.

Acute inflammation of the liver usually terminates in resolution, but sometimes it terminates in suppuration with abscess formation. This is more apt to be the case in hot climates. The amount of matter discharged from an abscess of the liver is sometimes enormous, and it is wonderful to see in what ways nature operates in getting rid of it.

There are several channels through which the pus may be sent out of the system. The inflammation may extend upward until an adhesion to the diaphragm is accomplished. A dense wall of scar tissue is first formed around the abscess. The abscess then extends through the diaphragm to the lungs, which become adherent to the diaphragm. Liver, diaphragm and lungs form one solid piece. A tight union of these organs prevents the pus from pouring into the peritoneal or pleural cavities. A hole is eaten through the lung and the pus is poured into a bronchial tube and is coughed up, emptying the abscess and leaving a clean hole. The wall of scar tissue thrown up around the path of the abscess grows stronger and contracts until, finally, only the scar remains, it having closed the hole, and the patient is well.

The abscess may be directed downward or to the side of the liver. In such a case the process is the same except the liver becomes united to the stomach, the intestines or the walls of the abdomen by adhesions produced by inflammation. If it adheres to the stomach or intestine, the abscess will perforate into these and the pus will pass out in the stools. If it becomes adherent to the wall of the abdomen, the abscess will "come to a head" under the skin and the pus will be discharged on the surface of the body. In either case cicatrisation follows and the patient is well. In some cases the abscess discharges into the gallbladder and passes from there into the intestine. It has also been known to "point" on the back.

It sometimes happens in weak individuals that nature is not able to make proper connections along the line of march and the pus ends up in the pleural cavity, resulting in empyema, or in the abdominal cavity, where it results in peritonitis and, usually, death.

Another daring engineering feat is often accomplished by nature in the case of gallstones that are too large to pass through the bile duct directly into the small intestine. She frequently causes the gallbladder to adhere, by means of inflammation, to the wall of the intestine. An ulcer forms, making a hole through both the wall of the gallbladder and the wall of the intestine. The stone slips through into the intestine and passes out with the stools. The hole heals up and all is well again. In other cases the stone may be sent out through the abdominal wall and skin, on the outside of the body.

An unusual piece of engineering which shows, in a remarkable manner, the ingenuity of nature in her efforts at prolonging life in spite of every obstacle, is recorder by J.F. Baldwin, A.M., MD, F.A.C.S., in a surgical paper dealing with blood transfusions. He performed an operation on a middle-aged woman who had been having frequent hemorrhages from her bowels for several years. He says: "At the operation I removed a snarl of small bowel making the usual anastamosis. Examination of this snarl showed that there had been an intestinal obstruction, but nature had overcome it by ulceration between adherent loops of the bowel above and below the obstruction. The ulcer persisted, however, and it was its persistent bleeding that caused her anemia. She made an excellent recovery and got fat and hearty."

It looks like a real intelligence at work when nature causes two folds of the bowels to adhere together and then ulcerates through them in order to make a passage around an obstruction. There cannot be the slightest doubt that the ulcer would have healed, leaving a passage, and the bleeding stopped, had the opportunity been afforded it. Nature probably cried out day after day in unmistakable language for the cessation of feeding long enough for her to complete her engineering feat. But this was never given her. The ulcerated surface was kept constantly irritated with food and drugs as well.

Abscesses everywhere in the body are limited and walled off by the formation of a thick wall of granulation tissue. Gangrene is also walled off in the same manner. The necrosed portion then sloughs off; nature grows new tissue to take the place of the destroyed tissue and the place is healed.

Encapsulation is the process of surrounding a body or substance with a capsule. A cyst or capsule consists of a cavity lined according to its origin by endothelium (in preexisting cavities of connective tissue-exudation cysts) or epithelium (in pre-existing epithelial cavities-retention cysts) with a fluid or semi fluid content.

Retention cysts are due to the obstruction of the excretory ducts of glands. The cavity becomes filled with the secretion of the gland, which later becomes altered and circumscribed by a fibrous wall. These may develop in any glandular structure, as pancreas, kidneys, salivary glands, and mammary glands, sebaceous glands (wens).

Around a foreign body like a bullet such a capsule forms. There is first inflammation and perhaps suppuration. But if this fails to remove the bullet, a capsule of tissue also containing fluid is formed, and the bullet is rendered innocuous.

The encapsulation of exudates, excretions, extravasions, disintegrating tissues, germs parasites, bullets and other foreign bodies renders them harmless. The process and structure it evolves are plainly defensive measures. They once more remind us of the may and varied emergency measures the body has at its command.

The formation of gallstones and other stones is in itself an engineering feat that serves a useful purpose and even extends and saves life. In the lungs, for instance, in those who have tuberculosis, the affected spots are often the seats of the formation of stones. When this takes place, the disease in that part ends. Medical authorities consider that nature employs this means to wall up the tubercle bacilli.

The formation of stones in the gallbladder and kidneys, just as in the lungs, is the end result of inflammation and undoubtedly serves a definite and useful purpose. Sometimes, it is true, they are made so large that they are the source of much trouble, but it is safe to assume that they are never made larger than the gravity of the situation demands. Most gallstones are small enough that they pass out without causing pain, and the individual is never aware that they had them. They never cause trouble until they go to pass out and only then if they are small enough to get into the gall duct but too large to make the entire passage. A stone that may easily travel through the common duct may be forced, with extreme difficulty, through the small opening of the duct into the intestine. This causes severe pain. As soon as the stone is forced through, the pain ceases. (The sufferer then things that it was the last treatment he employed that relieved the pain and "cured" his troubles.)

A thrombus is a small blot clot formed inside a blood vessel. The condition is called thrombosis and the vessel is said to be thrombosed. They are the result of injury and inflammation and may completely plug the vessel.

In the intestines are many small glands composed of lymphoid structure just as are the tonsils of the throat. They are known as Peyer's patches. In typhoid fever these patches are swollen or enlarged (hypertrophied), and frequently they suppurate. They may slough off. This peeling off may result in a hemorrhage or it may not, depending on whether or not all the vessels in that locality are tightly thrombosed. If they are all tightly thrombosed, no hemorrhage occurs. If the work of sealing the vessel is not complete or perfect, then a hemorrhage occurs with more or less loss of blood before it finally ceases. This is but another evidence of nature's engineering work. These thrombi may later be swept into the general circulation and carried to some vital spot where they are too large to pass through the artery and may there cut off the blood to parts of the organ, causing it to die of starvation. Starvation would only occur in cases of stopping of an "end artery." '"Anastamosing" arteries would soon establish sufficient collateral and compensatory circulation to supply the part with blood.

If heat or friction of sufficient intensity and duration is applied to the skin, a blister forms; that is, a watery exudates or serum is poured out of the surrounding tissues and circulation into the "space" between the dermis and epidermis and detaches the dermis from this, raising it up and thus protecting the tissues beneath. The accumulated fluids holds back the heat or, in the case of sunburn, the actinic rays, and protects from the friction. This little piece of engineering work is quite obviously a defensive work. In both sunburn pigmentation occurs to protect from future sunburn.

Of a similarly defensive nature are corns and calluses that form on the feet and hands or any other surface of the body that are subjected to constant friction. The clerk who deserts the store for manual labor finds his hands are tender and blister easily when he handles tools. However, before many days have passed, the skin on his hands has become thickened and hardened, ultimately becoming almost horn-like. When this occurs, he finds that no reasonable amount of hard work blisters his hands.

Tumors likely begin in this same manner. They probably begin as hardening and thickening of the tissues at a point of irritation as a means of defense.

Hardening and thickening of the tissues occurs in any and all parts of the body to resist constant irritation. This can be seen in the mouth, stomach and intestines of those who employ salt and condiments. It is seen in the constant use of drugs. Silver nitrate, for instance, if repeatedly employed, converts the mucous surface upon which it is used into a kind of half-living leather. Other organs harden and thicken as a result of toxic irritation. Toxemia, with or without the aid of external irritation, often necessitates, at certain points of the body, the erection of greater than ordinary barriers against it. When the normal cells of a local spot become so impaired that they no longer successfully resist the encroachment of toxins, not only are the usual defense processes brought into activity, but also, since a more than usual condition is to be met, nature calls into play her heavier battalions. She begins by erecting a barrier of connective tissue cells. Then, with a slowly yielding fight against the toxins, she continues to erect her barriers. This may continue until the tumor becomes so large as to constitute a source of danger itself. Were it not for the erection of this barrier, the causes against which it is erected would destroy life long before they ultimately do. The tumor actually prolongs life.

A process similar to this is seen in plants that have been invaded by parasites. The large, rough excrescence seen on oak tress form about the larva of a certain fly. This fly lays its eggs beneath the bark of the tree. The larvae, which develop form the eggs, secrete a substance that results in the formation of the huge *tumorous* mass. Large tumor-like masses form on the roots and stalks of cabbages as a result of parasitic invasion. The olive tree also develops tumors from a similar cause, while cedar trees present peculiar growths called "witches' brooms" as a result of a fungus growing on them. There are many other examples, and they are all quite obviously protective measures. Tumor formation is undoubtedly due to a variation in the complex relations determining normal growth and is of a distinctively protective nature. A tumor is not a source of danger until it begins to break down.

In inflammation of the kidneys due to the impairment of kidney function, the normal constituents of the urine are decreased. They remain in the blood instead of being eliminated. Due to the necessity of removing from the circulation, the salts, etc., that are normally eliminated through the kidneys, and due also to the necessity of keeping these in dilute solution so long as they remain in the body, and to the equal necessity of removing them from the circulation, edema develops in various portions of the body, particularly in the tissues immediately under the skin. It may also collect in the cavities of the body. When kidney function is restored, the endemic fluid is gradually absorbed into circulation and eliminated.

An aneurism is an inflated portion of an artery. If the walls of an artery become weak at a given place, they either burst, some of its coats are strengthened or else it becomes bulged out due to the pressure of the blood from within. The body at once sets about to protect itself by forming a wall of new tissue around the aneurism. Should it rupture so that the blood finds its way along between other organs, a wall of scar tissue is thrown up around the aneurism to limit the escape of blood. This is called a dissecting aneurism.

Thus we might continue giving example after example of the wonderful engineering feats of the body and show with what marvelous powers and works it meets emergencies and protects its own vital interests. When we consider the wonderful mechanism of the human body, the certainty with which all organs perform their allotted work, the marvelous ingenuity with which the body meets emergencies, its almost limitless powers of repair and recuperation, we develop a large respect and admiration for the healing powers of the body and learn to view with contempt and disgust the means that people employ in unintelligent efforts to "cure."

SO MY BODY IS POISONED -- NOW WHAT?

Well by now you should be feeling hopefully a little bit better. The thing that was hardest for me to deal with while I was ill was the **'not knowing'** what was causing me to be so sick. The fear of the 'unknown' was at most times worse than the debilitating pain itself. The worry that I was dying from some rare disease that Medical Science just didn't have a name for yet haunted me. It was impossible fighting an invisible force. Once I knew what the underlying cause of my illness was I was able to fight it.

The battle isn't over yet though. The fight has just begun. Now you know that you are sick because you are toxic. I am assuming the question you are asking now is, "But WHAT made me toxic?" If that is what you are asking yourself, BRAVO!! You're ahead of the game. You now have to find out **what** is poisoning your body.

There are many things that can poison your system. Many people can be diagnosed with the same disease and yet have developed that same disease for completely different reasons. I will devote the next chapter entirely to giving you information on some of the many ways that we poison ourselves.

Chapter 4: TOXIC OVERLOAD: The Many Ways We Poison Ourselves

As I dove deeper into my research on drugless healing, fasting, and curative eating (healing through diet), I kept seeing many references being made to something called Natural Hygiene. Not knowing what it was, I did further research.

WHAT IS NATURAL HYGIENE?

Natural Hygiene is a philosophy and a set of principles and practices based on the fact that only the body itself can reverse disease and only if we set forth for it the proper dietary and lifestyle conditions for it to do so. All other alternative healing practices, such as naturopathy, homeopathy, chiropractic, acupuncture, reflexology, massage therapy, E.F.T. (emotion freedom therapy technique), etc. rely on special treatments and/or some type of vitamin or herbal supplementation in order to cure the body. I tried countless alternative therapy methods and **none** of them cured me. I lost a lot of money, but I didn't get well. I soon found myself bouncing from one alternative medicine healer to another spending money on everything they 'prescribed', to try and get well. But all I was doing was running into brick walls, just as I had been doing with conventional medicine and the doctor's prescription drugs. Millions of people worldwide are having this same problem. Their desperate for a cure, but for many the alternative therapies are failing them just as the conventional therapies are. It is for these people that I am writing my book.

I finally found out WHY conventional medicine and the alternative therapies I tried could not "cure" me. This is the information I will be sharing with you in this book, in particular in extensive detail in the next chapter. Right now let me share some more information with you on Natural Hygiene.

Simply put, Natural Hygiene teaches you the diet and lifestyle changes that must take place in order for your body to heal itself from disease. In fact, Hygienists believe that the so-called "disease" itself is actually the process of your body curing itself. This is explained in great detail in Dr. Sniadach's Essential Natural Hygiene Course. Dr. Sniadach explains how the formation of gallstones, abscesses, ulcers, blisters; even tumors are actually processes that the body takes to save itself.   I was so impressed with this information that I contacted Dr. Sniadach to ask if I could share it with you, my readers, and he graciously agreed.

You'll be relieved to know there is no 'selling' of any treatment or pill involved with Natural Hygiene, so you can get well and NOT have to spend money on a variety of 'magic pills' and treatments to do so. You'll be relying on your body to heal you, and you already have a body ... so other than the right foods, and you already have to buy food anyway, there's nothing else to buy!

Natural Hygiene teaches that disease is brought on by the body as an emergency measure to purify and repair itself. Disease is a result of our body working to fight off toxins.

I didn't start researching "Natural Hygiene" until I had already successfully reversed the majority of my pain. It wasn't until I was already on my way to getting well that I heard the words, Natural Hygiene. I started to do some research on the subject of NH, and I was truly amazed to see that the same steps I had personally achieved success with, to reverse my so-called "incurable" disease, were basically the same steps that are taught in Natural Hygiene. Knowing from my own personal experience that these principles DO work, I was simply thrilled to find that there was an entire healing science premised on these steps!

THE 2 SOURCES OF TOXEMIA:
Endogenous & Exogenous Toxins

You may wonder why I am talking about 'Natural Hygiene' in a chapter that I've titled - TOXIC OVERLOAD: The Many Ways We Poison Ourselves. The reason I am doing so, is because Natural Hygiene teaches that there are two ways we become toxemic, or poisoned. We can become auto-intoxicated (self-poisoned) by endogenous (originating from inside the body) and/or exogenous (originating from outside the body) toxins.

- endogenous - toxins originating from inside the body
- exogenous - toxins originating from outside the body

SOME OF THE WAYS WE BECOME POISONED BY ENDOGENOUS & EXOGENOUS TOXINS

ENDOGENOUS TOXINS originate from the following:

- Natural, normal, on-going metabolic waste; toxic by-products at the cellular level

- The normal and natural death of our cells, from the natural aging process

- Normal emotional and mental stress

- Emotional & mental stress in unnatural excess

- Physical fatigue, both in excess or in normal amounts

EXOGENOUS TOXINS originate from the following:

- Unnatural food & drink typical of The SAD Diet (**SAD** = acronym for **Standard American Diet**) i.e.: processed foods, refined foods, junk foods, and even some foods that have been deranged by cooking

- Improper food combinations that result in Endogenous Toxins upon digestion

- Drugging by taking prescription drugs

- Drugging by taking herbal or other 'natural' supplementation

- Tobacco, alcohol & all forms of recreational drugging

- Environmental and industrial pollutants

- Impure air

- Impure water

For your reference some great web sites on Natural Hygiene can be found at the web sites below...

http://www.angelfire.com/ia/sniadach/
http://www.doctorgraham.cc
http://www.anhs.org/aboutus.htm
http://free.freespeech.org/nhn/
http://members.rotfl.com/sidhwa/
http://www.healthfullivingintl.com

Now let me continue by sharing with you some of the ways we are poisoning ourselves ...

WAYS WE ARE KNOWINGLY AND UNKNOWINGLY POISONING OURSELVES

Dr Samuel Epstein, co-author of ***The Safe Shoppers Bible*** says, "Since 1965 more than 4 million distinct chemical compounds have been reported in the scientific literature; of these, 70,000 are in commercial production and have been completely untested or inadequately tested, which raises questions about their safety."

As you can see, there are many different ways you may be poisoning your body. In the world we live intoday, we experience a toxic overload of unnatural and dangerous chemicals from almost everything we come in contact with; i.e., our food, water, air, house-cleaning supplies, beauty/healthcare products, dental work, and dry-cleaned garments, just to name a few. My intention isn't to scare you, only to inform you. Below I will go into deeper detail on some of the many ways you may be poisoning your body and causing future disease to set hold.

Endogenous Toxins in Detail:

This topic, endogenous toxins, is pretty self-explanatory, but it should not be overlooked. Everyone is going to eventually die. It is a normal, inevitable path that we will all travel. Living life out to an old age is one way our body becomes poisoned by endogenous toxins -- normal wear and tear on our body's cells that comes through the aging process.

You can also become poisoned by endogenous toxins from a direct result of **physical or emotional stress**. I find this is something that we all know, but usually just don't grasp the seriousness of it is usually too late. Excess stress DOES kill.

If you are under immense physical or emotional stress you need to realize that you are causing much harm to your body. You will need to remove the stress from your life if you want to remove your disease. I know it is easier said than done. I know it is a very complicated topic. Entire books and self-help programs are created to help people learn how to get the stress out of their lives. I don't want to try and oversimplify things, but I think the keys to de-stressing come through two major avenues: 1) prioritizing one's life and/or 2) learning to forgive and let go of things you have no control over. I can't possibly go into great detail on this topic, for if I did, I would end up writing an entire other book. I will however cover it in a little more detail in the next chapter. On a positive note please let me assure you that once I took the steps I took to reverse my disease I learned how to keep excess stress out of my life. As I became well it became very clear to me what was really important in life. I have found many others that have also had this happen to them too. As you get 'physically' well, you get 'mentally' well too. Getting physically well and de-stressing seem to go hand in hand.

Exogenous Toxins in Detail:

There are many ways we become auto-intoxicated through exogenous toxins. I'll try to touch on some of the most common ways we become poisoned by exogenous toxins.

ARE RX DRUGS KILLING YOU?

"If prescription drugs are so bad for us, then why do some of them seem to work?" Sometimes you may be given a prescription drug that seems to work. You take it, it alleviates your pain, and you are thankful. So doesn't that mean prescription drugs work? You'll get no argument from me that prescription drugs work. They do. Prescription drugs do exactly what they are intended to do. They were created to ease or eliminate the pain while you are ingesting them. They are intended to suppress pain. Prescription drugs do work if all you are looking for is suppression to the problem. But, if you are looking for a CURE to the problem, prescription drugs are NEVER the answer. There is no magic pill that can cure disease, NOT ONE.

You also have to ask yourself, what further damage is this drug causing to my system? What is the long-term side effect this drug is going to have on me? Are you trusting that the doctors or the drug companies or the FDA is going to protect you? If so, you might want to THINK AGAIN! Many of the severe side affects I suffered from, and thousands of other of women are suffering from because of the birth control injections, aren't even listed on the Material Safety Data Sheet for the those injections. But even though those side affects aren't listed, thousands are still suffering from the same or similar 'symptoms'. These thousands of women are not lying. So never trust with 100% certainty that all of the information is being given to you.

100,000 DIE EACH YEAR FROM RX DRUGS! In 1998 the New England Journal of Medicine reported that properly prescribed legal drugs kill 106,000 Americans every year -- 20 times more than illegal drugs do. Prescription drugs also seriously injure an additional 2.1 million every year, far more than most people realize. Now keep in mind that those are the ADMITTED numbers of deaths from Rx drugs.

In a press release found online at **http://www.geocities.com/socialspit/prescribe.htm**, one of the interviewees named Dasbach points out, **"The government admits that aspirin killed twice as many people last year as PCP and LSD combined!"** He went on to say, **"But don't expect a war on *aspirin*. The government is less interested in protecting lives than in protecting the jobs of the government bureaucrats and law enforcement personnel who are on the Drug Prohibition payroll. "**

Again, there are no arguments from me that prescription drugs do work. They are doing their job; they are **suppressing** your problem, which makes you happy because you can't feel the pain. But what if you could see what real damage was happening to your body as a result of taking these drugs? Out of sight, out of mind. You can't see it, so you don't think about it. But if you want to get well this is something you have to start thinking about.

The cure is worse than the disease! The allopathic doctor's cure -- *prescription drugs and surgeries* -- is often times much worse than the disease itself! Moore, the author of Prescription for Disaster: The Hidden Dangers in Your Medicine Cabinet states... **"Of the 50 top-selling prescription drugs, only four are ''safe,'' says Thomas J. Moore, a medical writer and senior**

fellow in health policy at George Washington University Medical Center. Numerous others, he claims, can cause addiction, cancer, or heart problems. And the number of Americans killed by pharmaceuticals is quadruple the number of people who are murdered and double the number who die in car crashes. Moore says at least a million each year are "severely injured" by their medications. An additional 2 million are harmed by drugs administered during hospital stays." Moore's claims are backed up with references to studies conducted by the U.S. Food & Drug Administration and others.

I disagree with Moore that even 4 of the Rx drugs are safe. I believe all are dangerous. But, this information isn't coming from someone like me who opposes all Rx drugs; it is coming from someone working for a medical center.   Someone from the inside even admits that almost all prescription drugs are unsafe!

Doctors are told in medical school that all drugs are toxic! I was horrified to read in the book Fasting and Eating for Health that Dr. Furhman was told, during his first pharmacology lecture in medical school, that they should **never forget that all drugs are toxic**. That statement shocked me. The very basis of conventional medicine is to treat with drugs and surgery. If all drugs are toxic doesn't it just make sense that you shouldn't try and TREAT someone with a toxic substance?

URGENT NOTE: *If* you are on prescription drugs right now and want to get off, do NOT just stop taking them. A professional must wean you off your medications!! Tell your doctor you want to be weaned off your medications. More than likely your doctor will tell you that you **need** to be taking the medications you are on. In fact, if they don't tell you that then I would be delightfully surprised. But don't worry; I will give you access to information on doctors who will help you get weaned off your medications.

I don't care if you are taking 10 or more different medications; you don't have to be doped up. You can be drug free!

DID VACCINATIONS OR IMMUNIZATIONS POISON YOU?

Your illness may even stem from early childhood vaccinations or immunizations. Below I have listed for you numerous web sites that discuss the dangers of vaccinations.

WEB SITES ON THE DANGERS OF VACCINATIONS

SV-40 A DEADLY CURE?
http://www.viewzone.com/sv40.html

HOW SAFE ARE VACCINATIONS?
http://www.ties.org/sarah/msnbc/

SOPHIE'S STORY: A TERRIBLE, TYPICAL TALE
**http://www.vaccinationnews.com/DailyNews/February200
2/Sophie'sStory.htm**

VACCINATION NEWS: Online Reporting of All Sides of the
Vaccination Controversy
http://www.vaccinationnews.com

AUTISM AND VACCINATION
http://osiris.sunderland.ac.uk/autism/vaccine.htm

VACCINES CAUSE BRAIN DISORDERS IN CHILDREN
http://www.bsuccessful.com/vaccines.htm

VACCINATIONS ARE THEY WORTH THE RISK?
http://www.survivalcenter.com/Vaccinations.html

AUTISM AND MERCURY
**http://www.mercola.com/2001/feb/24/autism_mercury.h
tm**

MAN ALLEGEDLY WRONGLY GIVEN LIFE IMPRISONMENT
AFTER VACCINES KILLED HIS CHILD. (a disturbing read!)
http://www.iahf.com/free_alan/20010904.html

On Dr. Lorraine Day's web site **http://www.drday.com** she
states that waivers for vaccinations are still available. You can get
the information from your public health department, or if they do
not help you, you can educate yourself by ordering a pamphlet
called **"Vaccine State Laws and Vaccine Exemptions"** available
from New Atlantean Press. Call 505-983-1856.

IS YOUR DIET KILLING YOU?

YES, our wrong diets, our **SAD** (Standard American Diet) diets,
are every year slowly killing millions worldwide. Out of all the

endogenous and exogenous toxins that are poisoning our system, the SAD diet, is by the far the largest contributor to our #1 cause of death -- disease!

Processed and refined foods that have indigestible chemical additives and preservatives are killing people. The meat that people eat today is not the same meat that our grandparents ate. Most of our meat has been injected with hormones, steroids, and antibiotics and is responsible for causing disease.   Even dangerous chemicals like pesticides, insecticides and preservatives that are sprayed on our produce, to make it bigger and to make it last longer, are harmful. People who are already sick will be the most affected by these chemicals.

Why are 57% of Americans currently listed as clinically obese? I believe the answer lies with the U.S. Agriculture Department. One of the first events that made the average Americans health start to take a dive was the consumption of the mass-produced soft drinks that began in the 1890's. With this new introduction into society, the average American's sugar intake increased from around 12 pounds per year to nearly 120 pounds per year by 1928. By 1996, this had grown to 152 pounds of sugar intake per year! Can you even fathom that?

Another event that compounded our health decline was the introduction of mass-produced white flour in that same decade. From that time on things really started going down hill.

Another thing we are using today that was not used years ago is food preservatives. Food preservatives are used to prolong shelf life and improve the taste of processed foods. Additives can be simple substances as salt or sugar to artificial chemicals used as antioxidants, anti-microbial, or artificial colors for better eye appeal. Currently there are over 3000 additives used in processing that have a variety of functions. But what **long-term** studies are done on these additives? How can they tell you what is going to happen to you 20 or 30 years done the road if they have not had the majority of these additives around long enough for long term studies to have been conducted?

Prior to 1912 the heart attack or coronary occlusion was totally unheard of. Today it kills 50% of us. Sugar has absolutely no nutritional value and is deadly. If it were a new product submitted to the FDA for approval, it would be banned in an instant. Excess sugar in the body is converted and stored as fat.

The number of people getting cancer has increased from 1 in 33 in 1900 to 1 in 2.5 people today. It is estimated that in about 20 years 1 in 2 people will be diagnosed with cancer and half of them will die. According to the American Heart Association (AHA) statistics, there are 53 million Americans with cardiovascular diseases, which include arteriolosclerosis, high blood pressure, and strokes. What has changed so drastically from 1900 until now? Our DIET. There were no Coca-Cola, no Ding-Dongs, and no TV dinners, etc., back then. But take a look around in the supermarkets today. The amount of frozen, packaged, boxed, and canned foods is unbelievable! How are these foods able to sit on the shelves for so long? They are filled with chemical additives and preservatives, that's how. These additives and preservatives are killing people.

There is no doubt that our society is addicted to fast foods, junk foods, and even healthy, **cooked** foods. If I had it my way parents that let their children eat junk food on a daily basis would be considered guilty of child abuse. There is no nutritional value in the fast food and junk food that people are not only stuffing into their own mouths, but also putting into the mouths of their own innocent children. We are dying of an inadequate diet in a country where our surplus of food is astounding.

We are eating to socialize, we are eating to relax, we are eating because we are depressed, but very few people are eating for the reason God intended for us to eat; to sustain a healthy body.

The fast food chains sell foods that are mostly high in fat, salt, sugar, and cholesterol content. All of those things are bad for you. Despite studies showing a link between consuming those types of foods and obesity, diabetes, coronary heart disease, high blood pressure, strokes, elevated cholesterol intake, related cancers, and other health problems, people are still eating this way.

But it is not just the fast food joints you have to avoid. The majority of the food in your supermarket is completely devoid of any nutrition too. By eating these things you are only filling your body with empty calories. You remain 'hungry all the time', because your body is not getting the vitamins, minerals, and nutrients it so desperately needs to survive.

Many people walk around in the dark believing that, because it is sitting on a store shelf, it can't be harmful. That is not true. Once we start learning about the toxins that we are ingesting, even in such 'healthy' foods as our fruits and vegetables, we can then make a conscious decision of what we want to put, and what we **don't** want to put, in our bodies. As consumers it is our demand that creates the supply. If we start choosing organic food products over inorganic food products the farmers and food producers will meet our demand.

HOW YOU CAN KEEP YOUR DIET FROM KILLING YOU

In the next chapter I will devote an entire section on what foods you should eat and what foods you shouldn't eat if you want to 1) remove your disease and 2) prevent it from coming back.

IS HOW YOUR FOOD IS COOKED KILLING YOU?

Even how we COOK our food can be responsible for our disease.

Microwaving Food:

Do you have any knowledge of the alteration food goes under through cooking processes such as microwaving? Do you know what the long-term affects of eating microwaved food can do to your body?   Some say the long-term effects of eating this "altered" food are unknown, others say it is not only dangerous but can be deadly. Something you may want to ask yourself is how long has the microwave been around? If you don't know the answer let me tell you. In 1947, Raytheon demonstrated the world's first microwave oven and called it a Radarange. Sometime between 1952-55, Tappan introduced the first home model priced at $1295. Technological advances and further developments led to a microwave oven that was polished and affordable for the consumer kitchen. In the late 70's is when they started to really take off and become more common household accessories. How on earth can you give me the LONG-TERM side affects of using something when it isn't that old to begin with?

Radiolytic compounds are compounds that are formed in food that has been microwaved. Radiolytic compounds are mutations that are unknown in the natural world. Ordinary cooking also causes the formation of some radiolytic compounds (which is why it is much better for us to eat a diet high in *raw* fruits, vegetables, sprouts, nuts and seeds), but microwaving cooking causes a much greater number.

There have been very few studies done on microwaving foods and its effect on our health. One prominent study that was done on the effects of microwaved food was done by two researchers by the names of Blanc and Hertel. Before starting their research Hertel worked as a food scientist for several years with a major Swiss food company. He was fired from his job for questioning procedures in processing food because they denatured it. He got together with Blanc of the Swiss Federal Institute of Biochemistry and the University Institute for Biochemistry to conduct tests on the effects of microwaving foods.

After taking blood samples from volunteers over a two-month period in 1992, the two researchers found that the nutrients in all the milk and vegetables that were heated in a microwave oven were degraded, causing significant changes in the blood chemistry of consumer. Their tests also showed that consuming microwaved foods caused cholesterol levels to increase, white blood cell numbers to increase, and red blood cell numbers to decrease. Hertel and Blanc also deduced that glowing bacteria indicated that high amounts of energy were being transferred to food, and to consumers of microwaved food.

Hertel's findings about the effects of microwaved foods being consumed appeared in an article published in issue number 19 of the Journal Franz Weber. Hertel noted that the consumption of food cooked in microwave ovens caused cancer-type effects in the blood.

As soon as Hertel and Blanc announced their results, they were attacked. A powerful trade organization, the Swiss Association of Dealers in Electro apparatuses for Households and Industry, known simply as FEA, struck swiftly. They forced the President of the Court of Seftigen, Canton Bern, to issue a "gag order" against Hertel and Blanc. Scared that he would face hefty fines or up to one year in prison Blanc quickly recanted his support. Hertel stood his ground and battled it out in court.

In March 1993, the court handed down this decision based to prohibit Dr. Ing and Hans Hertel from declaring any public statements or talks that food prepared in the microwave oven is dangerous to health and leads to changes in the blood of consumers.

Hertel continued to fight, and in 1998, that decision was reversed. The European Court of Human Rights held that there had been a violation of Hertel's rights in the 1993 decision. The Court of Human Rights decided that the "gag order" issued by the Swiss courts against Dr. Hertel, prohibiting him from declaring that microwave ovens are dangerous to health, was contrary to the right of freedom of expression.

A few others have written about the dangers of microwaved foods too. In the April 1992 issue of Pediatrics Journal, they reported on a Stanford study showing that microwaved breast milk loses important vitamins and antibodies that fend off malevolent microbes. Yet this information isn't common knowledge and many mothers warm their baby's bottles in a microwave.

I did some research online and found quite a few web sites discussing the dangers of microwaving our food. I, for one, no longer use my microwave. If you want to do some further reading on this topic please check out the following web sites. The top web site is an absolute MUST read for anyone concerned about the dangers of microwaving food.

http://www.rfsafe.com/cookingmicrowaves.htm
http://www.rifeenergymedicine.com/Microwaving.html
http://www.health101.org/art_microwaving.htm
http://www.manbir-online.com/htm3/new.48.htm
http://www.besthealth.com.au/microwaveart.htm

Irradiating Food:

Besides microwaving there is also something going on called *"irradiation"*. We are irradiating meat to destroy pathogens, insects and bacteria! Who is irradiating our meat and why? It was the beef lobby that decided to start irradiating meat. They did so because of all the tainted hamburgers that were causing people to fall so desperately ill. The FDA publicly had to recall a lot of tainted beef, which of course was really BAD publicity for them, and you know they can't afford bad publicity. Just look at what they tried to do to Oprah when she said she wasn't eating a hamburger ever again. So here you have these meat guys trying to think up way to stop the sickness. Then all of a sudden... VIOLA! Someone says, **"Let's just expose it to radiation!"** The radiation will kill the bacteria, but they don't think about what it will do to the consumer. By us allowing meat irradiation to take place, this allows the food industry to continue to sell dirty, contaminated products to the public without cleaning up their practices! Irradiated food is still contaminated; the contamination is merely sterilized.

The Cornell University in 1977 irradiated some sugar and fed it to rats. **The type of cell damage shown on post mortem was the same as if the rats themselves had been irradiated!** This is what is happening to you when you eat irradiated meat!

At the University of Illinois, the Department of Medicine fed radiated food to mice. Seventeen percent had to be killed or died because of respiratory problems so severe they couldn't even move around their cages. They did autopsies. The hearts of the mice had enlarged to twice to three times normal, and in some cases had burst.

Researchers at the Medical College of Virginia fed rats radiated beef to study the effects of eating radiated meat. Within 34 days all the male rats died of hemorrhagic syndrome. "Hemorrhagic" means excessive discharge of blood from the blood vessels; i.e., profuse bleeding. They investigated the effect of hormones by castrating a group of male rats and then feeding them with radiated beef. They all died within 63-days. All female rats died as well.

If you want a more detailed horror story about the process of irradiation, I would suggest you read **"The Food That Would Last Forever"** by Dr. Gary Gibbs, an authority on food radiation.

Irradiating even harms beneficial nutrients -- about 30% of Vitamin C is destroyed; milk is known to lose 70% of vitamin A, B1 and B2 when radiated; vitamins E, K, the entire B group, amino acids, and essential fatty acids are all known to be adversely affected by irradiation.

Thinking the FDA is going to protect you? Thinking that food that is irradiated is labeled? If so, THINK AGAIN! The FDA requires a label to be put on irradiated food only if "whole food" is radiated and then sold unchanged. But if the food is processed in any way for example if it has had any other ingredients added to it, no label disclosure is required!

To date, FDA has approved irradiation of raw meat, raw poultry, spices, fresh shell eggs, and seeds for sprouting

Grilling Food:

Even cooking on the grill has been proven to be harmful for you. My nutritionist shared with me a strange story about one of her clients that use to grill on a weekly basis. When this woman was going through the detoxification process she actually started to smell just like the 'burnt' smell that you get when barbecuing foods. This lasted for days. The husband of the lady this happened to even confirmed that his wife smelled like 'grilled' meat. This story popped into my head while writing this chapter and it prompted me to search the internet for some similar stories. The web site below has some interesting information on the dangers of 'grilling' out.

Is It True That Grilling Out Causes Cancer?
http://www.howstuffworks.com/question253.htm

Frying Food:

What happened with the report that was all over the news for a few days about French fries having a chemical in them that caused cancer? The chemical they were referring to was called acrylamide. Acrylamide is a chemical that is used to make plastics and dyes, and it is proven to cause cancer in animals. The food industry managed to get that story hushed up in a hurry didn't they? Scientists in Sweden tested more than 100 food items and discovered that some potato and cereal products that were fried, oven-baked and deep-fried contained high levels of acrylamide.

The two web sites below have additional information on acrylamide for those who want to investigate it further.

Acrylamide: The food toxin that could cause cancer.
http://www.health-freedom-nutrition.com/articles/020918acrylamide.html

ABCNEWS.COM WHO To*(???)* Evaluate Deep-Frying Cancer Link
http://abcnews.go.com/sections/living/DailyNews/WHO_acrylamide020625.html

The Cooking of Food in General:

Other methods of cooking food, such as simply baking it or warming it on the stove also cause great changes in the composition of the food to take place. Some not near as harmful of others of course but changes nonetheless, changes that take all of the nutrients out of the foods.

Why do we eat? We must eat to sustain life. The majority does not eat for that reason however. They eat to be social, they eat because they are stressed or depressed, happy or sad. Very rarely do people stop to realize that the reason we should eat first and foremost is to provide our bodies with the vitamins, minerals and nutrients they need.

A very small percentage of people never stop to realize that by cooking food, such as our precious vegetables, they become completely denatured. Cooking makes food, in a word, "worthless". Enzymes are lost when we cook at temperatures above 116 degrees.

So what is the purpose of eating food if we cannot gain any nutrients from it? Do you see the great importance of adding fresh, raw fruits and vegetables into our diet? I will provide more information on this topic, Cooked Food vs. Raw Food in **Chapter 7: Cooked Food Vs. Raw Food: The Facts**

Preserving Food:

Most people never once turn over the bag of chips, cookies or canned foods to read the ingredient list. Others who may be concerned for their health might do so, but they quickly stop looking because it all looks like a bunch of gibberish.

What you need to know is that most food additives are made out of chemicals. It is also important for you to understand that many of the chemicals used in additives and preservatives put into your food have not been tested on a long-term basis in humans. And, what about the dangers of eating combinations of various additives/preservatives? No long-term studies there either I'm afraid. By blindly ingesting these chemicals, as the majority of our society is doing, you are submitting yourself as a guinea pig. Just take a look around at society. It seems almost everyone is sick, overweight, or on drugs for some type of health condition.

Our bodies are not designed to ingest these chemicals (additives/preservatives). Clearly, anyone who has the slightest desire to avoid disease or heal themselves must avoid the most toxic substances, such as: Monosodium glutamate or MSG (and it's secret label names: MSG, hydrolyzed proteins, autolyzed yeast,

yeast extract, caseinates, "natural flavors"), Olestra, and Aspartame. But, the dangers go well beyond those three.

For most people that need to detoxify toxins out of their bodies to reverse their disease, it is imperative that they gradually and completely eliminate all preservatives, additives, coloring, artificial sweeteners (e.g., Sunnette/acesulfame-k, Splenda/sucralose, saccharine, NutraSweet 2000, etc.), and other dangerous and unhealthy ingredients from their diet. I know at first, especially if you are a junk food junkie, this will seem to be a daunting task, but the process becomes relatively easy once you start to feel better from eliminating these things from your diet. As your health starts to improve you will soon see the detrimental effect eating these chemically laden foods has had on your body.

As you progress in changing your diet, the task of eliminating these processed and preserved foods is made even easier if you make the decision to only purchase bagged and or canned foods from a health food stores, or the 'healthy' section of your grocery store. Keep in mind however: Even if you do purchase your foods from these areas, you STILL should be careful to read the labels. You will find that most health food stores won't carry anything with harmful chemicals in them. If you **must** buy canned foods, choose ones that have only ascorbic acid (vitamin c) or sea salt as their only preservative. If you follow the steps I lay out for you in my next chapter the majority of the food you buy will be fresh fruits and vegetables so you won't have any labels to worry about.

For those of you who want more information on the subject of food additives and preservatives I will be adding information as I gather it to my online message boards at
http://www.rawandjuicy.com/messageboard.html.

IS WHAT YOU'RE DRINKING POISONING YOU?

What's in your water? Water is the best thing for you right? Well, that depends on of course what is IN the water you are drinking.

What comes out of the tap is spiked with chlorine, a known carcinogen, and with fluoride, which has been found to break down the collagen in the bones, the glue which gives them strength and flexibility.

But there's more than just chlorine and fluoride in some people's water. I've read literally hundreds of online articles on this subject. On the web site
http://www.waterwater.net/news6.htm it states, "**Are your children drinking harmful pesticides? That depends on where you live. A new study, released in August by the Environmental Working Group (EWG), discovered that tap water in many Midwest cities contains potentially dangerous levels of pesticides. Out of 29 cities tested over the summer, 18 had traces of weed-killers, such as atrazine and cyanazine that exceeded the EPA's safety standards. Children and infants - who drink more water in relation to their body weight than adults - may be especially at risk because they're still going through critical stages of development, says J. Routt Reigart, MD, a professor of pediatrics at the Medical University of South Carolina and past chair of the American Academy of Pediatrics Committee on Environmental Health.**"

Also on that web site the question, "Is lead a danger in our drinking water?" is answered by stating, **"It can be, and those who are most susceptible to its ill effects are infants and children younger than 6. Exposure to the substance can cause developmental problems, learning disabilities, and lethargy. While the main source of lead poisoning in children is from paint in houses built before 1980, lead can get into drinking water from faucets or pipes. The EPA estimates that 15 percent of the nation's households have lead in faucets, pipes, or well pumps. People living in houses built before 1930 are at highest risk, since lead pipes were used in plumbing at that time. But any house built before 1988, before lead laws were implemented, may have lead solder in its pipes."**

Pure water is essential to life. Without it man would soon die. Notice I stressed the word *"pure."* Is your water pure? In my opinion the best book you can read on the dangers of your tap water, is Paul Bragg's book, **Water: The Shocking Truth**.

The following is an excerpt from that book.

TEN COMMONSENSE REASONS WHY YOU SHOULD ONLY DRINK PURE DISTILLED WATER!

1: There are over 12,000 chemicals on the market today . . . and 500 are being added annually! Regardless of where you live - in the city or on the farm, some of these chemicals are getting into your drinking water.

2: No one knows what effects these toxic chemicals may have upon the body and what and how many toxic combinations are created. It's like making a mixture of colors; one drop can change the color.

3: No equipment has been designed to detect these harmful chemical combinations and may not be for years.

4: The body is made up of approximately 70% water, the essential fluid of life. Therefore, don't you think you should be wise about the type of water you drink?

5: The Navy has been drinking distilled water for years!

6: Distilled water is chemical and mineral free. Distillation removes all the chemicals and impurities from water that are possible to remove. If distillation doesn't remove them, there is no method known today that will.

7: The body does need minerals, but it's not necessary that they come from water. There is not one mineral in water which cannot be found more abundantly in food! Water is the most unreliable source of minerals because it varies from one area to another. The food we eat - not the water we drink - is our best reliable source of organic minerals!

8: Distilled water is used for intravenous feeding, inhalation therapy, prescriptions and baby formulas. Therefore, doesn't it make common sense that distilled water is good and healthier for everyone?

9: Thousands of water distillers have been sold throughout the United States and many foreign countries to individuals, families, dentists, doctors, hospitals, nursing homes and government agencies . . . and these informed, alert consumers are helping protect their health by using only pure distilled water.

10: With all of the chemicals, pollutants and other impurities in our water, it only makes good common sense that you should clean up the water you drink the inexpensive way, through distillation.

It's not just impure water that you should be concerned about. If you are drinking coffee, pop, or other 'bottled' juices or drinks you need to ask yourself, "What's inside this, and is it causing me any damage?" Many of these things are loaded with things like caffeine and sugar, or artificial sweeteners, which are not good for healthy bodies, let alone sick ones.

The DANGER of Aspartame! - This FDA approved sweetener is now being linked to a long list of diseases, including but NOT limited to: Gulf War Syndrome, MSL and Alzheimer's. I think many people know that aspartame is dangerous, even deadly. Unfortunately there are still many who are in the dark on this subject. Just do a search on the internet about aspartame and you will find thousands of web sites touting the dangers of this deadly FDA-APPROVED chemical. Some web sites for those of you interested in going online to learn more are...

http://www.aspartamekills.com - Aspartame Kills

http://holisticmed.com/aspartame - Aspartame Toxicity Information Center

http://web2.airmail.net/marystod/index.html - Aspartame Consumer Safety Network

http://presidiotex.com/aspartame - Aspartame victims support group

Diet soda is even more dangerous than regular soda but both will poison your system with things your body is not designed to digest and assimilate. Be aware of what you are putting into your body.

People are not drinking enough water. If you are not eating a Natural Hygiene-type of raw food diet you should be drinking at least eight 8-oz. glasses of water each day. I will touch on the importance of drinking enough water in a later chapter. My water intake is much less than that because I am on a diet that is very water-sufficient. If you take my advice and make the same dietary changes I have you too will be getting much of your water needs from the fresh fruits and vegetables you eat. Unfortunately 99% of you who will read my book do eat a diet that is mostly cooked foods and when this is the case your body will require a minimum of eight 8-oz glasses of water each day. Until the time you transition to the same diet I am on, make sure you drink your PURE water and plenty of it.

Note: Do NOT rely solely on the water treatment company you may be using to tell you if there are dangerous chemicals in your water. Have a non-partial outside source test your water.

IS TECHNOLOGY KILLING YOU?
Microwaves, High-Voltage Power Lines, Computers, Cell Phones... Are They Causing Cancer??

The following information was written by Neal Lawrence and was taken, with permission, from Midwest Today Magazine's (P.O. Box 685 - Panora, Iowa 50216). Their web page can be viewed at...

http://www.midtod.com/9603/voltage.phtml

It was sort of a funny story when we first heard about it a few years ago: A dairy farmer living in Wisconsin near high voltage utility company transmission lines couldn't turn out the lights in his barn. Even with the switches in the off position, night after night after he had finished his chores, he'd go back out to the barn to find the light bulbs still glowing from the electrical charge hovering in the air. The cows were none too happy about it either, because the constant light prevented them from sleeping, and they gave less milk.

But the story doesn't seem so funny any more -- not after the spate of recent reports of children developing deadly illnesses or adults dying prematurely of rare diseases -- all apparently because they had the misfortune of living near high amounts of electrical current.

A growing body of scientific evidence suggests that invisible electromagnetic fields (EMF's) -- created by everything from high-voltage utility company lines to personal computers, microwave ovens, TVs and even electric blankets -- are linked to a frightening array of cancers and other serious health problems in children and adults.

Though it received scant attention from the mainstream press, a report leaked last October from the U.S. National Council on Radiation Protection said there is a powerful body of impressive evidence showing that even very low exposure to electromagnetic radiation has long-term effects on health.

The report cited studies that show EMF's can disturb the production of the hormone melatonin, which is linked with sleep patterns. It said there was strong evidence that children exposed to EMF's had a higher risk of leukemia.

This follows on the heels of three epidemiological reports released in 1994. One indicated a tie between occupational exposure to EMF's and Alzheimer's disease. Another suggested a link with Sudden Infant Death Syndrome (SIDS). The third study indicated a tie with amyotrophic lateralsclerosis.

Now a surprising new report released in February by physicists at Britain's University of Bristol shows that power lines attract particles of radon -- a colorless, odorless gas irrefutably linked with cancer.

What's this all about? And why have the media failed to report with the appropriate emphasis the implications of these significant health risks?

Shortly after her son Kevin was diagnosed with leukemia, Julie Larm, of Omaha, NE, began to notice other children at the local pool who had lost their hair or had surgical scars. As her suspicion rose, she began talking to other parents. One person she contacted was Dee Hendricks, whose son was also undergoing cancer treatment. Together they collected the names of eleven children in the area who had cancer.

When they plotted them on a map they were surprised to see that all lived within one mile of each other and an electric power substation.

"If there was nothing to worry about, why does our utility have an EMF committee...which was in effect long before we came and started making noise?" asks Larm, a member of the Omaha Parents for the Prevention of Cancer. "Why do they need such things if there's nothing to it?"

The group's efforts have been buttressed by Paul Brodeur, a campaigning environmental journalist who had in his day taken on asbestos and chlorofluorocarbons and is the author of two books on the subject of EMF's. Brodeur is convinced that EMF's are one of the greatest environmental threats facing the nation.

"Never before has there been this much epidemiological evidence of the carcinogenicity of any agent," says Brodeur, "and that agent declared to be benign."

Robert Becker, MD, author of *Cross Currents* (Tarcher, 1990), who has studied this subject since the 1960s*(,)* warns, "EMF's could turn out to be a far worse environmental disaster, affecting far more people than toxic waste, radiation or asbestos." **For the rest of this story please go to the web page:**

http://www.midtod.com/9603/voltage.phtml

When something is new, or fairly new, how can anybody tell you it is safe? We don't know the long-term side affects of living near such things as high-voltage power lines. We also don't know what can happen from using such things as our computers or using our cell phones. I found equally disturbing information on that too. There are no long-term studies to research, because there are no long-term studies done. If this is a concern for you, limit the time you spend using these products, or eliminate the use of them all together.

If this topic is of interest you, you may find the following web sites very informative...

Are You Killing Your Brain With Your Mobile Phone
http://www.rocknroll.force9.co.uk/science/mobiletelephon es.html

Microwaving Your Food Isn't Safe
http://www.wellbeingjournal.com/microwaving.htm

ABCNEWS.COM 20/20 Are Cell Phones Safe?
http://abcnews.go.com/onair/2020/2020_000526_cellpho nes.html

Are EMF's dangerous?

The following is from the Center For Disease Control's Government web site at

http://www.cdc.gov/niosh/emf2.html

"**What Are EMF's?** EMF's are invisible lines of force created whenever electricity is generated or used. EMF's are produced by power lines, electric wiring and electric equipment and appliances. The frequency of EMF's is measured in hertz (Hz, or cycles per second). People are exposed to both electric and magnetic fields, but scientists are most concerned about magnetic fields. This fact sheet deals only with magnetic fields that have frequencies near 60 Hz, the frequency of electric power in North America."

"**Do EMF's cause cancer or other health effects?** Studies have shown that some workers exposed to high magnetic fields have increased cancer rates. But such associations do not necessarily show that EMF exposures cause cancer (any more than the springtime association of robins and daffodils shows that one causes the other). Scientists have looked carefully at all the EMF evidence, but they disagree about the health effects of EMF's except to say that better information is needed."

For me personally, hearing the statement 'better information is needed' is enough for me to try and keep my contact with EMF's to a minimum.

The web pages I've just listed are only a tiny fraction of what is available on the internet on this subject. If you feel compelled please feel free to go online and do your own further investigation.

IS THE INDOOR AIR YOU'RE BREATHING KILLING YOU?

Many of us get very little fresh air. It is said that the average adult spends 90% of their time indoors. We go from our homes, to our cars, to our workplace back into our homes. We need to get more FRESH AIR! I will cover the importance of fresh air and sunshine later in this book. Often when I was little, I would run to my mom and moan, "Mom what can I do? I'M BORED!" Her reply was always; "Go outside and get the stink blown off you." That is what we ALL need to do. Okay, I don't really know where the 'get the stink blown off you' part comes from, but we can all benefit from the first part of my mother's message to me... 'GO OUTSIDE'.

What are indoor air pollutants? Just some examples of indoor air pollutants are carbon monoxide, nitrogen dioxide, and other combustion pollutants, including secondary tobacco smoke. Bacteria and viruses, mold, pet dander, insect parts (dust mites or roaches), and chemicals found in some arts and craft supplies, household cleaning supplies, and even our personal care and beauty products. Some other examples of indoor air pollutants are faulty furnaces, mold growing in carpeting, or even a freshly painted room. Even burning candles can emit small amounts of toxins such as acetone, benzene, lead and mercury into the air. Some cases, like one that I viewed on a television talk show recently, was a woman who became desperately ill because of the chemicals used in the dry-cleaning of her bedspread! Her doctors couldn't help her. Worse yet, the doctor eventually called her husband into tell him that he needed to have his wife admitted to a mental hospital because she was crazy! When she told that story I really felt her pain. No doctors came out and told my husband or me I was crazy, but I sure felt like they did because they could never find a 'source' to my pain. When the doctor's kept saying, "Your tests say you are fine," I felt like they thought I was lying about being in pain.

This women, who was having a reaction to the chemicals used in the dry cleaning of her bedspread, was only cured once she found the cause, eliminated it and then detoxified her body.

Pollutants from outside the home can even come into your home and be an indoor air pollutant. One example is a car running in the garage attached to the house. More examples are burning leaves or trash, or radon coming into your house from the ground below.

What Are The Risks of Indoor Air Pollutants? - Breathing indoor air pollutants can lead to a myriad of problems. Some of which are asthmatic reactions, allergic reactions, and infections. In the case of the women above who was poisoned by the dry cleaning chemicals she suffered from a plethora of symptoms like muscle pain and weakness, fatigue, inability to breathe, and so much more. Things like headaches, nausea, vomiting, brain damage, and even death can occur when high enough levels of carbon monoxide are inhaled. Exposure to radon may increase the risk of lung cancer. Exposure to VOC's (Volatile Organic Compounds) may affect the lungs, brain, and nervous systems.

How do Indoor Air Pollutants Affect Your Health? - Some people may be affectedly greatly while others are not affected at all by indoor air pollutants. How indoor air pollutants affect us depends on a number of factors. One factor is the overall health of a person. Healthy individuals will of course not be affected as severely, if at all, by the same indoor air pollutant that can make an ill person even sicker. Age is another factor. Infants and the elderly are usually much more sensitive to indoor air pollutants because their immune systems are either not yet fully developed, or are weak. Regardless of health or age however, there are two other factors that will determine how your health can be affected by indoor air pollutants. Those two things are: 1) the amount of pollutant you inhale and 2) the length of time you are exposed to the pollutant.

How Can I Reduce Exposure to Indoor Air Pollutants In My Home? - A few tips on how to reduce indoor air pollutants are listed below. This is not an all-inclusive list. The following information was taken, with permission, from the Vermont Department of Health web site at:

http://www.healthyvermonters.info/hp/airquality/indoorair.shtml

To decrease the risk of exposure and health effects, a number of actions can be taken. In general, decrease or remove the source of pollution, stop or reduce the pathways that pollutants may take and increase ventilation (fresh air).

- Install a carbon monoxide detector that meets UL rating 2034 and be aware of possible sources of carbon monoxide pollution in your home. Have your furnace, boiler, and gas stove checked and serviced once a year, or more if necessary. Have stove pipe and chimneys checked and cleaned as often as needed, especially if you burn wood. Don't idle your car's engine in an attached garage. Don't operate a space heater (kerosene, etc.) unless it's vented to the outside. Don't smoke in the house.

  You can see a fact sheet on carbon monoxide at their web site.

- Test your home for radon, the second leading cause of lung cancer.

  You can see a fact sheet on radon at their web site.

- Increase ventilation. In some cases, opening the windows and doors to provide fresh air from the outside can do this. Installing exhaust fans in bathrooms and kitchens and properly maintaining air filter systems will also help air quality.

- Keep your home in good repair. Prevent or repair roof, pipe, and basement leaks. Prevent or reduce mold growth and the spread of mold spores by venting the clothes dryer, the bathroom, and the area by the kitchen stove to the outside of the house. Limit the use of humidifiers and maintain and clean them regularly and frequently. Using a dehumidifier in high moisture areas such as the basement can help. Discard water damaged porous items (sheetrock, paneling, carpets, furniture, etc.) especially if repeatedly dampened or wet for more than 24 hours. Regularly clean the drip pan under your refrigerator. Keep your home warm enough to prevent moisture buildup or condensation (and mold growth), especially in poorly insulated areas. Properly insulate and correctly install a vapor barrier in wall and ceiling areas. In winter, do not allow the indoor relative humidity to go over 50 percent.

You can see a fact sheet on mold at their web site.

- Limit the use of carpeting, an easy gathering and possible growing place for biological pollutants like mold, dust mites, and bacteria. Do not use carpeting directly on cement floors or in damp areas like the basement. Consider limiting where pets, (dogs, cats, etc.) can travel in your house or not allowing pets to occupy carpeted areas of the house.

You can see a fact sheet on carpeting at their web site.

- Care for carpeting. Use a HEPA (High Efficiency Particulate Air) filtering vacuum cleaner daily. Leave shoes by the entry door. Do not saturate your carpeting if wet-cleaning it. Use 140 degree F water with an extractor to reduce the amount of water remaining in the carpeting. Limit or do not use high solvent cleaners when cleaning the carpet. Use fans and a dehumidifier in the carpeted room in order to dry it within 24 hours.

- Reduce your use of household chemicals. When you have a choice between two products that produce the same cleaning results, choose the least toxic. Look at ingredients on the label, or obtain an MSDS (Material Safety Data Sheet) from the company. Under "Health Hazard Rating," which gives a rating between 0 and 4, consider choosing the one with the lowest number. Consider alternate hobbies, or alternate hobby-related products, if the hobby could expose you to harmful fumes or vapors.

- Store chemicals properly in an area not normally occupied by people, such as a garage or shed, and safely out of reach of children. Buy only the amount you need and store in original container so that safety information is not lost.

- Read and follow directions for use on the label. Do not mix any cleaning products unless directed on the product label. When instructions read, "Use with adequate ventilation," strongly consider using the product outside the building. If the product is used inside the building, increase ventilation by opening a window and using exhaust fans.

Other tips I want to add on this subject ...

- Buy items that don't need to be dry-cleaned WHENEVER possible. You don't know what chemicals or how many chemicals they are using for sure. Some people, especially already enervated, elderly or small children may have violent reactions to these chemicals.

- Buy organic household cleaning supplies. There ARE organic solutions, and the products work just as well, and in my opinion some of them even BETTER than those containing chemicals. Like the organic window cleaner I have for instance. Windex cannot compare to this stuff!! Don't know where to buy them? No worries, I'll tell you. At the end of this chapter I will list for you the web sites that I use to buy my household cleaning supplies, health care and beauty products! (And in case any of you are wondering: **No, I do not get paid on the sale of any of these products.** This is a non-biased opinion of products I actually use and recommend.)

- If you use a wood stove or fireplace clean the chimney regularly. Burn only dry wood, and do not use synthetic logs or newspapers.

- If you are doing any painting in your home make sure you paint with paint that leaves the mold retardant and fungicides out. When painting, use only paint with low VOC (volatile organic chemicals) levels, like Sherwin Williams

HealthSpec™ Low Odor interior latex paint, wear a mask and have proper ventilation.

- Let fresh air into your house as often as possible. Some in warmer climates may never have to use an air conditioner or furnace. Others, who do have to use air conditioners and furnaces, give them a break whenever possible. Spring, summer, and fall. Keep your windows open as often as you can and breathe in that fresh air.

- While real plants are beautiful, they can also cause problems. Mold can often grow in the soil after the plant is watered. In the book Natural Detoxification, by Jacqueline Krohn, MD and Frances Taylor, MA, it recommends that you use Impregnon or taheebo tea (both available at health food stores) added in your houseplant water to retard the growth of mold in soil of your houseplants.

- Keep a clean home. Vacuum carpets daily. Dust frequently. Don't let the dust build up! Dusting regularly will also help prevent mold growth.

INDOOR AIR QUALITY TESTING SERVICES

Home Test Kits

The following web sites offer home test kits for testing such things like asbestos, radon, carbon monoxide, mold and mildew, VOC's, and formaldehyde.

http://www.air-techinternational.com/Testing%20Kits.html

http://www.homestoreproducts.com/cart/index.html?mid=HomeStore

http://www.inspect-ny.com/sickhouse/bulksamp.htm

http://www.healthgoods.com/Shopping/Home_Test_Kits/Indoor_Air_Quality_Testing.asp

Other Indoor Air Quality Resources

U.S. Environmental Protection Agency
Indoor Air Quality Information Web Site
http://www.epa.gov/iaq

Indoor Air Quality Information Clearinghouse
Phone: 800-438-4318
or email: iaqinfo@aol.com

National Radon Information Hotline
800-SOS-RADON
800-767-7236

National Lead Information Center
800-LEAD-INFO
800-532-3394
http://www.epa.gov/lead/nlic.htm

Healthy Indoor Air For America's Homes
406-994-3451
http://www.healthyindoorair.org

ARE YOUR HOUSEHOLD CLEANING SUPPLIES POISONING YOU?

Take a look at look at the ingredients on labels of your household cleaning supplies. First thing you notice is that the print is so very tiny. The reason it is so very tiny is because the list is like a mile long. Do you know what these chemicals are? Do you even recognize what a few of them are? Do you know anything about the harmful side affects of short-term or prolonged exposure to these chemicals? More than likely your answer is no.

I threw away all of the cleaning supplies from my home. The Pledge, the Windex, the "scrubbing bubbles." I tossed out our laundry detergents, fabric softener, and dishwashing detergent. I threw them all out because not only did they all contain chemicals with names I couldn't even pronounce, but I had no idea what the chemicals were or what harm they could cause. Who knows the long-term side affects of using these products? I don't, and I am not going to trust someone else's tests. I've learned that lesson the hard way. The FDA-approved birth control injections that I took were supposed to be "safe." Yet I, and thousands of other

women, were poisoned by these FDA-approved injections. And
even though thousands of horror stories are being documented on
just my web site alone,
http://www.abcinternetmarketing.com/depo-provera the FDA has
still done nothing to take this drug off the market. So, if you think
that something is available to the public only because it is perfectly
safe, you are dreadfully wrong.

I replaced all of my household cleaning products with safer,
chemical free alternatives. There is a plethora of chemical free
home cleaning supplies on the internet. I use the BI-O-KLEEN
products. I do not sell them. I am not a representative for the
company. I make absolutely no money off of mentioning their
name. I just want to get that out of the way for any skeptics who
may be reading my book.

I've used the BI-O-KLEEN products for months now and all the
ones I have used work great. The glass cleaner is actually better
than any other chemically laden glass-cleaning product I have ever
used.

You can find the retailer of BI-O-KLEEN products that is nearest
you by visiting their web site at http**://www.bi-o-kleen.com**

BI-O-KLEEN does not sell direct to the public, so you do have to
purchase from one of their distributors.

There are many other companies that sell safe household cleaning
supplies too. It is just a matter of what you want to buy. NOTE:
Just because a web site uses words like "all natural," it can still
have chemicals in it. You still must be sure to read the ingredient
list of the products you are buying, regardless of what it says on
the front. "All natural" doesn't necessarily mean anything. I found
some web sites that claimed to have all natural products, yet they
didn't offer ingredient lists for their products. Make sure you read
the ingredients first before buying! Do some research on your
own. If you are at all curious about the long-term side affects to
your or your family's health from using these products, know there
are safer alternatives.

WHAT'S REALLY INSIDE YOUR
PERSONAL CARE & BEAUTY PRODUCTS?

Every day you entrust your safety to a host of manufacturing
companies. You are trusting that they care about selling you

products that are 100% safe. The majority of companies sell products with one sole purpose: To make money.

You may be bathing with a soap that contains chemicals known to be carcinogens. You might be using a skin lotion that contains anti-freeze. Your shampoo could contain chemicals that are used in many industrial de-greasers. The deodorant you and your family are using may contain aluminum, an ingredient known to cause Alzheimer's disease. All I am saying is be aware of what you are putting into your body. While you shouldn't expect to drop over dead after applying your deodorant, the long-term use of it could cause you to become diseased. Many products that contain aluminum are being linked to such serious diseases as Alzheimer's disease.

Would you be disgusted to know that diseased animal parts can be used in your cosmetics and soaps? I was! In the book, MAD COWBOY: Plain Truth From The Cattle Rancher Who Won't Eat Meat, the author, Howard F. Lyman explains in great detail how the remnants of cows, (such as the intestines, the head, the hooves, the horns, and their bones and blood), are sent off to rendering plants, as are other farm animals and even animals that are euthanized at animal shelters and roadkill. The rendering plants mix these animals together, grind them up and steam-cook them. In Mad Cowboy, Howard Lyman states, **"There is simply no such thing in America as an animal too ravaged by disease, too cancerous, or too putrid to be welcomed by the all-embracing arms of the renderer."**

The result of the grinding and steam cooking of these animals and animal parts leaves a fatty material that floats to the top of the surface. They refine this fatty material that floats to the top and use it in such things as cosmetics, lubricants, soaps, candles, and waxes. But don't expect to see "roadkill" when you flip over your bottle of foundation ladies, it doesn't have to be listed like that. Unless I myself would have fallen ill I would still NOT know these things. That is why in the first chapter I said that having those birth control injections poison my body were the worst thing, and ironically the best thing that could have ever happened to me.

The average American women, while getting ready for work, a hot date, or even just a night out with the girls will shampoo and condition; she will apply deodorant and skin lotion; she will put on all of her make-up -- her foundation, her blush, her eye shadow, her mascara, her lip liners, lipsticks, and sometimes a nice gloss for that "pouty" look. She will also mouse, gel and/or spritz her hair with hairspray. If she hasn't had them already professionally painted, she will also paint her nails to top off her 'look'. In just the very short time it takes for a woman to doll herself up, she has usually exposed herself to **over 200** different chemicals! Most of the chemicals are the type that are very dangerous to her long-term health.

I've taken the following paragraph from the web site...

http://freelife.com/sites/bewell/redir.cfm?page=info/pers onalcare/areyoupoisoningyourself/body.cfm

"Every day we use products that we think are safe; but the truth is that products are NOT always safe - and manufacturers don't have to tell us so. Ever since 1938 - when the FDA granted self-regulation to the cosmetics industry - such products can be marketed without government approval of ingredients, regardless of what tests show. Most of the 25,000 chemicals used have not been tested for long-term toxic effects. In a typical day, you might be exposed to over 200 different chemicals, many of which are suspected of causing cancer or juggling hormones. EPA tests conclude that ingredients in personal care products and home care products may be playing havoc with hormones that control reproduction and development."

I have also taken, with permission, the following information on hazardous chemicals lurking in our personal care and beauty supplies...

START CHECKING ALL PRODUCT LABELS:
AVOID THESE HARMFUL, HAZARDOUS "TOUCH-ME-NOT" INGREDIENTS!

Alcohol, Isopropyl (SD-40): A very drying and irritating solvent and dehydrator that strips your skin's moisture and natural immune barrier, making you more vulnerable to bacteria, molds and viruses. It is made from propylene, a petroleum derivative and is found in many skin and hair products, fragrance, antibacterial hand washes as well as shellac and antifreeze. It can act as a "carrier" accelerating the penetration of other harmful chemicals into your skin. It may promote brown spots and premature aging of skin. A Consumer's Dictionary of Cosmetic Ingredients says it may cause headaches, flushing, dizziness, mental depression, nausea, vomiting, narcosis, anesthesia, and coma. Fatal ingested dose is one ounce or less. Alternative: BGSE

DEA (diethanolamine), MEA (Monoethanolamine), & TEA (triethanolamine): Hormone-disrupting chemicals that can form cancer-causing nitrates and nitrosamines. These chemicals are already restricted in Europe due to known carcinogenic effects. In the United States however, they are still used despite the fact that Americans may be exposed to them 10-20 times per day with products such as shampoos, shaving creams and bubble baths. Dr. Samuel Epstein, Professor of Environmental Health at the University of Illinois, says that repeated skin applications of DEA-based detergents resulted in a major increase in the incidence of liver and kidney cancer. The FDA's John Bailey says this is especially important since "The risk equation changes significantly for children." No Alternative Necessary.

DMDM Hydantoin & Urea (Imidazolidinyl): Just two of many preservatives that often release formaldehyde which may cause joint pain, skin reactions, allergies, depression, headaches, chest pains, ear infections, chronic fatigue, dizziness, and loss of sleep. Exposure may also irritate the respiratory system, trigger heart palpitations or asthma, and aggravate coughs and colds. Other possible side effects include weakening the immune system and cancer. Alternative: Lonicera Japonica

FD&C Color Pigments: Synthetic colors made from coal tar, containing heavy metal salts that deposit toxins onto the skin, causing skin sensitivity and irritation. Absorption of certain colors can cause depletion of oxygen in the body and death. Animal studies have shown almost all of them to be carcinogenic. No Alternative Necessary.

Fragrances: Mostly synthetic ingredients can indicate the presence of up to four thousand separate ingredients, many toxic or carcinogenic. Symptoms reported to the FDA include headaches, dizziness, allergic rashes, skin discoloration, violent coughing and vomiting, and skin irritation. Clinical observation proves fragrances can affect the central nervous system, causing depression, hyperactivity, irritability, inability to cope, and other behavioral changes. Alternatives: Aromatherapeutic, Organic Essential Oils.

Mineral Oil: Petroleum by-product that coats the skin like plastic, clogging the pores. Interferes with skin's ability to eliminate toxins, promoting acne and other disorders. Slows down skin function and cell development, resulting in premature aging. Used in many products (baby oil is 100% mineral oil!). Alternatives: Moisture Magnets (Saccharide Isomerate) from beets; Ceramides, Jojoba and other vegetable oils, etc.

Polyethylene Glycol (PEG): Potentially carcinogenic petroleum ingredient that can alter and reduce the skin's natural moisture factor. This could increase the appearance of aging and leave you more vulnerable to bacteria. Used in cleansers to dissolve oil and grease. It adjusts the melting point and thickens products. Also used in caustic spray-on oven cleaners. One Alternative: Planteren™.

Propylene Glycol (PG) and Butylene Glycol: Gaseous hydrocarbons, which in a liquid state act as "surfactants" (wetting agents and solvents). They easily penetrate the skin and can weaken protein and cellular structure. Commonly used to make extracts from herbs. PG is strong enough to remove barnacles from boats! The EPA considers PG so toxic that it requires workers to wear protective gloves, clothing and goggles and to dispose of any PG solutions by burying them in the ground. Because PG penetrates the skin so quickly, the EPA warns against skin contact to prevent consequences such as brain, liver, and kidney abnormalities. But there isn't even a warning label on products such as stick deodorants, where the concentration is greater than in most industrial applications. Alternatives: Water, Water-Extracted herbs, Essential Oils, etc.

Sodium Lauryl Sulfate (SLS) & Sodium Laureth Sulfate (SLES): Detergents and surfactants that pose serious health threats. Used in car washes, garage floor cleaners and engine degreasers - and in 90% of personal-care products that foam. Animals exposed to SLS experience eye damage, depression, labored breathing, diarrhea, severe skin irritation, and even death. Young eyes may not develop properly if exposed to SLS because proteins are dissolved. SLS may also damage the skin's immune system by causing layers to separate and inflame. When combined with other chemicals, SLS can be transformed into nitrosamines, a potent class of carcinogens. Your body may retain the SLS for up to five days, during which time it may enter and maintain residual levels in the heart, liver, the lungs, and the brain. Alternative: Ammonium Cocoyl Isethionate.

Triclosan: A synthetic "antibacterial" ingredient with a chemical structure similar to Agent Orange! The EPA registers it as a pesticide, giving it high scores as a risk to both human health and the environment. It is classified as a chlorophenol, a class of chemicals suspected of causing cancer in humans. Its manufacturing process may produce dioxin, a powerful hormone-disrupting chemical with toxic effects measured in the parts per trillion; that is only one drop in 300 Olympic-size swimming pools! Hormone disruptors pose enormous long-term, chronic health risks by interfering with the way hormones perform, such as changing genetic material, decreasing fertility and sexual function, and fostering birth defects. It can temporarily deactivate sensory nerve endings, so contact with it often causes little or no pain. Internally, it can lead to cold sweats, circulatory collapse, and convulsions. Stored in body fat, it can accumulate to toxic levels, damaging the liver, kidneys and lungs, and can cause paralysis, suppression of immune function, brain hemorrhages, and heart problems. Tufts University School of Medicine says that triclosan is capable of forcing the emergence of "super bugs" that it cannot kill. Its widespread use in popular antibacterial cleansers, toothpastes and household products may have nightmare implications for our future. Alternative: BGSE

Besides throwing out all of my cleaning supplies I threw out my soap, my make-up, my skin lotions, my toothpaste, my deodorant, my nail polishes, and my shampoo and conditioners. That was my choice. You make your own informed decision.
I can also comment on the products from the other three web sites below as I purchase our personal care products; toothpaste, deodorant, shampoo, and soap, and my beauty products; foundation, cleansers, toners, and make-up, from them.
I want to make it clear that the safest thing for us to do is to refrain from the use of all make-ups, skin lotions, soaps, etc., **even the safer ones** that I am listing for you below, because anything that is not natural and is ingested or applied to the body cannot be used and has to be eliminated. The less work you make for your body the better. I am a realist however, and I do know that the majority of people will not forego these products altogether. So for those of you looking for safer alternatives I've listed some web sites for you that may be of help:

http://www.abundantearth.com

http://www.nonieofbeverlyhills.com

http://www.bareescentuals.com

http://www.bewellstaywell.com

http://www.burtsbees.com

I am not affiliated with any of those web sites, and I do not get paid for telling you about them. Those are the products I recommend because they are the ones that I have used or do use currently.

ARE THE CANDLES & AIR FRESHENERS
YOU ARE USING POISONING YOU?

What are you trying to cover up? Is the smell really that bad in your house that you need to cover it up? Don't get me wrong, I love candles. But for some people burning candles causes them to become sick. My mother has never been able to burn candles in her house because they've always given my father violent headaches. When he would moan and groan and tell her to blow them out my mom and I would just look at each other and roll our eyes. We didn't believe him. He wasn't lying, though; they do make him sick. At the time I didn't realize it, but having done research for this book, I found that some people cannot have candles burning in their homes, because they cause such things as headaches and breathing difficulties. The people who usually have the most problems with these things are those who are elderly, infants, and/or individuals who are ill.

I took the following information about burning candles in the home, from The American Lung Association of Washington's web site, with their permission. To go to their web site go to:

**http://www.alaw.org/air_quality/information_and_referral
/indoor_air_
quality/candles.html**

Although candles create a warm, inviting feeling within the home during the holidays and throughout the year, there are studies showing that candle usage can create problems for your home's interior. Burning candles can emit small amounts of toxins such as acetone, benzene, lead, and mercury into the air.

Choose beeswax candles, instead of scented or slow-burning candles with metal in the wick or candles that are greasy to the touch. Keep wicks trimmed to less than ¼ inch to minimize sooting. Keep candles away from drafty places. Vacuum more often during periods of high candle use with high-performance vacuum bags that catch micro-particles. Use a good filtration system on your furnace and replace filters more often during periods of high candle use.

IS YOUR WORK PLACE TOXIC?

For some, the exposure to toxins in their workplace is inevitable. For those that do come in contact with these dangerous chemicals for eight hours a day or longer, it is important for them to learn how to prevent serious injury to their health from being exposed to these chemicals. Some may find that the only way to remove disease is to change professions all together and remove the source of disease from their life entirely.

If you are saying, "I can't just quit my job. How will I provide for my family?" I completely understand the seriousness of this statement, as it too is something my husband and I are struggling with ourselves. My husband works in an extremely toxic environment every day as a heavy equipment operator in a mill. He has medical problems that we believe are, in part, related to his workplace environment. The paychecks he brings home are wonderful, but at what cost? I would rather give up all of our monetary possessions than to compromise the health of either one of us. He too shares this same feeling. Do we have debt? Yes, we do. Will it be difficult for us when he leaves his job? Yes, it will. However it is something that we as a couple have decided is best.

It is up to you to decide what is best for you and your family. If you know that your workplace is the cause of your illness or disease you have to make the choices that are right for you. You have to ask yourself, what is more important, your health or the lifestyle you are accustomed to? What is more important to your family, the things you can buy for them or you? The answer is always the latter. I believe that when we live the way God intends for us, he will provide for us, if we have faith.

Below I've listed for you just some of the professions that are at risk of disease from the chemicals or air pollution they are surrounded by on a daily basis.

- Pharmaceutical Workers
- Chemical Manufacturers
- Steel Mill Workers
- Asbestos Removal

- Road Construction Workers
- Painters
- Mechanics
- Gas Station Attendants
- Welders
- Beauticians
- Dentists and Dental Hygienists
- Coal Miners
- Military Professionals
- Truck Drivers, Taxi Drivers, Bus Drivers
- Maids/Janitors
- Dry-cleaners
- Pilots/Flight Attendants
- Computer Programmers/Web Developers (anyone who spends many hours each in front of computer screens and exposes themselves to dangerous EMF's.)

Not all employers comply with the law. The majority of employers themselves may not even know that they are putting you in harm's way. Do not trust your health to someone else. The best prevention is to know for yourself if your job is a hazard to your health. Knowing can save your life.

DID A DENTAL PROCEDURE POISON YOU?

There is so much evidence that dental procedures can cause serious illness. I too suffered from a root canal gone bad. The birth control injections were definitely the main cause to the seriousness of my deterioration, but there were other factors too, such as a bad root canal, and a poor diet. And when I say poor diet I am referring to one that by society's standards would actually be considered healthy!

The first book I read on drugless healing was Fast Your Way To Health, by Lee Bueno-Aquer. Lee became deathly ill because of a dental procedure gone wrong. At the time she didn't realize it was the dental procedure that caused her to become ill. She was eventually diagnosed with vascular rheumatoid arthritis. As she found her way to drugless healing and started healing herself, she realized that it was a dental procedure that caused her to become 'diseased'. There are many people that report they have become ill and diseased as a direct result of dental procedures.

There will be some people that read my book that may also have a dental procedure to blame for their illness. For those of you who are questioning this, I encourage you to pick up the book, Root Canal Cover-Up EXPOSED: Many Illnesses Result - Dr. Meinig

Dr. Meinig, up until about two years ago, was not only performing root canals himself, but he was also teaching the technique of root canals to dentists across the country. When he retired he decided to read all 1,174 pages of the detailed research of Dr. Weston Price, D.D.S. Dr. Meinig was startled and shocked at the valid documentation Dr. Weston provided that proved that systemic illnesses were resulting from latent infections lingering in filled roots. With his new knowledge he wrote the book Root Canal Cover-Up EXPOSED: Many Illnesses Result.

IS YOUR VANITY KILLING YOU?

Breast implants, teeth bleaching, steroids to enhance your muscles, liposuction,
Botox injections, etc. – To whom are you entrusting your safety, the FDA? HA! GOOD LUCK! Are breast implants really safe? Are botox injections really safe? What are the long-term side effects of these cosmetic procedures? Do you know? More importantly, do you care? If you don't care, so be it, continue on with what you are doing. If you do care however, and you believe these things are only on the market because they are perfectly safe, you are in for rude awakening!

Just because the FDA approves something, by no stretch of even the most vivid imagination, does that mean it is safe. If that was the case Depo-Provera would not be on the market, Norplant birth control that was subsequently **removed** from the market would have never made it to market, silicone breast implants would never have been on the market, etc., etc., etc. I could go on and on and on. You have to start asking questions, real questions. You need to start asking doctors to show you the PDR, or Physician's Desk Reference, and look up any drug and the REAL information they have on it before putting it into your body. Then, keep in mind that all of the side affects of a drug aren't even necessarily listed in the PDR. Always remember that even every doctor is taught that all drugs are toxic.

Also keep in mind that when you opt for these new cosmetic procedures that no **long-term** side effects have taken place because, quite frankly, they haven't been around long enough for long-term side effects to be done. If you are only concerned about the here and now, this is fine. If you are concerned about what you are doing to your body 10, 20, or 30 years or more down the road, then my advice to you is start obeying God's laws. Eat fruits, vegetables, legumes, whole grains, nuts and seeds -- not junk food. Drink pure water, not colas and alcohol. Get fresh air and sunshine. Don't lock yourself indoors.

I'll cover this in more detail in the next chapter, but I can tell you honestly that when you eliminate all of the chemicals from your life you will undergo an unbelievable physical and mental transformation. I've watched it happen to myself, as well as those around me who are now doing what I have done to get well. Soon you will be happy with what God gave you, not disgusted by what you created through a lifetime of wrong foods, drugs, and an unhealthy lifestyle. As you get free from disease, your physical appearance and mental attitude will change. You'll undoubtedly start to look better, but mentally you will change too. You will soon learn to be satisfied with what God gave you instead of feeling overwhelmed to be the best-looking person in the world.

Web Sites on the health risks of breast implants:

Saline implants are deadly bombs, too. Don't let anyone tell you differently, they are lying.

**http://www.cancerpage.com/cancernews/cancernews2696
.htm
http://news.bbc.co.uk/1/hi/health/277602.stm
http://community-
2.webtv.net/lany25/GlamourMagazineNov/page2.html
http://www.info-implants.com/ALB/Hope/05.html**

Ilena Rosenthal, Author of Breast Implants: The Myths, the Facts, the Women, has been connecting, supporting and educating women harmed by breast implants for over 5 years. As director of The Humantics Foundation for Women based in San Diego, she created and heads the largest Breast Implant Support Group in the world. E-mail: ilena2000@hotmail.com phone: 858/270-0680. Her web site is **http://www.BreastImplantAwareness.org**

A word about Botox: In an editorial published in the British Medical Journal (BMJ), it sternly warns that many aspects of Botox's long-term impact on health have never been explored, especially on the nervous system. **"Robust evidence for the action of botulinum toxin on sensory neurones is lacking,"**

according to the editorial, written by Peter Misra, a consultant at the National Hospital for Neurology and Neurosurgery in London. **"Animal experiments have shown that botulinum toxin affects the transmission of afferent nerves,"** he said, referring to nerves that relay signals from the limbs to the central nervous system. Other studies, among rats, have shown that Botox can block the release of nerve-signal chemicals called neurotransmitters in rats, he said. **"It is easy to forget that botulinum toxin is a potent neurotoxin and that its very long-term effects are still unknown,"** he warned.

If you are concerned that your gastric bypass surgery which has a death rate of 1 in 200, or liposuction surgery, or other 'vanity' procedure, has caused your illness, trust your instincts. Do not rely on a doctor or the FDA to tell you the truth because more than likely they don't know much more about it than you do.

KNOW WHAT YOU ARE PUTTING INTO YOUR BODY.. And Ask Yourself, "What Damage Can This Cause?"

By no means are the items that I've listed in the **exogenous toxin** category an all-inclusive list of the things that can poison your system. But, the things I've listed are the main ones. You need to become aware of what you are putting into your body. Ask yourself is there is any potential damage you may be causing yourself, either immediate or long-term, by either ingesting or coming in contact with the *item* in question.

Some exogenous toxins that poison our systems are obvious. For example, we know smoking, illegal drugs, alcohol, and junk food diets are all no-no's and are harmful to our bodies. But I hope this chapter convinces you that you need to start taking a look at the other not so obvious things that can be causing you to be sick. The processed foods, the coffee, the pop, the hair dye, the nail polish, the fumes you ingest from your household cleaning supplies, the dry cleaning you have done, the high-voltage power lines running by your home, or even your cell phone can perhaps be part of the cause of your illness/disease. Make yourself aware as to the dangers of these toxins and their effect on your health.

LONG-TERM EFFECTS

The poisoning that takes place in our body from this chemical overload doesn't happen overnight. Because you don't get sick from a product immediately, it is easy to believe that it is perfectly

safe. As more and more poisonous chemicals are absorbed into
your body, your sensitivities will increase in their severity, which
can result in chronic, debilitating diseases.

Symptoms from chemical poisoning often include headaches,
nausea, fatigue, depressed immune responses and joint pain. The
more severe symptoms can include birth defects, attention deficit
disorder (ADD), emphysema, asthma, skin diseases, cancers, and
even multiple sclerosis. In The Safe Shopper's Bible, Dr. Epstein
sums it up by saying that the process, *the poisoning*, is so gradual
that the cause is not established.

WHAT CAN WE DO TO PROTECT
OURSELVES FROM THIS CHEMICAL INVASION?

I believe it is impossible to be 100% chemical free, living in the
modern world that we live intoday. We can however take
responsibility for our health by following the advice of experts and
others who have healed themselves from so-called "incurable
diseases." We can start by eating as much organic food as
possible, with a high percentage of the food intake being raw. We
should beginto read food and product labels, and know that, if it
isn't something we can ingest, we shouldn't be breathing it; i.e.,
household cleaning supplies, hair spray, etc. We should try and
avoid as many harmful ingredients as possible by substituting
them with safer alternatives. I think anyone can benefit by reading
the book entitled, **The Safe Shopper's Bible**.

I am in no means suggesting we all go and live inside bubbles.
Not everyone will want to get all of the chemicals out of their lives.
The choice is yours. For me it was something I had to do because
I wanted to have optimum health. I was sick of being sick. I
learned what makes us sick. Toxemia makes us sick. Ingesting
toxins into our body, be it through eating wrong foods, applying
make-up daily that is made with chemicals, etc., causes toxemia.

What things you choose to eliminate out of your life is up to you.
Since toxemia or autointoxication is the one cause for disease it
was imperative that I share the information in this chapter with
you. Many people are poisoning themselves without even realizing
they are doing so.

Once this too becomes common knowledge to society as a whole,
the prices of these 100% organic, environmentally-friendly
products (everything from organic food to organic cleaning

supplies) will drop and become more readily available. Our demand creates the supply.

The purpose of this chapter is **not to alarm** you, but to bring you factual information on the role chemicals and food-cooking procedures are now playing in the long-term health of hundreds of millions of people all over the world. Only when you are armed with *all* of the information can you make an informed decision.

In the next chapter I will reveal to you the cure to disease, and my detailed, 12-step program of how I reversed my own disease that had me crying in pain on a daily basis.

Chapter 5: The One Cure To All Disease REVEALED!!

There have been many teachers, doctors, and natural Hygienists throughout the years that have taught that there is only one cause and one cure to all disease. Having researched thousands of stories of individuals throughout the world who have cured themselves from almost every type of disease possible, all using the same natural methods, I too believe there is but one cause and one cure to all disease. Using the same principles that have cured others from cancer, diabetes, arthritis, obesity, heart disease, lupus, and a long list of other diseases, I have reversed my so-called incurable disease -- fibromyalgia.

You'll be happy to know that you don't have to "buy" the cure. The one cure to all disease doesn't come in a pill; it isn't a surgical procedure; it isn't in the form of a homeopathic drop or herbal supplementation. No! The CURE to disease is simply the natural healing power of our bodies. Our bodies are designed to be able to reverse disease. If this seems too impossible to believe, don't worry. I found it impossible to believe too, until I cured myself from the pain that had taken over my body and my life.

HOW TO SET THE CONDITIONS FOR YOUR BODY TO HEAL ITSELF

There are two *MAIN* steps to setting the proper conditions for your body to heal itself:

1) Remove ALL of the causes that are making you diseased!
2) Detoxify your body!

YOU DO NOT NEED TO MAKE THIS CONFUSING!

I can make it a lot more confusing for you, but I don't have to, and I don't want to. I have read literally hundreds of books, studies, and newspaper and magazine articles on the subjects of detoxification, reversing disease, etc. Almost everyone whom I've read who has successfully reversed their disease through drugless healing has had the same basic plan for doing so. **Why? How could so many diseases be cured by the same plan?**   The reason one person with diabetes, another person with fibromyalgia, and another person with a heart disease can cure themselves all using the same or very similar plans, is because there really is only **one** way to **cure** disease. The one way to reverse disease is to set the proper conditions for your body to heal itself!

If it were really as difficult a task as the medical community and the drug companies would have you believe, you would need a pill for every problem. And, surprise, surprise, WE HAVE ONE! But the majority isn't getting well taking these prescription drugs, they are getting worse. The prescription drugs are simply not working. If we did need a different drug for every problem, as the doctors would have you believe, then explainto me how is it possible for millions of people to have SUCCESSFULLY REVERSED THEIR DISEASE by using the same, or very similar methods, as the others who successfully reversed their so-called "incurable diseases?" The medical community and the drug companies will have no answer for you as to how that is possible. Most will tell you it is impossible.

My main goal is to help you get the information you need to reverse your illness through this natural, miraculous healing process. I have read some books on the subject of 'natural detoxification' that make the disease reversal process unnecessarily confusing. If I bore you, if I make it hard for you, you will not do it. It is NOT hard. I have done this myself. I am not just someone that is writing about experiences that I have read others go through. I can tell you honestly I have used the exact information I am going to share with you in this chapter for myself, and it worked. When everything else failed me -- a myriad of prescription drugs, surgery, and even homeopathic treatments, this is what worked, **period**.

Keep it simple. It isn't hard. The two hardest things about the 12-step program I personally used to reverse my disease, and have outlined for you below, are making the decision to actually **do it**, and then **stick to it**!

By following the steps below exactly, I have reversed my disease of so-called "incurable" fibromyalgia. I'm not just talking about curing flu-ike symptoms here. I'm talking about curing pain that was so severe I wanted to kill myself. I am talking about severe migraines, chronic muscle pain and weakness, loss of libido, hormonal imbalances (low DHEA and progesterone through the roof!), painful intercourse, fibrocystic breasts, shortness of breath, unexplained irregular heart beat, dizziness, and inability to bend over without feeling that I was being strangled and would pass out, lymph nodes in my neck so swollen and sore it would hurt to tilt my head back or down or turn my head, weight gain, and leaky gut.

Now: Daily migraines - GONE! Daily muscle pain and weakness - GONE! Daily pressure in my head - GONE! Daily joint pain - GONE! Nightly insomnia - GONE! Daily pain in my lymph nodes in my neck - GONE! Inability to bend over without feeling of strangulation - GONE! Leaky gut - GONE!

MY 12-STEP PLAN FOR REVERSING MY SO-CALLED incurable DISEASE

Step 1) DIETARY CHANGE. I had to make a strict dietary change to a Natural Hygiene, raw food diet. First I was on a 75% high raw (fruits & veggies) and meat and dairy diet at the request of a homeopathic doctor who had me on Eat Right For Your Blood Type Diet. I saw him for months, but I did not get well. That diet didn't work. I was told that such foods and drinks as mozzarella cheese, wheat bagels, wine, yogurt, turkey, and coffee for example were okay or **highly beneficial** for my A blood type, yet all of those foods, and others that were 'approved' for my blood type, made me very sick. The ER4YT diet also said that I had to avoid such things as tomatoes, which I loved and knew I had no problems with. I just didn't get well. It simply did not work and I followed it faithfully, from 95% to 100% (mostly 100%) for months. There were days when I would eat some chips, or an ice cream cone, I won't lie, but all in all I followed it for months at 100% with nothing but severe pain. It failed miserably.

Thankfully, however. the doctor who had me on the Eat Right For Your Blood Type diet was the first one to tell me about fasting, raw foods, etc., and if it was not for him I may have never gotten to the path, the correct path, that led me to great health. Seeing I was not getting well he told he told me I needed to go have a colonic. In doing so I ended up with a wonderful nutritionist Paula, who introduced me too the 100% raw food diet.

Paula put me on a 30-day, **limited** raw food diet, followed by a 2-week juice fast, followed by a 3-day water-only fast (however I only made it two days and drank fresh squeezed juice on the third day). I stress that it was a **limited** raw food diet because during this time she wanted me to also avoid nuts and avocados, which, even though they are indeed raw, I had to omit from my diet. The reason I had to leave these two foods, nuts and avocados, out of my raw diet was because toxins store themselves in our fat cells, and avocados and nuts are both very high in fat. Even though they are considered good fats, and not bad fats, they are still fats and they will impede the detoxification process.

So, for 30 days I dined on nothing but fresh fruits and vegetables. Was it tough? Yes! The first few days were brutal, I won't lie. However, I was so ill and I had such a desperate desire to get well I had 110% determination to stick it out and do it. And I did. I didn't cheat once.

My meals were simple. Breakfasts and lunches or brunches were usually fruit. However some lunches were salads as were all of my dinners. Usually I ate about four meals a day, two large fruit meals and two large vegetable meals were the norm. I also did indulge in smoothies for desserts too when I felt I was still hungry. Also, there were many days I did eat six meals if I was hungry. I had no limit to the quantities of food I could eat at each meal, so I ate until I was full.

During that 6-week period I had witnessed such an obvious and very dramatic change in my health, I knew that I was finally on the right path. After that 6-week period, in which I had such unmistakable improvement, I was given permission to add cooked vegan (no meat, no eggs, no dairy) foods back into my diet. As I did this I soon started to feel myself taking steps backwards. Hmmm … what was the problem now? It was obvious to me it had to be the cooked foods because it was the only thing I was doing differently.

Don't panic! I know the thought of giving up cooked food has you probably ready to throw this book right into the trash can but trust me, my goal is not to turn every human into a Hygienist raw foodist. My goal is to teach you the great importance raw foods plays in our health. What level you take it to is up to you. All I can share with you is the truth about how raw food was an imperative step in the reversal of my disease.

In the next chapter I will discuss with you in great detail what the ideal diet for humans is suppose to be and why. I will also discuss the topic of raw foods vs. cooked foods so I can shed some more light on this highly controversial subject for you.

Step 2) FASTING (Some will not require this step). I have undergone a few smaller duration water-only fasts (2 to 4 days) to give my body the time, energy, and reserves it needs to repair the injuries my body has sustained. I also underwent a weekly 24-hour to 36-hour water-only fast for about six months. All fasts really must be professionally supervised. I did them on my own as they were shorter duration fasts, however at the time I did them I did have a nutritionist with whom I was working and at my disposal. In Chapter 8, my chapter on fasting, I provide you with a list of professional fasting clinics throughout the U.S.

Some may never need to fast in order to reverse their disease. For some, proper dietary change may be all it takes for them to reverse their disease. A few people may even find that they have conditions that will prevent them from being able to fast. (I will list these conditions in Chapter 8). With that said however, fasting is perfectly natural and safe for almost everyone, so long as that person is informed on the subject and is also supervised by a professional trained in fasting. I can't tell you how truly grateful I am that I have learned the truths about, and the powers of, fasting. My fasting experiences, while I've only underwent those of smaller duration, were a substantial part in the reversal of all of my pain and disease.

Step 3) FRESH AIR. Get plenty of fresh air daily (at **least** 30 minutes a day). Even if it is winter and you are in a cold climate, just bundle up if you need to, and get outdoors. Of course there are exceptions. If it is dangerously cold and the weather experts tell you to stay indoors, then do so. Use common sense. We absolutely must have fresh air, however. This is imperative.

People who are lying in hospital beds dying don't get this necessary fresh air. That is just one of the reasons hospitals are such improper places for the ill and diseased. There is no fresh air in our hospitals. The air in hospitals is filled with chemicals that are released through drugs given, germs from the sick people in the hospital, and the cleaners used to keep the hospital sanitized. The air inside hospitals is probably the worst air of all!! Yet, this is where we send our sick people.

In the spring, summer, and fall open the windows. Shut off your air conditioners and let the fresh air flow through your house. Spend as much time outdoors as humanly possible.

Don't take this step lightly. Pure air is essential to life. We can survive a few days without water and many weeks without food, but cut off our air supply, and we will die within minutes. This proves that respiration must be considered the primary function of our bodies. It is also true that fresh air is the best air for us to breathe. The fewer toxins we take into the body, the less work we cause for the body.

In Dr. Sniadach's Essential Natural Hygiene course he states, "At each exhalation the lungs discard enough gases, consisting of carbonic lactic, hydrochloric, phosphoric and other acids, to poison a barrelful of air. In every 24-hour period, the amount of carbon dioxide eliminated by the lungs is equal to a lump of charcoal weighing eight ounces. With this in mind, consider also that every person in a room needs 3,000 cubic feet of fresh air an hour to insure purity. In the case where several occupy a room not adequately ventilated, we inhale the exhalations of others and ourselves, and the amount of carbon dioxide contained in the air increases, making it more dangerous to breathe." Keep that thought in your mind the next time you go into an unventilated health club or sauna.

I've already discussed with you in a previous chapter the importance of your indoor air quality and filters. However we should get as much fresh air as possible. Thankfully I live in a very rural area with little pollution and our windows and doors are open day and night.

One last note, with the diet that I am on currently the heat and humidity simply do not bother me like they did when I was ill. As you become healthy, your body adjusts to the temperatures, high and low, and humidity. I do not have that need for air conditioning, as I used to. The heat/humidity simply does not affect me like it did at one time.

Step 4) SUNSHINE. Get adequate amounts of sunlight. Never stay in the sun long enough to cause your skinto burn, use common sense here, too. But don't STAY OUT OF THE SUN because you are afraid of skin cancer. Doctors have most of us fearful of going into the sun. But we NEED sunlight!!

Sunlight gives our bodies the absolutely essential vitamin D. Vitamin D helps our bodies absorb calcium. Don't substitute going outside for taking a multi-vitamin that has vitamin D. There is NO comparison. For one, your body may not even be digesting and assimilating that multi-vitamin and secondly, you need fresh air anyway, so you have to go outdoors. No excuses. Sunlight will decrease the triglycerides in your blood. Sunlight also stimulates the immune system.

Think about those poor hospital patients again. Not only do they not get fresh air, but also they don't get sunlight either. Just another reason to stay out of the hospital.

Just 30 minutes a day of sunlight will do wonders for your health. The best times to go outdoors to soak up the sun's rays are (before 10:00 am or after 4:00 pm).

Step 5) EXCERCISE. Get exercise daily. If you do steps 3 & 4 daily to get fresh air and sunshine, as you must, you will have the perfect opportunity to take care of this step, Step 5. While you are outside for your fresh air and sunshine, do some walking. Walking is the perfect exercise for those who may be too weak at first to do other types of exercising.

There will be some that are so ill, however, that they will not be able to get outside because they are bedridden. In these severe cases don't worry, as your health increases you will gain the energy needed to exercise. Most will be able to get some exercise, even if at first all you can do is make movements with your arms or legs.

Through daily movement and exercise, your strength will increase at amazing rates when you follow these steps! Soon you will not just have to exercise daily, but you will WANT to exercise daily! I exercise for about an hour to two hours a day broken up into 1/2 hour to 1 hour in the morning, and 1/2 to 1 hour at night. I get much more exercise a day if I find myself just sitting around doing nothing. For example if I am watching TV in the evening, I just pull out my exercise ball or yoga mat and put my spare time to use. You don't need to just sit on the couch to watch TV. Make **good use** of your spare time. As you become healthier, your energy level dramatically increases. Don't worry if right now you feel like you can't move a muscle. This will all change for you as you change your diet and lifestyle to incorporate these 12 steps.

When it is warmer outside, I love getting my exercise through walking and jumping on my trampoline. Jumping on a trampoline is excellent for your lymph system. When I cannot go outside to exercise I enjoy yoga, Pilates, and walking on my treadmill.

I've owned seven different yoga tapes. My two favorites are:

1   Rodney Yee's Yoga Journal's Yoga for Strength and Energy
2   Ali McGraw's Yoga Mind and Body

I know all of the yoga asanas (poses) by heart, so many days I just do yoga with no tapes, and no distractions. I really enjoy doing yoga outdoors. I also own a Pilates machine that I absolutely love! If you want an exercise that you can do for the most part while lying down, you'll love having your own Pilates machine. The machine I have is the Pilates Premier XP. I purchased it QVC.

If you can't afford a Pilates machine, but you do want to start Pilates exercises, I recommend Denise Austin's DVD - Mat Workout Based On The Work Of Pilates. There are two sections to her DVD, a Pilates section and a yoga section. It is an excellent DVD. I use it even though I do have a Pilates machine. With some of her Pilates routines, I can feel my core muscles getting an even deeper workout than they do with my machine.

I also use an exercise ball, which I like because it allows me to do sit-ups without putting a lot of strain on my neck. One of the things that happened to me, as a result of the birth control injections, was that my neck muscles were severely weakened. Doing normal sit-ups were impossible for me to do without hurting my neck. My Pilates machine and my exercise ball allow me to work on my stomach muscles without causing added strain on my neck. I am happy to report however that I have gained much strength back in my neck over the past few months following my methods I am sharing with you in these 12 steps.

The important point to remember in regards to exercising is for you to do something you enjoy. Do a few different activities, so that you do not get bored. By doing a variety of different things, I look forward to my exercise time; I don't dread it. If you dread it, then you need to find some other types of exercise that keep you interested.

Step 6) REST & SLEEP. For optimal health, it is imperative that you get not only proper sleep every night, but that you also get ample rest during each day as well. The body needs rest for the **cells of the body,** and it requires sleep for the **brain and the nervous system.**

Rest: For the Cells of the Body
Sleep: For the Brain & Nervous System

Rest is inactivity while being conscious. Sleep is basically inactivity while being unconscious. However, being in a coma of course is not "sleep." Both rest and sleep are equally important to reversing your illness/disease and maintaining good health.

First I must define rest. Rest as defined by Dr. Robert Sniadach in his course, Essential Natural Hygiene, is "a period of inactivity during which the faculties can restore expended nerve energy." He also states, "Essentially rest is the curtailment of energy expenditure and waste generation. This permits the body to redirect energies to cleansing and restoration."

Rest doesn't just mean plopping yourself down in front of the television and sitting still, lying down while reading a magazine, talking on the phone, or watching television. When I tell you to "rest," I mean you must refrain from all draining activity that is either mental and/or physical. Turn off the television. Turn off any noise. Let the stress of your life leave your body. Easier said then done, I know. I've been there, but it is a key step in setting the proper conditions for your body to heal itself.

Just one 20 to 30 minute nap in the middle of the day will do you a world of good. If it were possible for you to **rest** for 5 to 10 minutes out of every hour, that would be ideal!

Doctors, such as Dr. Nathaniel L. Kleitman, have concluded that the body builds nerve energy while we sleep and that is the actual purpose of sleep is to build nerve energy. Dr. Sniadach stated the following about the purpose of sleep, "Sleep is primarily for the purpose of generating nerve energy or low-level electricity. Many other beneficial purposes are also served during sleep. The physiological rest obtained during sleep is extraordinarily valuable. During the prolonged rest of sleep, the body restocks its cells and organs with fuel, replaces cells that have lost their vitality, often increases digestive processes and rids itself of extraordinary toxins that may not have been eliminated the previous day. Thus, the value of sleep is manifold. The benefits of sleep may be chronicled as follows: The regeneration of nerve energy; refueling the liver and cells with glycogen; destruction of old cells and replacement with new cells -- multiplication of cells occurs during sleep at a rate of more than twice that during waking hours and the body expels more debris and wastes during sleep and rest than when active; there are increased secretions of anabolic hormones, such as human growth hormone, during sleep."

Having myself suffered for years from insomnia I can tell you that it really can drive you mad. For several years I did not get more than two to three hours maximum of sleep a night, and it was never a continuous sleep but 20 minutes here, 20 minutes there. The majority of people do not get the type of long, uninterrupted, peaceful sleep they need for their body to repair itself.

I can tell you honestly that when you follow the diet that I am following, and you do not eat for at least three or preferably four or more hours before you go to bed, you will have the most peaceful, restful, and recuperative sleep you can imagine. You will truly sleep like a baby!!

Take time in the middle of every afternoon to get some uninterrupted rest, even if it is for only 15 minutes. No noise, no interruptions. Just close our eyes and rest. Get to bed early and go to bed at the same time every night. Don't force your body into staying up past that point of being tired. While you are getting well, while you are detoxifying, you may have nights where you feel tired at 7:00 p.m. If that is the case, listen to your body. Your body knows what it needs, and you have to learn to listen to it.

I realize many of you have children or evening jobs, etc., and you may think it is impossible to get to bed early. My answer to you is everyone has a story, and there are others out there in worse off situations than yours and they can manage to get to bed early to get proper rest and sleep. Try not to make excuses, but just to apply these steps to your life. It may take time to incorporate it into your life, but work at it consistently until you accomplish your goals.

Remember that there are millions out there who have it worse than you do. We have to learn to stop whining and to start taking control of our health. If you have children and you need to go to bed early, put them to bed early too. If you feel you can't do that then hire a babysitter or ask a friend or a family member to help you out.

Rest and sleep are of extreme importance to reversing disease. During rest and sleep our bodies undergo the much-needed recuperation and repair process. Don't make apologies for this. Don't feel like a failure if you get tired or feel weak during the detoxification process. Your body knows what it needs. If it tells you it is time to take a nap, do it. If it tells you it is time to go to bed, listen to it.

Step 7) ELIMINATE STRESS. Eliminate all stress from your life. I cannot possibly go into great detail on this step. There are things people are going to argue, like "My job stresses me, but I must have a job." This is like the meat-eating topic. I am not going to debate it. If you are stressed you must eliminate the sources of your stress. You already know this. It is common sense. When we are stressed our heartbeat increases, our muscles tighten, and our blood pressure rises. None of these things are good for us. You have to get out of that stressed state.

I had to remove the stresses from my life, and I have done it. You must do it, too. No excuses. How you do it is up to you, but it must be done. Remember everyone has their own "poor me" story. Yours is no more tragic than some others out there. Sometimes we need to "suck it up" and deal with it. There is always someone worse off than me – I try to remember that. Do what it takes to remove the stress from your life.

Two excellent ways to eliminate stress are through meditation and exercising, especially exercises that focus mainly around your breathing like yoga, tai chi, and Pilates.

When you feel your blood pressure starting to rise and your muscles starting to cramp, remove yourself from the situation that is stressing you. If possible, retreat to an area where you can lie down or do some exercising. Go outdoors and lie down on the ground or in a hammock or lawn chair. If you can't go outdoors, retreat to the bedroom or lie in bed and listen to a relaxation CD.

When lying down take deep breaths and concentrate on nothing but your breathing and your health. While you are lying there realize what harm you are causing yourself by letting things bother you. Is it worth it? When exercising, preferably with yoga, Pilates, tai chi, or walking, also concentrate on your breathing and your health. Learn to not let things bother you. Your health is of the utmost importance. Without good health all of the fame and fortune in the world are useless. You can't control everything in life, so don't try. Learn to stop taking things that aren't so serious, so seriously. Eventually your only goals will be to live a healthy lifestyle, to help others who are less fortunate than you are, and to work at a job you enjoy, regardless of the income level. As you reduce your stress levels you will soon see that the only truly important things in life can never be bought.

Step 8) DITCH THE NEGATIVE ATTITUDE AND BE THANKFUL.
To help successfully reverse your disease you need to eliminate negativity from your life.

For most people their negative attitude stems from their being sick. It is hard to be upbeat and smiles when you feel like you are on your deathbed. The great thing about these steps is that as you follow them everything just starts moving in the right direction, almost effortlessly. Even if you aren't really focusing on being more positive, you will notice your negativity starting to vanish as you change your diet and get more fresh air, sunshine, and exercise.

One of the most tragic parts of a negative attitude is that misery loves company. Negative people will search out others and attempt to bring them down to their level. This is how negative attitudes spread.

NOTE: You may find that in order for you to eliminate the negativity in your life, you may need to remove yourself from certain individuals in your life. In some cases this may even be close family members or best friends. Stay away from negative people! Stay away from the people who make you unhappy or depressed. Do you have that certain friend who always puts you in a bad mood after talking to them? Do you have a family member or friend that is so unhappy with his or her life that they try to bring everyone down around them? If so, stay away from these people.

Most miserable people are miserable because they too are sick. Usually they don't feel good because they are also suffering from autointoxication of the wrong foods and/or drugs. Their bad attitude is not your problem. Don't try changing them, especially if they do not ask for your help. Your main concern should be getting your health back on track. This means staying away from those that want to bring you down.

It is easy to wake up in the morning cursing your body, your doctors, or even God because you don't feel good. You have to remember that no matter how sick you are there is ALWAYS someone who is much worse off than you are. If you are not blind, be thankful you can see. If you are not deaf, be thankful you can hear. If you are not paralyzed, be thankful you can walk. Be thankful for what you DO have, do not be unthankful for what you DON'T have.

It is important for you to thank God every day for the things you **do** have. Consider all those who are suffering a fate much worse than yours that would gladly change places with you. Keep a positive attitude and learn to let go of the negativity.

Step 9) CHARITY: BE A GIVER. Stop focusing on your own problems. Caring for and helping others can give you a feeling that is unlike anything else. Realize that there are others in this world that are less fortunate than you are and need your help.

Many times you hear people say, that *the problem is too big, I'm only one person. I can't make a difference.* But one person can do a lot. With a little faith you can move mountains! If we all just helped one person can you imagine the result? We could cure disease; we could end hunger, and we could end so much needless suffering, if we all pitch in.

Helping others also makes you feel good about YOU. Helping someone else can take your mind off your problems, too. Lend a helping hand or volunteer some of your time to help someone who is less fortunate than you are. Do a good deed for a neighbor or friend. You'll be amazed at how good it makes you feel. By helping others, you really do help yourself.

"You have not lived a perfect day... unless you have done something for someone who will never be able to repay you." - Ruth Smeltzer

Step 10) ENEMAS OR COLONICS (Many will not need this step). Some authors on the subject of detoxification do not mention anything about keeping your bowels or colon clean, others have said they don't recommend it, and still others say it is an essential part of the reversal of disease. Colonic therapy was a step I took. Looking back I do not know whether or not it was something I needed. I now know that only our bodies can repair themselves, and they can only best do that when we leave them intelligently alone.

The reason I do have this step in my 12-step program is not only because it is a step I have taken, but I also realize there may be some very severe cases that simply do not have time for dietary and lifestyle changes to take effect. For some, colonics may be a treatment that for them can mean life or death, and for that reason I have included it. Most individuals, even those who are quite gravely ill, as long as they do make the dietary and lifestyle changes I have listed, will not need this step.

The Difference Between Enemas and Colonics: There are three main differences between enemas and colonics:

- The amount of water used.
- The depth of the cleaning and the water pressure used.
- The method used.

First, the amount of water used in an enema is about 1 to 2 quarts. With a colonic the amount of water used is about 12 to 15 gallons. The cleansing effect of one colonic is the equivalent to about 12 to 15 enemas.

Secondly, the difference between an enema and a colonic is the amount of water pressure that is used and how deeply the water enters into the body. During a colonic, the 12-15 gallons of water used by the therapist travels the length of the colon (6 feet) and activates cleansing from the sigmoid to the ascending colon. The water in an enema does not travel that far and only addresses cleansing of the lower colon.

Third: The Method Used.

The enema allows the water to enter into your colon slowly. You lie down on your side to take the water in. You insert a tube anywhere from a few inches to 20+ inches into your rectum. How far you insert it is of course up to the individual. The further the tube is inserted the deeper the cleaning. You go to the toilet to release the water after about 15 to 20 minutes, or longer if you can hold it.

The colonic is similar to the enema but on a bigger, more effective scale. A professional, unless you purchase a home colonic kit, will administer most colonics. With a colonic you lie down on your back as opposed to your side. There is one tube inserted a few inches. You do not go to the toilet to release. With a colonic your waste will also exit through a separate area of the tubing that also inserts the water. The therapist assisting you will insert a soft, disposable plastic tube into your rectum, which will remain in place during the entire session.

First, the therapist gently pumps a measured amount of body-temperature, filtered water into your colon. Then, the therapist may gently massage your abdomen to help release the impacted fecal material from the intestinal walls. Finally, the pump is reversed, and the water is gently vacuumed back through the same tube and into a closed waste system. There is no mess or foul odor.

The process is repeated many times during the session, which lasts about an hour. Approximately 12 to 20 gallons of water will be used, but unlike an enema, the therapy does not require any "race to the toilet" afterward, since most of the water is removed by the end of the session.

Some people report feeling lighter and more energized after colonic irrigation. Others may experience nausea, headache, or flu-like symptoms. These symptoms generally pass within a few hours. I was very ill during most of my colonics, and it would take about 15 to 20 minutes for me to start feeling better afterwards. Some people do not get sick at all during the treatment. I did because I was in such a highly toxic state.

I had undergone I believe about 8 colonic treatments, 1 a week for about two months. I have also used 1 coffee enemas, and 3 lemon water enemas. I've used the enemas at home. I used the coffee enema, before I went to Paula for my colonics.

Anything in excess is not good for you! Once you start having treatments such as enemas or colonics continually over extended periods your body could eventually lose the ability to do the work on its own. So, these are things to consider. As I stated earlier, most will not need this step if they make the very necessary and permanent dietary and lifestyle changes as I am laying out for you in my book.

Step 11) PURE WATER. I am simply flabbergasted at my cooked-food friends who don't drink water. I don't even know how they survive. It is amazing to me. If you are someone who eats mostly cooked food and very little amounts of fresh, RAW fruits and vegetables and says, "I hate water, and I won't drink it", you are in for a rude awakening. It is imperative to good health that you drink an ample amount of pure water every day or be eating a water-sufficient diet. Our bodies need pure water.

While watching Dr. Lorraine Day's VHS tape Cancer Doesn't Scare Me Anymore, I was shocked to learn that we lose, out of our bodies, the equivalent of 8 to 10 glasses of water just through every day living. We lose water through our skin, through our breath, through our perspiration, etc. This water has to be replaced if you want to achieve optimum health!

Our bodies are made up of 75% water. Our brains are made up of 80.5% water. Our blood is made up of 90.7% water! I don't know if people actually comprehend this. If you are not drinking water, where are you getting your water? Many people who are diseased are diseased simply because they are dehydrated. They are not getting enough water for their bodies to function properly. To meet your body's water requirements, the ideal thing to do is follow a water-sufficient Natural Hygiene raw food diet, and if you are not going to do that you must drink sufficient amounts of pure water.

The naturally ripened fruits we eat contain up to 80 to 90% of the purest distilled water. Vegetables also have high water contents. If one is eating sufficient amounts of fresh raw fruits, melons, and vegetables little to no water is needed. Very few however do transition to this ideal diet, so be aware of your body's daily pure water requirements and make sure these are met either through your intake of fresh, raw fruits and vegetables, and/or by drinking distilled or reverse osmosis water.

There are things you need to know about distilled water too. My editor and one of my message board moderators, Lisa OBorne, shared a post on my internet message boards that distilled water that comes in plastic jugs that have a number on the bottom of anything less than a #7 are dangerous because the plastic from the container can leech out into the water. When buying distilled water take this into consideration. I was horrified to know that my distilled water was in #2 plastic jugs. Uggghh! While trying to do a good thing, I've been drinking plastic. No worries however, you can get a water distiller or reverse osmosis filters for your home and not have to resort to purchasing your distilled water in plastic jugs. We use reverse osmosis filters in our home for our drinking water.

If you want to look into distilling your own water be sure to look for the highest quality steam distiller and make sure it uses glass or stainless steel components and not plastic. One web site I found that may be of use to you is **http://www.water-distiller.com**

HOW *MUCH* WATER DO I NEED?

Your body's daily requirements for pure water depend almost entirely on your diet. Those eating a SAD diet, (the Standard American Diet), for example need to drink large amounts of pure water daily in large part because of the high sodium content. Even if you don't pick up the salt shaker and physically salt your food, it doesn't matter. Canned foods, frozen foods, boxed foods, and bagged foods are all loaded with sodium. Because our bodies are so very wise, when we eat these foods with such high salt contents, your body will dilute the salt so that it won't harm the tissues and cells in our body. For this dilution process, the body requires large amounts of pure water. Ever swell up or experience bloating after a meal? Ever wake up in the morning and the ring that was too big on your finger the day before now is cutting off circulation in your finger? The culprit is SALT. You swell up as a defense mechanism to keep the salt from causing damage to your body's tissues, cells, etc.

On a Hygienic, diet I do no longer suffer from bloating. This is fact.

Those individuals who follow a water-sufficient, Natural Hygiene raw food diet may find that they need to drink very little to no water because their diet, consisting of ample amounts of fresh fruits and vegetables, provides them with their body's daily water requirements. Of course if one is on a water-sufficient Hygienic diet but is doing heavy labor or exercise for example, then it may be necessary for them to drink more pure water. The key is to let your natural thirst be your guide.

As a general rule anyone on a cooked food diet with a little to no fruit or vegetable intake should drink half their body weight in ounces of water every day to provide their body with its MINIMUM water replacement requirements; i.e., a women on the typical SAD diet that weighs 120 pounds would need to take in **at least** 60 oz. of pure water daily.

In the beginning, even if you switch cold turkey to a proper raw food diet, you may still find that you feel thirsty and need to drink more water. Listen to your body. When we have days that we are undergoing heavy detoxification (elimination of toxins), our bodies may require additional water intake. The body is a miraculous machine. If the toxins that get stirred up for elimination during the detoxification process are too great, your body will try and dilute the toxins by holding onto water so that the detoxification process causes the least amount of damage to your body.

If you feel thirsty, drink, but ONLY reach for pure water (distilled or reverse osmosis). Don't reach for that can of pop, cup of coffee, or glass of iced tea. Pure water only should be used, as your body has no need for any other type of drink. Meet your body's needs and it will take care of you.

"Dehydration of certain organs will result in symptoms which are often misdiagnosed by physicians. The message is: Drink your way to health with volumes of pure water." That is a quote from F. Batmanghelidj, MD, author of Your Body's Many Cries For Water: You Are Not Sick, You Are Thirsty!" Dr. Batmanghelidj attributes many diseases, such as: Asthma, allergies, arthritis, hypertension, depression, headaches, diabetes, obesity, and MS to persistent dehydration. Dr. Batmanghelidj also says that drinking enough pure water daily can actually prevent and reverse aging, cure asthma in a few days, eliminate pains, including heartburn, back pain, and migraine headaches, and much more.

You absolutely can't ignore this step. You can't ignore any of these steps, but this one I think most people will try to put off because a lot of people simply don't like to drink water. If you don't like drinking water your only other alternative, and by the way the best way to meet your daily water requirements, is to greatly increase your fresh, raw fruit and vegetable intake. It is crucial to optimum health! You have to do it; you have to take in ample amounts of pure water each and every day. If you won't do it through dietary changes then the next best way is through drinking it.

If you are still asking, "Why should I drink water," below are a few good reasons for doing so. I took the following information, with permission, from the web site **http://www.harmonikireland.com/index.php?topic=needwater.**

- Water is the substance of life. Life cannot exist without water. We must constantly be adding fresh water to our body in order to keep it properly hydrated.

- The body is comprised of over 70% water. This ratio must be maintained for good health. Water is the most important thing we can put inside our bodies.

- It is difficult for the body to get water from any other source than water itself. Soft drinks and alcohol steal tremendous amounts of water from the body; however, even other beverages such as coffee, milk and juice require water from the body to be properly digested.

- Water plays a vital role in nearly every bodily function.

- Water is essential for proper digestion, nutrient absorption and chemical reactions.

- Water is essential for proper circulation in the body, and flexibility of the blood vessels.

- Water helps remove toxins (acidic waste) from the body, in particular from the digestive tract.

1 Water regulates your body's temperature. Imagine a car running without water in the radiator. Consistent failure to drink enough water can lead to Chronic Cellular Dehydration. This condition where the body's cells do not

get hydrated enough leaving them in a weakened state, and vulnerable to disease processes. It weakens the body's overall immune system and leads to chemical, nutritional, and pH imbalances.

Dehydration can occur at any time of the year, not only during the summer months when it is hot. The dryness that occurs during winter can dehydrate the body even quicker than when it is hot. The first reason for this is the dry atmosphere in the home from the use of central heating. The second reason being simply not eating a water-sufficient diet or drinking enough pure water. Many diseases such as cholera are caused primarily through dehydration.

For more information on this topic you can go to the main web page of this site at **http://www.harmonikireland.com.**

If you go to the web page **http://www.ca.uky.edu/enri/pubs/enri129.pdf** you can view a chart that shows you the water content of fruits and vegetables.

The diet I am on now is very water-sufficient. My water in take is down considerably from where it was a year ago because I am a much healthier state, and I am getting my water from the abundance of fresh raw fruits and vegetables that I eat. Some days I drink less than 16 oz of pure water a day, and I'm not thirsty because my body is getting its water needs met through my diet.

Step 12) FAITH. Have faith in God. I know this is a very touchy subject. Nobody wants to be told what to believe or how to worship -- ME included! However it is important for me to share with you what I have experienced myself and everything that was required on my part to reverse **my** pain and disease.

I am not what society would consider an overly religious individual. I do not attend church. I do not claim to be part of a religion, even though I was raised a Catholic. But, I do speak with God daily. I am not here to tell you to go to church; I am not telling you what name to use to call HIM by. I am here to tell you that without faith in God, **my** recovery would not have happened. I am here to tell you that the majority of individuals whom I have read, who also have reversed their so-called incurable diseases, have also stressed that their faith in God was a crucial part of their recovery.

When I was at the lowest points of my illness I often questioned God. Why am I so sick? What have I done? Why aren't you helping me? I prayed every night for him to heal me, yet nothing. Why wasn't he listening to me? Was there even a God at all? I shudder even typing those words for I know with undeniable certainty that there is a God, but my illness had me so toxic I was questioning whether or not He really existed.

As I did my first four day water-only fast, I put my faith in God one last time and prayed and fasted and read from the book Fast Your Way To Health (by Lee Bueno-Aquer - an absolutely fascinating read). Some will argue that it was my dietary change and fasting alone that reversed my disease. That is fine; everyone is entitled to his or her opinion. What it is very important for those people to remember however is when we give up our addictions and make a change to a natural diet of fresh raw fruits, vegetables, nuts and seeds, and partake in the occasional fast, we are actually obeying God's laws. So is it only the dietary change and fasting that cures us? Or, is it the fact that by eating a plant-based diet and fasting, we are doing what God asks of us and expects of us? I believe it is both.

Some fast and pray for reasons of spiritual awakening alone. While that is not why I fasted, I did witness it. Everything in your life, both the good and the bad, I believe happens for a reason. Perhaps I suffered so that I could write this book and help just one person reverse their disease. If I can help save just one life, I will feel very accomplished. Perhaps you are sick so that you can find God's natural cure to disease, ***the miraculous healing power of our own body***, and also go on to share this information and help someone else.

Keep your faith and don't be afraid to ask God to help you. If you obey all of his laws, and not just pick and choose which ones you want to obey, and ask him for help, he will answer your prayers. I see people preaching thou shalt not kill, thou shalt not commit adultery, yet they themselves commit the sin of gluttony every day, yet wonder why they become diseased. We cannot break the laws of nature and not pay the price.

IT'S REALLY ABOUT GETTING BACK TO THE BASICS

None of these steps I've detailed for you in my 12-step program to reversing my disease gives you profound or new advice. We know we should eat well; we know we should get fresh air; we know we should exercise; we know we need sunlight; we know we should eliminate stress from our lives, etc. Unfortunately most of us ignore these basic and essential steps that are completely responsible for optimum health. It's really all about getting back to the basics -- obeying the laws of nature.

That's it. Those are the 12 steps I took to help me reverse my so-called incurable fibromyalgia, and long list of other symptoms. It is true that the simplest things in life will make us the happiest. It is also true that the simplest things in life make us the healthiest!

Most of you reading this are probably still thinking, "Raw? She doesn't eat cooked food? Is she nuts?" That is okay to feel that way; it is quite a normal reaction. When my nutritionist Paula put me on that first 30-day raw food diet,I was so sick I didn't question it. But after it was all over, and I started entering cooked vegan foods into my diet, and started to notice the back peddling that was going on, I started to do some research into raw food. Imagine my surprise when I found out there were tens of thousands of raw foodists around the world, many of which have been raw foodists for decades! Take it slow if you need to. Transition from your SAD diet to a vegetarian diet, then to a vegan diet, then to a raw diet. Or, go cold turkey if you can. Do what is comfortable for you.

Having personally experienced a diet of all raw food, in particular a Hygienic raw food diet, I can tell you the unmistakable health benefits that will come to you from an all-raw diet is simply awesome! If you can personally speak to just a few of these raw foodists I guarantee you that their stories will inspire you! In fact, the raw foodists I've met on my road to recovery have inspired me so much I am compiling their stories into a new book I'm working on currently, entitled Raw and Juicy: The Healing Power of Raw Foods.

Knowledge is power. Take the time to read some other books on raw foodism. I was thrilled to see tons of resources on the internet about raw foods. Just do a search on any search engine for raw foods and the number of results you get back will really astound you.

RAW FOODS RESOURCES:

http://www.rawandjuicy.com (my web site)
http://www.douglasgraham.cc

http://www.transformationinst.com
http://www.transformationinst.org
http://www.at1withnature.com
http://www.livingintheraw.com
http://www.livingnutrition.com
http://www.therawworld.com
http://www.shazzie.com
http://www.davidwolfe.com
http://www.paulnison.com
http://www.rawfood.com
http://www.biopia.net/../USA/altmed/rawfooddiet.htm
http://www.rawvegan.com/faq_various2.html
http://www.godsdirectcontact.com/vegetarian/abc/tenadvantages.htm
http://www.living-foods.com
http://www.sunfood.net
http://www.tanglewoodwellnesscenter.com
http://www.justeatanapple.com
http://www.waldorfhomeschoolers.com/rawtransition.htm

There are literally thousands of other web pages related to 'raw food' on the internet. If those are not enough to satisfy your curiosity please just surf around for some more.

URGENT NOTE: When you initially start eating a raw diet and you are doing so for **detoxification purposes**, you may not want to follow the recipes in the raw food recipe books just yet. Some things such as sea salt, Nama Shoyu, certain herbs, and even just the combination of the foods may cause irritation. Those who go raw to get well need to know that the majority of those who reversed their illnesses with raw food were following a more Hygienic raw food diet.

ALL DETOXIFICATION DIETS SHOULD INITIALLY BE PERSONALLY SUPERVISED

In my nutritionists, Paula DuVall's book, A New World of Eating she states, "All detoxifying diets should initially be professionally supervised." I completely agree with this. I had so many questions, and experienced so many strange things during my detoxification diet that I can't imagine having done it without being able to talk to Paula about the different things that were happening. I had an hour period where I could smell an intense smell of paint fumes. It was overwhelming. I had about a year prior to this painted our entire house with a spray machine. I actually detoxed this out of my body. I had many similar things like this happen to me. I woke up in the middle of the night to the smell of perm solution. I had not permed my hair in a few years, and had not dyed it in two years prior to this event. I had many evacuations that were equally bizarre. I used to lay in tanning beds in high school. If you've ever laid in a tanning bed you might know what I am talking about when I say my skin would smell after getting out of the tanning bed. For a couple of weeks I would smell this odor. I kept telling my husband to smell my skin. He couldn't smell anything. The smell was unmistakable. It was exactly how I would smell when I would get out of a tanning bed. I also experienced many pains as I still do very occasionally because I am still detoxing.

Additionally, depending on how toxic you are, you might detox too fast if you change your diet too strictly too quickly. This can be dangerous if you are extremely toxic, so have someone help you. You have the secret information now. You have the information that can help you start to reverse your disease so you can start living life again. Don't mess it up by not following the steps correctly. Seek professional assistance. I only needed help for a couple of months and then I was flying solo! You can do it too.

I know you probably don't want to put your faith or trust into one more professional -- I KNOW THAT FEELING! I didn't want to believe another word anybody told me. But please, take it from me, someone who has been in somewhat similar shoes to what you are in now, professionals in the Natural Hygiene field, or any profession that is trained to heal SOLELY through dietary change, fasting or juicing, can be of great assistance to you. I will do my best to try and help you find these types of professionals. I will list some of them for you in the next chapter dedicated to fasting. Also, as I find professionals who train by Natural Hygiene methods, I will add their contact information to my web site in the **resources** section on my message boards. http://www.rawandjuicy.com/messageboard.html

HOW TO DEAL WITH CRAVINGS AS YOU TRANSITION FROM AN UNHEALTHY DIET TO A HEALTHY DIET

It is very important for you to understand WHY you have cravings. I found for me personally that there are three things that cause me to have cravings.

1   Foods leaving my body from detoxification

2   Not getting enough of the proper nutrients
3   Not eating enough calories

As a certain food, for example dairy, starts to be detoxified from your body, it can cause tremendous cravings. It is just like a person in rehab who is addicted to cocaine or any other drug. You've probably heard stories that while the drug addict is in rehab they cry that they **need** the drug. They crave it; they say they **have to have it**! And, while they detox the drug they will want to do everything in their power to get more of that drug into their system. When you are detoxing junk food, the exact thing that makes the drug-addict crave drugs will make you crave the food(s) you are addicted to. We are addicted to food. It should not be treated in any other way; it should be treated like an addiction because that is **exactly** what it is.

I know for me, my biggest weakness through the detoxification of my dietary change was cheese. I would get cravings so bad I would swear I could actually commit murder for a slice of pizza or lasagna, or anything else that was really cheesy! I have been through this for several months, and I have experienced numerous cravings. I think part of the reason I craved dairy, especially cheese so tremendously, was because for two years I was following the extremely DANGEROUS high-protein diets! Following the high-protein diets was the worst thing I could have done to my already sick and enervated body.

These cravings you will experience are just tricks. Don't give in! Let it pass. Know and understand why you are having the cravings. Below are some tips that were helpful to me when the cravings would come ...

- Remove yourself from temptation. If someone is eating "bad" things in front of you, get up and walk away. Just do I -- remove yourself from the temptation.

- If TV is loaded with commercials sending you signals to go eat junk, SHUT OFF the television. It is sickening how many food commercials there are. Ironically there seem to be just as many prescription drug commercials. Hmmm, the two really **DO** go hand in hand.

- Drink the ample amounts of pure water for your body. (Divide your body weight in half to get the number of ounces of water you should be drinking.) Staying hydrated will curb your appetite and help you deal more effectively with the cravings. *If you eventually transition to a Natural Hygiene raw foods diet, your need for water in take will decrease. On a Natural Hygiene raw food diet your daily water requirements are met in large part, or wholly, by your diet. This diet is referred to as a water-sufficient diet.*

- Reach for a healthy alternative. Two healthy alternatives that helped me enormously in the beginning when cravings would strike were bananas and avocados. If you are craving something sweet try and eat a banana. If you are craving something 'greasy' eat an avocado. One thing you have to be careful of when going raw is the overeating of fats. I did use avocados for months. Dr. Douglas Graham states that when we are craving sweets we are under-eating on fruits. When I follow his advice and increase my fruit intake this always knocks my sweet cravings out!

- Stay active! If you start craving something take note of what you are doing at the time the craving hits. More than likely you will be unoccupied, perhaps just watching TV. If you aren't doing anything productive when the craving hits, get active. If you are able to, clean house, or do some exercising, walk the dog, etc.

- Stay motivated! I find it so helpful to keep motivational reading material on hand. When you see how others did it, it helps to show you that it really is obtainable. If cravings strike, I like to read books on raw food diets and veganism; they keep me super motivated.

The other reason you will get cravings is because you are not getting the proper nutrients. When you are eating a lot of fresh fruits and veggies, you will find that your cravings will go away. The reason this happens is because you are finally getting what your body needs. I have also found that when I am eating correctly, and paying attention to my body, it will actually tell me what to eat. Your cravings actually change from "eat some pizza" to "eat a mango", or "drink some grapefruit juice," etc. This takes time. It is a process. Learn to work with your body.

REVERSING DISEASE IS NOT IMPOSSIBLE & IT IS NOT NEW!!
Don't Be Brainwashed Into Thinking It Is!

Is it really this simple? Can you really reverse disease by 1) eliminating the source of the poisoning and 2) detoxing the body? YES! A thousand times, YES! There will be some rare cases where a person is too far gone and their disease cannot be reversed. But for the majority, even for some with advanced stages of cancer, disease can absolutely be reversed if you make the necessary changes it will require for your body to cure itself. For most of you reading this book your disease reversal will seriously be as easy as undergoing a permanent dietary and lifestyle change. By "lifestyle" I mean, one that focuses on the importance of proper exercise, outdoor life for fresh air and sunshine, and proper rest for your body when it is needed.

If you think reversing disease simply can't be this easy, don't worry. Neither did I. Had I not done it myself I don't know if I would have really believed it. Seeing is believing. So, what have you got to lose? If you are reading this book it is because you have not received any help so far with conventional medicine. If you are reading this book it is more than likely because you are sick and tired of being sick and tired. If you are sick and tired of only 'suppressing' your pain, if you are scared that the prescription drugs you are on are causing further damage to your system, if you are willing to try a natural alternative to getting well, give this a shot. You have nothing to lose and truly everything to gain!

12 STEPS, 10 STEPS, 5 STEPS, 2 STEPS
MANY STEP-BY-STEP PROGRAMS
BUT MOST SHARE THE SAME BASIC INFORMATION

Dr. Day, who cured herself of advanced breast cancer, has a 10-step program that is similar to my 12-step program. The late Paul Bragg, N.D. and his daughter Patricia, who is still spreading her father's word, also have a 10-step program that is similar to the 12 steps I used to reverse my disease. The entire principle of "Natural Hygiene" is similar to the steps I followed to reverse my disease. I have read accounts of many others that have also created their own step-by-step plans to curing their body of so-called incurable disease. All of them are a little different, but **ALL** of them require drastic, permanent dietary change and a means of detoxing the body to cure disease! Do you know why **all** of them have this same **basic information** in their plans? The answer is so simple, even a child could understand it. The reason to why they all have the same information is because, quite simply, there is only ONE cause of disease – AUTOINTOXICATION, and there is only one cure – removing the toxins from and detoxifying the body.

Remember, don't make it harder than it is! There are many books out there on curing disease that will have you needlessly running around in circles. This isn't complicated, so don't make it so. It may take a little tweaking and perfecting on your part, it may even require professional assistance, i.e., a doctor to monitor your prolonged supervised fast or a nutritionist to help set up for you a detoxification diet that is appropriate for your body, but it will work if you stick to the basics - **1) REMOVE THE CAUSE OF THE DISEASE and 2) DETOX THE BODY.**

Chapter 6: What Humans Are and Are NOT Designed To Eat

ARE HUMANS DESIGNED TO EAT MEAT?

If you are asking the question, "Why can't I eat meat?" Prepare yourself for the truth because I am going to share it with you. We truly are not designed to eat meat, and I am going to explainto you **exactly** why this is **fact**. But before I do, let the tree-hugging, PETA supporter in me say that eating meat is cruel, horribly cruel.

The majority of our meat comes from slaughterhouses on today's factory farms where animals are dehorned, debeaked, and castrated without anesthesia. These poor animals are crowded together in the least space possible, to maximize on profits, some spending their entire lives never moving more than a few feet, if that. Most suffer lameness, crippling leg deformities, or bone breaks because their legs can't keep up with their scientifically enhanced bodies. Finally, they are trucked without food or water, through all weather extremes, to a frightening and hellish death. Let me quote for you a disturbing quote from Paul Bragg, N.D., a man responsible for helping countless individuals reverse their so-called incurable diseases. (quote taken from The Miracle of Fasting) "Speaking of the slaughterhouse, what kind of chemical reaction do you suppose would occur in your body if somebody put a choke chain around your neck to keep you in line, shoved you onto a conveyor belt, and made you watch in horror as all of those inline in front of you were beheaded one by one? Well, your body would be pumped so full of adrenaline from all that fear you wouldn't know what hit you! Unused adrenaline is extremely toxic. If you think for a minute that most of the meat that you consume is not packed with this toxic substance, you're sadly mistaken."

As I researched drugless healing plans to cure myself from my disease I continually ran into information like the quote I shared with you by Paul Bragg above. I started asking myself questions like, "Would God work in a slaughterhouse?" Of course not. "Would I eat a dog or a cat?" Of course not. So I thought why do I think it is okay to eat a pig, cow, chicken, etc.? I asked myself if I support cruelty to animals, needless suffering, violence, and death, or didn't I?

By reading the two paragraphs you've just read above, you can clearly see that my opinions stated are made from the position that eating meat is **cruel**. Yes, I do think it is. **HOWEVER**, it isn't just a cruelty issue at all, it is the "danger" issue of eating meat that made me decide to never eat meat again! It isn't just the unused adrenaline that concerned me enough to make me change my diet to a vegan diet. There were many other reasons I made a change to a vegan diet. Let me share some of those reasons with you.

MORE REASONS WHY I NO LONGER EAT MEAT

Let me share with you some more of the information that helped me turn to a meat- less diet. But, before I share with you just a few of the reasons I no longer eat meat, please keep in mind that I was **NOT** a vegan a year ago. I was not even a vegetarian a year ago. I was **NOT** a vegan when I was sick, but actually quite the opposite! I, too, was a meat eater. In fact, for a period of two years I was on the ever-popular **high-protein** diets. During that time I consumed a lot of meat, cheese, and oils. Following those diets was absolutely the **WORST** thing I could have possibly done to my already sick and severely enervated body. Also keep in mind I am not demanding that you become a vegetarian *permanently*. I highly suggest it and I give it my highest recommendations, and it is what I chose for myself, however what you are going to do with your life is going to be up to you. I think that there will be people who will, no matter what I say, add meat back into their diet, AFTER they detox, and for those that are going to do that, it is my sincere hope that you do it as safely as possible. Later in this chapter I will give instructions on the safest ways to reincorporating meat back into your diet if that is what you

choose to do. Again, I do not recommend it. Below are just a few of the other reasons I no longer eat meat.

1) I don't want to eat unhealthy fat -- saturated fats and trans-fatty acids -- because eliminating these things from your diet are proven to help prevent disease.

Dietary fat can be classified into four groups: Saturated, mono-unsaturated, polyunsaturated, and trans-fats. Each group behaves differently inside the body. All four types of fat consist of fatty acids, which are made up of the molecules carbon and hydrogen in various combinations.

The amount and type of fat in the diet may result in the narrowing or widening of the arteries, which has the effect of altering the flow of blood. This may increase the tendency for blood to clot. These are important factors that influence the risk of developing cardiovascular disease.

Healthy Fat vs. Unhealthy Fat:

Healthy Fats are some types of **UN**saturated Fats. Unhealthy Fats are saturated Fats.

Health Fats = Unsaturated Fats
Unhealthy Fats = Saturated Fats & Trans-fatty acids

I'll give you one guess which category meat fat falls into.

You've probably also heard the terms polyunsaturated and monounsaturated. So what do these words "polyunsaturated", "monounsaturated" mean? Is it all Greek to you? Well, to understand these terms you do actually have to know a little Greek.

- Un means not: Unsaturated means not saturated
- mono means one: Monounsaturated means one unsaturated
- poly means many: Polyunsaturated means many unsaturated

What's The Difference Between Saturated and Unsaturated Fat?

All fats contain carbon, hydrogen and a little oxygen to form what are called "fatty acids." Fats are classified according to the proportion of **hydrogen** in the fatty acids. Saturated fats are fats that contain all the hydrogen possible. If the fatty acids are not completely full of hydrogen, fatty acids are termed unsaturated.

Animal fat tends to be highly saturated with hydrogen, while vegetable fats are unsaturated to varying degrees. However, all foods contain a mixture of saturated and unsaturated fats. Beef, pork, and lamb have about equal amounts of each, 50% saturated and 50% unsaturated. Vegetable fats, like corn oil, olive oil, sesame oil, soybean oil, and peanut oil, contain approximately only 14% saturated and 85% unsaturated fats. **Meat contains much higher levels of bad fat than fruits and vegetables do. Meat is 50% SATURATED fat.**

Some Sources of Different Types of Saturated & Unsaturated Fats:

Saturated fats - sources include beef, lamb, milk, cheese, other dairy products, and some processed foods containing hydrogenated vegetable shortening, such as pastries and fried fast foods.

Mono-unsaturated fats - sources include avocado, olive oil, canola oil, and peanuts.

Polyunsaturated fats - sources include fish oils, seafood and vegetable oils, especially safflower, sunflower, corn or soy oils.

Trans-Fatty Acids - sources include commercial baked foods, fried foods, most margarines, vegetable oils and hardened vegetable oils. Trans-fatty acids also occur naturally in small quantities in beef, pork, lamb, butter and milk.

To help foods stay fresh on the shelf or to get a solid fat product, such as margarine, food manufacturers hydrogenate polyunsaturated oils. Hydrogenate means to add hydrogen. This gives you a trans-fatty acid.

How Trans-fatty Acids And Saturated Fats Are Harmful:

Some say trans-fatty acids are more harmful than saturated fats; some say saturated fats are more harmful than trans-fatty acids. One thing everyone seems to agree on, however, is that a healthy diet should be one that greatly reduces or completely eliminates these two things types of fats altogether.

I've taken the following information from the web page **http://www.americanheart.org/presenter.jhtml?identifier= 4776.**

"In clinical studies, *trans-fatty* acids or hydrogenated fats tend to raise total blood cholesterol levels, but less than more saturated fatty acids. *Trans-fatty* acids also tend to raise LDL ("bad") cholesterol and lower HDL ("good") cholesterol when used instead of cis fatty acids or natural oils. These changes may increase the risk of heart disease. It's not clear if trans-fats that occur naturally have the same effect on cholesterol and heart disease as those produced by hydrogenating vegetable oils."

From the Heart Center Online, at **http://www.heartcenteronline.com/Types_Of_Fats.html**, I've taken the following:

"There are a variety of different types of fats. The most harmful to heart health are saturated fat and trans-fatty acids (*trans-fats*). Saturated fat is found in fatty meats (e.g., marbled steak) and dairy products (e.g., cheese). Trans-fatty acids are produced through a manufacturing process called *hydrogenation*, which attaches extra hydrogen atoms to unsaturated fatty acids to make them behave like saturated fats. Other types of fats are not as harmful, and are sometimes helpful. For example, they absorb and carry the **vitamins** A, D, E and K. However, the average American is getting far more total fat than is necessary for good health, raising the risk of heart disease."

"Choose a diet low in saturated fat: Fats contain both saturated and unsaturated (monounsaturated and polyunsaturated) fatty acids. Saturated fat raises blood cholesterol more than other forms of fat. Reducing saturated fat to less than 10 percent of calories will help you lower your blood cholesterol level. The fats from meat, milk, and milk products are the main sources of saturated fats in most diets. Many bakery products are also sources of saturated fats. Vegetable oils supply smaller amounts of saturated fat."

Just go online to the (AMA) American Heart Association's web site, http://www.americanheart.org, and you can read article after article of why you should eat diet low in saturated fat. Saturated fat has been proven for years in study after study to cause such things as clogging of the arteries:

Yes, even the AMA lists the meat, eggs, and dairy products as the foods that raise your cholesterol. See their page --

http://www.americanheart.org/presenter.jhtml?identifier=4582

On the National Children's Leukemia Foundation's web site, in particular at the web page --

http://www.leukemiafoundation.org/Prevent/prevent.htm

They list that one of the things people should do to reduce the chance of leukemia is: **Reduce saturated fat, such as meat and high-fat dairy products.**

Even the American Cancer Society has many articles within its database that link diets high in saturated fats to many different types of cancers.   The following page lists a diet high in saturated fats to Prostate Cancer.

http://www.cancer.org/docroot/COM/content/div_OH/COM_6_1x_Lets_Talk_About_It.asp

Another article from the American Cancer Society's web page --

http://www.cancer.org/docroot/MED/content/MED_2_1x_American_Cancer_Society_Releases_New_Nutrition_and_Physical_Activity_Guidelines.asp

It states, "According to the Society, nearly one-third of the more than 500,000 annual U.S. cancer deaths are attributable to diet and physical activity habits. The Society's newest guidelines, similar to earlier versions, stress adopting a diet with a wide variety of healthy foods that are primarily plant-based. They advise eating five or more daily servings of vegetables and fruits and

recommend eating whole grains over refined grains for more nutrients and fiber. In addition, based on evidence that cancer risk is influenced by the type of fat consumed, rather than simply the total amount, the guidelines recommend limiting the intake of foods high in saturated fat."
This isn't new information. Saturated fat should be eliminated or greatly reduced in our diets to prevent cancer, heart disease, and many other diseases. Just another reason I chose to eliminate meat from my diet.

How Much Fat Do We REALLY Need A Day?

According to Dr. Lorraine Day's VHS Tape You Can't Approve on God, we only need 50 grams of fat a day, and the average American eats **THREE TIMES** the amount of fat that is actually needed. You can choose to get your fat grams from unhealthy fats, the saturated fats such as meats and cheese. Or you can get your fats from HEALTHY FATS, such as avocados, raw nuts & seeds, etc. I chose the latter.

One avocado has about 30 grams of fat. Just 1/2 of a cup of whole, raw almonds has about 35 grams of fat.

Absolutely everything you could possibly want to know about olive oil can be found online at a web site called The Olive Oil Source at **http://www.oliveoilsource.com**

2) I Don't Want To Ingest Hormones, Antibiotics, or Pesticides.

I don't want to ingest pesticides, hormones and antibiotics. Most meat contains pesticides, hormones and antibiotics! These animals are eating pesticides and insecticides in their feed, and it goes into their body and ultimately into you. Most animals are injected with hormones to make bigger, meatier meat. The hormones get locked in the cells of the animal, and you eat them and it goes into your cells. Many animals are injected with antibiotics to prevent them from dying. Most need antibiotics because their living conditions are so horrible they would die if they were not injected with antibiotics. The antibiotics get locked in the cells of the animals, and if you eat them, that ends up in you.   No, thank you! I don't want pesticides, hormones and insecticides in my body.

3) I Don't Want To Eat Animal 'Waste'.

Many animals that you end up eating have been feed the waste products of other animals. To cut costs, many ranchers feed their animals ground-up, dead animals. They then slaughter these poor creatures and feed them to you! Some of these animals that **you** end up eating have been fed dogs and cats from the Humane Society that have been put to sleep or KILLED. And if that is not sick enough, they are also at times feed animals that have **died from disease**! If you eat meat, unless it is grass feed and you are 100% positive it is, you end up eating this too! Do you want to eat a diseased animal? Do you want to eat a dog or cat that was euthanized? I sure as hell don't want to.

Mad Cow disease started as a result of animals being feed other diseased animals. For absolutely must-read information on what the government isn't telling you about Mad Cow disease go to Dr. Lorraine Day's web page for more information.
http://www.drday.com/madcow.htm

4) I don't want to eat anything that will actually <u>lock toxins into</u> my body. I want my body to eliminate toxins, not lock them in.

The human body uses fat cells to store food. This was critical for our ancestors who had to hunt for each meal. Our body was designed to protect us. This storage is a protection mechanism in case of famine, food shortages, etc.

It is hard for me to explain how eating meat actually locks toxins in your body, so I've asked my nutritionist Paula to explain it to you.

Q. Paula, could you explainto my readers how eating meat actually locks toxins into the body and prevents detoxification from happening?

A. "Eating meat not only locks toxins in but adds to toxins that are already in the body. Toxins accumulate in the body because, for some reason, the body does not digest a food. When you eat a food, instead of digesting, assimilating and excreting the food, it will not digest or excrete but will become a toxin. The most difficult foods to digest are fat first and then protein. Flesh foods all contain a very difficult to digest fat as well as a difficult to digest protein. When you have taken a drug, the drug affects the digestive system in its digestion, assimilation and excretion processes. Therefore, your body becomes digestively hypersensitive in the digestive process. Heated fats are the most difficult foods. And all flesh foods have heated fats."

5) I've read the book MAD COWBOY: Plain Truth From The Cattle Rancher Who Won't Eat Meat.

Howard Lyman **was** a fourth-generation dairy farmer and cattle rancher. Mr. Lyman is now a vegan (does not eat any animal products), and was President of Earth Save International, an organization that promotes organic farming and vegetarian diet. He is the author of the book MAD COWBOY: Plain Truth From The Cattle Rancher Who Won't Eat Meat.

Some of you probably know Howard Lyman without even realizing that you know him. Who is Howard Lyman? Remember in 1996 when Oprah Winfrey stated on air that she'd never eat a burger again and a group of "MAD" Texas cattleman went ballistic and tried suing her and the guest that she had on her show that gave her information that made her say that she would never eat a burger again? Well Howard Lyman was the guest on that Oprah Winfrey show that caused such a ruckus with the cattle ranchers.

I do not see how anyone can read the truths that Howard Lyman shares in his book and still continue to eat meat. His story is phenomenal and the information he provides is priceless. In MAD COWBOY: Plain Truth From The Cattle Rancher Who Won't Eat Meat, Howard Lyman makes several points on why and how eating meat is not only bad for you, but for the environment as well. He also shows inhumane feedlot operations are and he tells of how very easily meat that is diseased can and does make it to your dining room table.

Mad Cowboy: Plain Truth from the Cattle Rancher Who Won't Eat Meat is an absolute must-read for **anyone** who eats meat! I believe it is an absolute must-read, too, for anyone who is trying to reverse his or her disease. It is my opinion that this book should be mandatory in schools. Children should be given this information so that they could make an informed choice as to what they are putting into their bodies.

Some of the other books that provided me with information that made me switch from a diet that included meat to a vegan diet are listed below,

- **Eating With Conscience -** By Michael W. Fox

- **Slaughterhouse**: **The Shocking Story of Greed, Neglect, and Inhumane Treatment Inside the U.S. Meat Industry -** Gail A. Eisnitz

- **Food Politics: How the Food Industry Influences Nutrition and Health -** by Marion Nestle, Ph.D., M.P.H

- **Diet for a New America: How Your Food Choices Affect Your Health, Happiness and the Future of Life on Earth** - by John Robbins

VHS Tapes That Changed My View About Eating Meat:

Cancer Doesn't Scare Me Anymore - VHS Tape. By Dr. Lorraine Day
http://www.drday.com

Web Sites That Changed My View About Eating Meat:

Why Meat Eating is Unnatural
http://michaelbluejay.com/veg/natural.html

How Humans Are Not Designed To Eat Meat
http://www.celestialhealing.net/physicalveg3.htm

The Problems With Meat And Dairy Products
http://home.iae.nl/users/lightnet/health/meat.htm

The Case Against Meat
http://www.emagazine.com/january-february_2002/0102feat1.html

Farm Sanctuary
http://www.farmsanctuary.com

People For The Ethical Treatment of Animals
http://www.peta.org

Earth Save International
http://www.earthsave.org - This is the web site for the organization of which Howard Lyman, author of MAD COWBOY:

Plain Truth From The Cattle Rancher Who Won't Eat Meat, is president.

I would like to share with you a quote from the book Mad Cowboy: Plain Truth From The Cattle Rancher Who Won't Eat Meat, by Howard Lyman. "Many people concerned about the health risks of a meat-based diet have adopted the half-measure of cutting down the red meat and eating more chicken and fish. Some people who consume fish and poultry while avoiding red meat entirely even call themselves "semi-vegetarian." Unfortunately for them, chicken and fish are not plants, and they are not health foods. It is not even clear that they are lesser evils than red meat. Only modern linguistic convention saves fish and poultry from the label of "meat" - for they are indeed meats, the flesh of animals. Substituting chicken and fish for red meat will not help you avoid any of the health risks associated with the meat of mammals. It will not save you from heart disease, strokes, diabetes, cancer, high blood pressure, or osteoporosis. Chicken and fish will in fact contribute to the danger of developing those conditions. They present the exact same threats to our well-being as red meat: They are high in fat (especially saturated fat), high in cholesterol, too high in protein, high in pesticide residue, and devoid of fiber and complex carbohydrates. There is a popular misconception that chicken and fish are low-cholesterol foods, or at least considerably lower than beef. A 3.5-ounce serving of beef contains 85 milligrams of cholesterol. The same-size serving of chicken (white meat, skinned) also has 85 milligrams of cholesterol. With equivalent servings of pork, trout, and turkey, you can clog your arteries with 90, 73, and 82 milligrams of cholesterol, respectively. There simply are no low-cholesterol flesh foods, and there are no plant foods with any cholesterol."

But besides all of those reasons above, I do not want to eat meat because the FACT is ...

HUMANS ARE NOT DESIGNED TO EAT MEAT!

When I started studying veganism, and raw foodism I kept hearing people say over and over again, "Humans are not designed to eat meat." When I would start to ask some people why this was so I found that many of them didn't have the answers to back up that statement. So, being the very inquisitive person that I am, I wanted to find out for myself, if the statement "Humans Are Not Designed To Eat Meat" was really fact or if it was just hype. To my great pleasure I found out that it is indeed fact. Humans are NOT designed to eat meat.

To break down protein, we need the enzyme pepsin and hydrochloric acid. We do have both the enzyme pepsin and hydrochloric acid. But, when we compare our levels of these enzymes and acid with, say, a true carnivore ours pale in comparison. In Dr. Sniadach's Essential Natural Hygiene course he stated that a tiger's stomach secretes a hydrochloric acid some **1,100% greater** than a humans!

But, if you are like me, you then ask the questions...

"But we **DO** have pepsin and hydrochloric acid so doesn't that then mean we are suppose to eat meat because our bodies make the enzyme and the acid for breaking down protein?"

and

"Perhaps we are just designed to eat smaller amounts of protein than tigers are?"

But the answer to both of those questions is NO. And, here is why... We need this pepsin/hydrochloric acid combo to break down protein, that is very true. However, you have to REMEMBER protein IS in such things as nuts, for example. Protein is even in fruits (however small the percentage may be). There is protein in fruit and vegetables!

But that wasn't what sunk the case for me as to why humans are not designed to eat meat. Another interesting thing I have learned is that the human body does not have the enzyme called **uricase** that animals do. Uricase is needed to break down the uric acid in meats. Humans simply do not make the enzyme uricase. "So what!" you say. I'll tell you so what -- when a human being eats meat they do not break down the toxic uric acid. When uric acid is in the human body it causes the body to use its precious reserves of alkaline minerals, like calcium, to neutralize the uric acid. In "Basic Arguments Against Flesh Foods" by T.C. Fry, he stated, "Because grain and meat-eating humans have a predominantly acid-forming diet, the body must often times get the necessary base minerals from its bones to neutralize the acids, The resulting calcium urates cause kidney stones, accretions in the joints that result in arthritis and, in all events, osteoporosis of both bones and teeth." After finding out information of this nature it did not shock me at all that a few years back, when on the ever popular high-protein diets for two years, my blood tests showed low calcium levels.

We simply are not designed to break down meat. We are designed to break down proteins, yes, in small quantities, and there IS protein in fruits, vegetables and nuts -- all of the foods that we are designed to eat. But the fact is we are not designed to break down meat because it has uric acid in it, and we completely incapable of breaking that down.

In Dr. Herbert M. Shelton's work "Proteins In The Fruitarian Diet" I read some information that fits so perfectly into this topic that I have to share it with you to drive the point home that there are things all species are designed to eat and not to eat. Dr. Shelton states, "Some plant substances are poisonous to some animals and not to others. An example is belladonna, which, highly poisonous to man, is non-toxic to the rabbit after it is six weeks old. After this age the rabbit secretes an enzyme that enables it to digest the two toxins in the plant. Man produces no such enzyme." I found that fascinating.

There are plants that are poisonous to humans. They are poisonous because we are not designed to eat them. People don't have a hard time accepting that concept. Try and tell a meat-eater that it is scientific fact that we are not designed to eat meat and they say "IMPOSSIBLE!" This reaction stems from their strong attachment to eating meat, not on facts. The fact is humans are not designed to eat meat.

Do you want to learn something else equally as fascinating as our inability to eat meat? Humans are also not designed to drink milk. Rennin is the enzyme that is needed to break down casein, which is what binds milk proteins, calcium and other nutrients. We do, interestingly enough, secrete rennin up until about the age of three. Is it a coincidence that this young age is the proper weaning age? No, it is no coincidence. Our bodies are wisely intelligent. The real problem is the average human being does not have a clue as to how the human body works, however. Instead of working with it, we are, usually from birth, working against it by filling it full of toxins that our bodies simply are not designed to digest, assimilate, and eliminate.

ARE HUMANS DESIGNED TO EAT GRAINS?

The following is a quote from T.C. Fry in response to the question, Are We Grain Eaters?: "Grains are grass seeds. The grains of today are rather small, but they're huge compared to the seeds from which they're developed. Grains have been cultivated and eaten by humans for only about 8,000 years."

In nature we did not eat grains or grass seeds. We did not develop any gathering or digestive equipment for grains. Natural grain eaters must be able to efficiently gather, grind, and digest grains. Humans fail on all accounts. Our teeth handle grains poorly. In fact, humans refuse to chew tasteless and hard grains. Even so, humans, not being starch eaters, cannot digest more than a handful of grains, if that much. True starch eaters secrete a plethora of starch-splitting enzymes in copious amounts. Humans secrete one starch-splitting enzyme, salivary amylase (ptyalin) which is quickly exhausted. After a mouthful or two of starch, the eater palls and stops. Nope, we're not grain eaters. The way we do eat grains by mechanical gathering, refining, cooking, etc., makes them palatable but more pathogenic.

WHAT HUMANS ARE DESIGNED TO EAT

Hopefully I've made it clear enough for you that humans are not designed to eat meat. So, if the human body isn't designed to eat meat, what is it designed to eat?

Our bodies are designed to eat fruits, vegetables, nuts, and seeds in their most natural, raw state. In all truth however, the body is best designed or equipped for a fruitarian diet. Don't panic! A fruitarian diet is much wider than the name itself suggests. Many vegetables are actually fruits, as are nuts. You can go to my message boards and read Dr. Shelton's work Proteins In Frutarian Diet for a detailed explanation of why many vegetables, legumes, and nuts are actually considered fruit.

Why is a fruitarian diet considered by Hygienists to be the ideal diet? An ideal diet, to me, is one that would require the body to do the least amount of work; one that would appropriately supply the body's vitamin, mineral, and nutrient needs, and one that would not put toxins into the body. You have to ask yourself which class of foods do humans most efficiently process. And, the answer to that question is fruits.

Illness and disease are created as the result of excessive toxins being introduced into the body faster than the body can eliminate them. Fruits, unless they are filled with pesticides/insecticides, leave no toxic residue in the body, none. Unlike meat, processed foods (even healthier processed vegetarian/vegan foods), and cooked foods that become toxic through the cooking process, fruits do not introduce toxins into the body. They are used by the body. Nothing more and nothing less.

The following information is from Dr. Herbert Shelton's work "Fruit Eating":

Dr. Herbert M. Shelton
Fruit Eating

"Fruit is real food. Indeed, fruits are among the few substances produced I organic nature that seem to be designed specially to serve as food ... Fruits supply the body with an abundance of minerals, sugars, and vitamins and, in the case of some of them, considerable high-grade protein. The sugar in fruit is ideally associated with minerals and vitamins and need not be rejected as one does (or should) refined sugars. Fruit sugar is superior as human nutriment to honey, which is so ludicrously lauded in many quarters. Indeed, honey, when compared with the sugars of fruits, ranks about on the level of white sugar.

Most fruits are abundant in minerals, also containing important trace minerals, so that they form important and vital ingredients in the diet of the growing child. Most of them are moderate to low in calcium, but this is easily compensated from other wholesome sources. Fruits are commonly rich in vitamin C but contain less of other vitamins. They are, however, on the whole, excellent sources of vitamins.

They are commonly low in protein, rarely containing over two to two and a half percent and many of them containing much less than this. The date, banana, avocado and a few other fruits contain small amounts of excellent proteins. Supplemented with nuts and green leaves, their proteins become valuable additions to the diet. A fruit and nut diet is improved by the addition of green leafy vegetables. A large green salad each day makes such a diet almost ideal.

Most fruits contain more or less acid - such as malic, citric, tartaric, etc. being present. The prejudice that has grown up around fruits is a revival of the medical prejudice against acid fruits. They were declared to cause "acid diseases", and were regarded as especially objectionable in rheumatism.

Fortunately, the body is able to oxidize the organic acids of fruits, at least of those fruits that we commonly use as food. These leave an alkaline ash upon being oxidized. There is sometimes difficulty with the acid of prunes, but there is no ground for the prejudice that has been revived against oranges, tangerines, lemons, grapefruit, tangelos, tomatoes, and similar citric-acid bearing fruits.

The acids of berries are also easily oxidized and these, also, leave an alkaline ash. The acid radical of organic acids is expelled as carbon dioxide through the lungs; the alkaline salts that remain help to alkalinize the blood. Teeth have been kept uninterruptedly immersed in lemon juice for as long as six months and the acid had no effect on their enamel. There would seem to be no foundation for the idea that eating oranges or drinking orange juice injures the teeth.

It should be generally known that when acids are taken into the mouth there is a copious outpouring of alkaline saliva, which bathes the membranes of the mouth and the tongue. This secretion of saliva is kept up long after the acid has been swallowed. Any acid left on the teeth or in the mouth is quickly neutralized by the alkaline saliva. We are too prone to overlook the body's own provisions for its safety.

In the late spring and summer, when such fruits as peaches, plums, apricots, nectarines, cherries, the various berries, cantaloupes, watermelons, grapes, figs, etc., are plentiful, it is well to make a large part of the diet fruits. In the fall, when pears, apples, persimmons, and the citrus fruits come into season, these should constitute a large part of the diet. Certain of these fruits, like the tomato, grapes, oranges, and grapefruits are plentiful throughout most of the year and may be eaten all the time. The avocado is abundant through most of the year, but is best eaten during the cooler periods of the year. Such sun-dried fruits as figs, dates, raisins, peaches, apricots, pears, etc., may be freely eaten during the winter months.

These melons make an excellent breakfast during the season of the year when they are ripening. They are best eaten alone. A large piece of watermelon makes an adequate breakfast, even for the physical worker. Cantaloupe, banana melon, casaba, Crenshaw and the Persian melon, in season, make a delightful and satisfying breakfast. If more food is desired for breakfast, it should be taken half an hour after eating the melon.

Nearly all of what we see of so-called allergy to fruits is indigestion resulting from wrongly combining the foods eaten. Fruits with starches, fruits with proteins, and similar combinations are prone to decompose, producing gas, discomfort, and skin eruptions. Melons with other foods may cause marked distress. Eaten alone, they digest with the greatest of ease. In very young children there may sometimes be a short period during the development of a child, when its digestive system cannot handle a certain fruit, for example, an apple. It is well to leave some fruits out of the child's diet until its development has progressed to a point where it can easily digest the fruit that gives trouble.

Great improvement in the ability to digest and handle foods follows a fast. It is no uncommon thing to find that an individual, who has trouble with a particular article of food, can take it with the greatest of ease after a fast. If we can learn that what is called allergy is not a permanent possession, but that when its causes are removed, it ceases, we can understand that it is possible for us to become able to enjoy any wholesome food. It amazes those who are "allergic" to strawberries, for example, to see no trouble develop if they are placed on a strawberry diet.

When fruit is eaten with a meal of bread, flesh, potatoes, butter and the rest of the usual meal, the fruit usually being taken at the end of the meal, but often at the beginning, the indigestion and discomfort that result from such combining of foods will almost certainly be blamed on the fruit, which is likely the only wholesome article of food in the meal. The discomforts following such a meal may range all the way from a little gas formation that scarcely attracts the attention of the eater, to a painful indigestion accompanied with nausea, vomiting and diarrhea. The fruit, kept away from the other foods, and eaten as a fruit meal will digest easily and result in no discomfort.

Fruits that are peeled and sliced and permitted to stand for long periods of time before eating are hardly wholesome foods. They change color, lose flavor, undergo oxidation with resulting loss of food value and tend to decompose readily. Fruits added to breads, cakes, pies and various other kinds of pastries can also occasion considerable indigestion and distress. In this latter case, not only is the food spoiled in preparation and cooking, but the combination is indigestible. Fresh fruits, with cleaning as the only preparation, are most easily digested. The addition of sugar, syrups, honey and other sweeteners to fruits can also result in indigestion and discomforts.

Fruits have fallen into disrepute with many people for the reason that they find that they suffer with discomfort after eating them. It was Dr. Dewey who said that fruits demoralize digestion. He was especially opposed to eating apples. This trouble with fruits grows out of the practice of wrongly combining them. Strawberries and melons are commonly singled out as "fruits that I am allergic to," and these foods are wholesome and toothsome. If taken alone, as in the case of melons, or properly combined as in the case of strawberries, they almost never cause any trouble, Sink rashes and intestinal disturbances that often follow the eating of fruit or that follow a particular fruit may, almost always, be traced to wrong combining. In the few cases where this is not so, correction of the way of life, so that normal digestive power is re-established, soon enables the individuals to eat fruit. I do not think that there is anyone who cannot eat freely of fruits if due care is taken in combining them."

William Esser, N.D, D.C., also taught that fruits are the ideal foods. In "Fruit - Best Food Of All" he stated the following:

Of all the foods that we can eat, fruits are the best in every respect. They are objects, which enchant the eye, delight the smell and thrill the normal taste beyond sensation incited by any other food. In itself, fruit is perfect. It requires no preparation of any kind other than cleansing, coring or peeling. Cooking, seasonings, additions and subtractions make it less, not more palatable.

Beyond its appeal to the senses, it possesses most of the essential proteins, minerals and vitamins necessary for maintaining health at its highest level. Obtained in large enough variety, fruits (with the addition of nuts which are also fruits) would be ample for the maintenance of ideal health."

Humans are designed to eat fruit. We have the enzymes required to digest fruit. We use ALL of the fruit. There is nothing in fruit that we cannot digest, assimilate and eliminate. Fruit, in so long as we eat a wide variety of it and in abundant quantity to meet our caloric needs, is meets all our nutrient requirements.

Chapter 7: Cooked Food Vs. Raw Food: The Facts

Why should we eat raw food? Is cooked food really that bad for us? When the nutritionist I went to for colonics put me on a 30-day raw food diet I didn't really question her. She explained that raw foods have all of their enzymes, vitamins, and minerals in tact and that is what my enervated body needed. It made perfect sense, so I followed her instructions to a T.

My health improved so much in those 30 short days that I knew that there really was something to this "'raw thing." It wasn't until I went back to eating cooked foods again, however, that I really started to ask the question, "Is cooked food good for us?"

In chapter 4, I've already touched on many of society's normal cooking methods, such as microwaving and grilling, which cause food to become toxic. But in this chapter, I just want to discuss all cooking in general and what happens to food when it is heated or cooked.

COOKING DESTROYS ENZYMES

When food is cooked, life-supporting enzymes are destroyed. If you are saying, "so what?" then what you need to comprehend is the fact that enzymes work as catalysts to our bodies make proper use the foods vitamins and minerals. It is true that when food is cooked it still does have some of its vitamins and minerals, and carbohydrates and proteins, etc., however they are put into an altered state by the cooking process. The phytochemicals and vitamins in foods are altered and diminished by cooking. The minerals in foods are made harder to dissolve. I've already discussed harmful trans-fatty acids with you in an earlier chapter. Fats are turned to trans-fatty acids through cooking.

By eating a diet high in cooked foods we prevent our body from working, as it is in continual motion doing, on keeping our body in its healthiest state. By filling our body with toxins, anything that is unnatural to the body, we make it divert its energy and attention from keeping us healthy. We burden and overwork our body by filling it with toxins and then when the real need arises for it to save us it is worn out from the continuous work it has been doing eliminating the barrage of toxins we are putting in it.

Cooking food greatly changes it from the form that nature intended it to have. These very simple facts alone make it a little easier to understand why we live in such a diseased society. We are cooked food eaters! Even though we may eat like pigs and be overweight or downright obese, we are in actuality suffering from malnutrition. We are essentially starving our bodies of their much-needed nutrients. The result of this starvation is disease; which, in fact, is a curative and restorative process of the body. If **it** was understood and the appropriate actions were taken when we become ill, i.e., strict dietary and lifestyle changes, people could reverse disease instead of die from it.

However, this is new and misunderstood.   So, instead of giving the body what it needs -- fresh raw foods, sunlight, exercise, rest/sleep, etc., we take the doctor's RX drugs and continue on our SAD (Standard American Diet) of cooked, processed, and chemically laden foods. Sadly, the majority of individuals eat very little if **any** fresh, raw fruits and vegetables. I'm hoping to change that J!!

But let's move beyond the obvious, or for some perhaps the not so obvious for a minute. What happens inside the body when we eat cooked food? Is there any difference inside the human body when one consumes cooked food or raw food? The answer is **yes**! There is an intensely, critical difference that takes place in our bodies when we eat cooked food as opposed to raw food.

WHAT HAPPENS IN OUR BODY
AFTER EATING A COOKED FOOD MEAL?

In the article, "Is Cooked Food Good For Us?" by T.C. Fry (taken from David Klein's web site http://www.LivingNutrition.com), Fry states, "Cooking renders food toxic! The toxicity of the deranged debris of cooking is confirmed by the doubling and tripling of white blood cells after eating a cooked food meal. The white blood cells are the first line of defense and are, collectively, popularly called 'the immune system'."

In his "Cooking is Pathogenic" section of his Essential Natural Hygiene course, Dr. Robert Sniadach states the following:

 Cooking creates diseases on several counts. The most salient are as follows: Cooking deranges and destroys nutrients. To the extent that this occurs, we are denied needed vitamins, minerals, proteins, essential fatty acids, and other nutrient factors.

The deranged nutrients become, via cooking, unusable substances that is toxic in the system. This is readily evidenced by the doubling and tripling of the leukocyte count in the blood in half an hour to an hour after eating a meal of cooked foods. Any poison or drug taken into the body occasions the same body response.

The body must expend tremendously of its nerve and other energies to expel the offending substances of cooked foods and to clear itself of their contamination. Cooked food eaters have "hangovers" and "withdrawal" symptoms just as do drinkers of coffee, tobacco smokers or other drug addicts who forego their regular round of stimulation.

The following article, COOKED FOOD EFFECTS, was taken, with permission from the editor, David Klein, from Volume 6 of his Living Nutrition Magazine:

COOKED FOOD EFFECTS
by Wes Peterson

During the past few decades there has been much research done in the area of nutrition. Some of this research casts light on some important insights regarding the foods Mother Nature offers to us in its whole, raw state, and what happens when we tamper with them.

What exactly happens to food when it is cooked? What happens to the body if we eat cooked food? Some key points are covered in this article. Due to space limitation, we can only but touch on the topic here; however, a brief overview is given below.

KEY POINTS REGARDING THE EFFECTS OF COOKING ON FOOD AND HEALTH

* The food's life force is greatly depleted or destroyed. The bioelectrical (energy) field is altered and greatly depleted (as is graphically demonstrated with kirlian photography). Live and bioactive (raw) food is rendered dead and inert.

* The biochemical structure and nutrient makeup of the food is altered from its original state. Molecules in the food are deranged, degraded, and broken down. The food is degenerated in many ways. Fiber in plant foods is broken down into a soft, passive substance, which loses its broom-like and magnetic cleansing quality in the intestines.

* Nutrients (vitamins, minerals, amino acids, etc.) are depleted, destroyed and altered. The degree of depletion, destruction and alteration is simply a matter of temperature, cooking method, and time.

* Up to 50% of the protein is coagulated. Much of this is rendered unusable. High temperatures also create cross-links in protein. Cross-linked proteins are implicated in many problems in the body, as well as being a factor in the acceleration of the aging process.

* The interrelationship of nutrients is altered from its natural synergistic makeup. For example, with meat, relatively more vitamin B-6 than methionine is destroyed, which fosters atherogenic, free-radical-initiating homocysteine accumulation (which is a factor in heart problems).

* The water content of the food is decreased. The natural structure of the water is also changed.

* Toxic substances and cooked "byproducts" are created. The higher the cooking temperature, the more toxins are created. Frying and grilling are especially toxin generating. Various carcinogenic and mutagenic substances and hordes of free radicals are generated in cooked fats and proteins in particular.

* Heat causes the molecules involved to collide, and repeated collision causes divalent bonding in order for new molecules, and hence a new substance, to form. In an ordinary baked potato, there are 450 by-products of every description. They have even been named "new chemical composites."

* Unusable (waste) material is created, which has a cumulative congesting/clogging effect on the body and is a burden to the natural eliminative processes of the body.

* All of the enzymes present in raw foods are destroyed at temperatures as low as 118 degrees Fahrenheit. These enzymes, named "food enzymes" are important for optimum digestion. They naturally aid in digestion and become active as soon as eating commences. Cooking destroys 100% of these enzymes. Eating enzyme-dead food places a burden on the pancreas and other organs and overworks them, which eventually exhausts these organs. The digestion of cooked food usurps valuable metabolic enzymes in order to help digest the food. Digestion of cooked food

is much more energetically demanding than the digestion of raw food. In general, raw food is so much more easily digested that it passes through the digestive tract in a half to a third of the time it takes for cooked food.

* After eating a cooked meal, there is a rush of white blood cells towards the digestive tract, leaving the rest of the body less protected by the immune system. From the point of view of the immune system the body is being invaded by a foreign (toxic) substance when cooked food is eaten.

* A general augmentation of white corpuscles in the blood and a change in the relative proportions of different blood cells occurs. This phenomenon is called "digestive leukocytosis".

* The natural population of beneficial intestinal flora becomes dominated by putrefactive bacteria (particularly from cooked meat), resulting in colonic dysfunction, allowing the absorption of toxins from the bowel. This phenomenon is variously called dysbacteria, dysbiosis, or intestinal toxemia (toxicosis).

* A buildup of mucoid plaque is created in the intestines. Mucoid plaque is a thick, tar-like substance, which is the long-term result of undigested, uneliminated cooked food putrefying in the intestines. Cooked starches and fats in particular are a major culprit in constipation and clogging of the intestines.

* A build-up of toxins and waste material in many parts of the body, including within individual cells. Some of these toxins and wastes are called lipofuscin, which accumulates in the skin and nervous system, including the brain. It can be observed as "liver spots" or "age spots."

* Malnutrition at the cellular level. Because cooked foods are lower in nutrients, in addition to containing wastes and toxins, individual cells don't receive enough of the nutrients they need.

* Tendency towards obesity through overeating. Because the cells don't get enough nutrients they are so to speak "always hungry" and hence "demand" more food. Cooked food is also less likely to be properly metabolized, which is another factor in excess weight gain.

* From time to time the body experiences detoxification crises (also called purification or healing crises). This happens when

toxins are released through the skin or dumped in the bloodstream for elimination by the liver, kidneys, and other organs. The symptoms may include headaches, fever, nausea, vomiting, colds, bronchitis, sinusitis, pneumonia, diarrhea, etc.

* The body can become so toxic that all kinds of particles, such as pollen, can cause detoxification crises, called "allergies". An estimated 80 million Americans suffer from such "allergies".

* The immune system, having to handle the massive daily invasions of toxins and toxic by-products, eventually becomes overwhelmed and weakened, a key factor in the aging process.

* Some of the waste material builds up in the arteries and clogs them, leading to high blood pressure, atherosclerosis, arteriosclerosis, strokes, etc. - killing an estimated 50% of Americans.

* The wastes, toxins, mutagens, and carcinogens that build up within cells, as well as the daily onslaught of excess free radicals, eventually cause some cells to become cancerous - killing an estimated 30% of Americans.

* In general, the natural aging process is accelerated by cooked food. People who switch to raw food often become biologically and visibly younger.

FROM CANCEROLOGIST BRUCE AMES (REGARDING "MUTAGENESIS, CARCINOGENESIS, AND THE DEGENERATIVE DISEASES OF AGING"):

Cooking food is plausible as a contributor to cancer. A wide variety of chemicals are formed during cooking. Four groups of chemicals that cause tumors in rodents have attracted attention because of mutagenicity, potency, and concentration:

1) Nitrosamines are formed from nitrogen oxides present in gas flames or from other burning. Surprisingly little work has been done on the levels of nitrosamines in fish or meat cooked in gas ovens or barbecued, considering their mutagenic and carcinogenic potency.

2) Heterocyclic amines are formed from heating amino acids or proteins.

3) Polycyclic hydrocarbons are formed from charring meat.

4) Furfural and similar furans are formed from heating sugars. Heating fat generates mutagenic epoxides, hydroperoxides, and unsaturated aldehydes, and may also be of importance.

References:

International Agency for Research on Cancer (1993) Some naturally occurring substances: Food items and constituents, heterocyclic aromatic amines and mycotoxins (International Agency for Research on Cancer, Lyon, France).

Gold, L. S., Slone, T. H., Stern, B. R., Manley, N. B. & Ames, B. N. (1992) Science 258, 261-265.

Gold, L. S., Slone, T. H., Manley, N. B. & Ames, B. N. (1994) Cancer Lett. 83, 21-29.

[Dr. Ames is a Professor of Biochemistry and Molecular Biology and Director, National Institute of Environmental Health Sciences Center, University of California, Berkeley. He is a member of the National Academy of Sciences and was on their Commission on Life Sciences. He was formerly on the board of directors of the National Cancer Institute (National Cancer Advisory Board). He was the recipient of the most prestigious award for cancer research, the General Motors Cancer Research Foundation Prize (1983), the highest award in environmental achievement, the Tyler Prize (1985), the Gold Medal Award of the American Institute of Chemists (1991), and the Glenn Foundation Award of the

Gerontological Society of America (1992). He has been elected to the Royal Swedish Academy of Sciences, the Japan Cancer Association, and the Academy of Toxicological Sciences. His 300 scientific publications have resulted in his being the 23rd most-cited scientist (in all fields) (1973-1984).]

LEUKOCYTOSIS AND COOKED FOOD

In 1930, research was conducted at the Institute of Clinical Chemistry in Lausanne, Switzerland, under the direction of Dr. Paul Kouchakoff. The effect of food (cooked/processed vs. raw/natural) on the immune system was tested and documented. Dr. Kouchakoff's discovery concerned the leukocytes, the white blood cells. Apparently, a well-known phenomenon occurred immediately after a person ate.

It was found that after a person eats cooked food, his/her blood responds immediately by increasing the number of white blood cells. This is a well-known phenomenon called "digestive leukocytosis", which means that there is a rise in the number of leukocytes, or white blood cells, after eating. Since digestive leukocytosis was always observed after eating, it was considered to be a normal physiological response to eating. No one knew why the number of white cells would rise after eating, since this appeared to be a stress response, as if the body was reacting to something harmful, such as infection, trauma, or exposure to toxic chemicals.

A REMARKABLE DISCOVERY

Back in 1930, Swiss researchers of the institute of Chemical Chemistry studied the influence of food on human blood and made a remarkable discovery. They found that eating unaltered, raw food or food heated at low temperatures did not cause a reaction in the blood. In addition, if a food had been heated beyond a certain temperature (unique to each food), or if the food was processed (refined, added chemicals, etc.), this ALWAYS caused a rise in the number of white cells in the blood. The researchers renamed this reaction "pathological leukocytosis," since the body was reacting to highly altered food. They tested many different kinds of foods and found that if the foods were not overheated or refined, they caused no reaction. The body saw them as "friendly foods." However, these same foods, if heated at too high a temperature, caused a negative reaction in the blood, a reaction that is found only when the body is invaded by a dangerous pathogen or trauma.

THE WORST OFFENDERS

The worst offenders of all, whether heated or not, were processed foods -- that had been refined (such as white flour or white rice), or homogenized (a process in which the fat in milk is subjected to artificial suspension), or pasteurized (also seen in milk, flash-heated to high temperatures to kill bacteria), or preserved (chemicals added to food to retard spoilage or to enhance taste or texture) -- in other words, foods that were changed from their original God-given state. Good examples of these harmful foods are: Pasteurized milk, chocolate, margarine, sugar, candy, white flour, and regular salt. The researchers found that if these altered, chemical foods were chewed very thoroughly, the harm to the blood could be lessened. In addition, another amazing finding was that if some of the same food in its raw state was eaten with the cooked counterpart, the pathological reaction in the blood was minimized. However, avoid these unnatural, processed foods; replace them with delicious whole foods for optimal health.

INCREASE YOUR RAW FOOD INTAKE

The body cannot build really healthy cells and tissues with poor quality materials. That which must be cooked to be palatable is not worthy of the human diet."

I am a realist. I realize that not everyone is going to become a 100% raw foodist permanently. At the very least I hope this chapter however encourages you to greatly increase the amount of fresh, raw fruits and vegetables that you are consuming. Remember, however, that whenever we put a toxic substance into the body we are causing unneeded stress and work on the body. When toxins are put into the body, whether they are from RX drugs or cooked food, they are still seen as foreign invaders, and the body will have to put its energy into the removal of the toxin.

If you are feeling ill or diseased, go raw! Try a Hygienic raw food diet for a few months and track your progress. Clear your body out, detoxify, get well. If you decide to add cooked food back into your diet at that point by all means do so, but do so as healthfully as possible, i.e., steamed vegetables.

I've already discussed with you the fact that humans are not designed to eat meat and that we stop producing the enzyme that helps break down milk at age 3. Our bodies are simply not designed to consume those foods. If you can't – no, let me rephrase that -- if you choose not to do a Hygienic, 100% raw food diet permanently, consider a vegan, predominantly high raw or a vegan, very high raw diet.

From my own personal experience, and the experience of countless others that I've spoken to who used raw foods to reverse their diseases, a Hygienic, raw food diet is a huge factor in successfully reversing so-called incurable disease and chronic illness.

Chapter 8: Where Do Raw Foodists Get Their Protein & Vitamin B-12?

WHERE DO VEGETARIANS, VEGANS & RAW FOODISTS GET THEIR PROTEIN?

If I had a nickel for every time I have been asked this question I would be a millionaire! When I first went raw, and then vegan, and then raw again J. This was a huge concern of mine. Where am I going to get my protein? Funny, I've been eating my entire life and the concern of where am I going to get my protein never entered into my head. I think of days in high school where I lived on frozen cheese pizzas, candy bars, and colas. Never once was I concerned about where my protein was coming from. When you go this route, you too are going to all of a sudden become quite concerned with where you're getting your protein. Well, I did the studying for you so you don't have to. Let me share with you some information on protein and our body's real requirements of protein.

First and foremost 70% of our body's protein needs are met through our body's own intelligent recycling ability. You'll never hear the authors of the high-protein diets sharing this information with you, and HELLO, why would they? They are making money off all of their "low-carb" products. Remember ... follow the money trail!

How do we recycle protein? Let me share with you another quote from Dr. Robert Sniadach: "When cells disintegrate from the action of lysosomes upon their death, the debris floats in the lymph. The lymph is the media of supply and drainage for the cells. Other cells may remove proteinaceous debris from the lymph by the processes of phagocytosis or pinocytosis (cell drinking or cell eating) if the amino acid supply is otherwise insufficient. The cells then break down the proteins into their amino acid constituents in a special little vesicle or stomach they have created for the process. Then the amino acids are diffused into the cells for use just as if they had been absorbed as amino acids from the intercellular fluids in the first place. The kidneys play a role in eliminating protein wastes normally, but, if there is a protein shortage, it will recover protein wastes and recycle them into the blood for reuse."

So besides the recycling of protein that takes place when cells disintegrate, how else do we get our protein? The next thing you have to realize is that the RDA's standard for protein requirements are actually much higher than what our **real** body's protein requirements are. To give you an example of what the RDA for protein:

The Recommended Daily Allowance (RDA) of protein according to U.S. government standards is 0.8 gram per kilogram (1 kilogram equals 2.2 pounds) of ideal body weight for the adult. So, if you followed RDA requirement for protein an adult male who weighs 154 pounds, he would require 56 grams of protein daily. A female whose weight is 110 pounds, needs 40 grams a day. Those are simply much higher than what is actually needed by the body. And, anything that the body does not use is eliminated. Keep in mind when following RDA guidelines that the meat and dairy industries do have much influence on their "requirements." Follow the money trail.

Many doctors from all fields including Natural Hygiene, naturopathy, homeopathy, and, yes, even conventional medicine are stating that our real protein needs are only approximately 25 grams a day. Studies have been done on men in other countries who live vigorous, high-activity lifestyles, yet take in only 15 grams of protein a day and they have superior health.

Dr. Lorraine Day, who healed herself of breast cancer states in her VHS Tape "You Can't Improve on God", that we need only about 30 grams of protein a day. In her tape she also says that the average American eats 125 grams of protein a day. She also notes that this additional protein we eat cannot be stored. The liver must break it down and the liver gets worn out trying to break down this extra protein.

Dr. Joel Fuhrman, in his book Fasting and Eating for Health states, "The United States Recommended Dietary Allowance for protein is 44 grams for a young woman. This includes a two-fold safety factor, which doubles the minimum requirements as determined by nitrogen balance studies. We do not need to eat any animal foods to meet these protein requirements. Strict vegetarians who eat no animal products get more than enough protein, and they do not need, selectively or scientifically, to mix and match foods to do so." Dr. Fuhrman also states, "The extra protein that we do not need merely adds stress to the system by increasing the acid tide in our blood-stream after a high-protein meal and forcing the body to deal with excess nitrogenous waste. The stress from excess protein results in premature aging of the kidneys and loss of excessive calcium when urinating. This inevitably weakens the bones as we age."

In Dr. Sniadach's Essential Natural Hygiene course he states, "Can we continue to say that fruits are protein poor? In view that, if protein is one per cent of our diet, our protein needs are amply met, and then fruits are protein adequate! When we've eaten some 2,250 calories worth of almost any fruit except apples, we also ingested some 25 to 40 grams of protein. Inasmuch as most fruits do contain all the essential amino acids, I would adjudge that fruits meet human needs for protein amply."

I will add many more quotes about our real protein needs to my online message boards for those of you who want further info. But it is fact that our protein requirements are really only 25 grams (and that is for the average man). The body cannot use more than it needs, and it must eliminate all that is in excess of its needs. When you are eating a high-protein diet you are working against the body, not with it.

Please do not forget that our fruits, vegetables, nuts and seeds **do** contain protein. Their protein percentages are low that is true, but we do not have the high-protein requirements, that the high-protein diet pushers and the heavily influenced RDA would have you believe.

Just to give you an example, if you were to eat 20 oranges in a day that would meet all of your daily protein requirements. In fact, having just completed a week of mono meals of oranges and grapefruits I can tell you honestly I had loads of energy and felt marvelous! Now that doesn't mean you have to subsist on oranges everyday for the rest of your life of course. That is just to give you an example. There is a wonderful, and FREE, online resource at http://www.fitday.com that allows you to type in the foods you have eaten throughout the day and it will give you your carbohydrate/protein/fat ratios for that meal or the meals throughout that day.

Vegans and raw foodists, as long as they are taking in enough calories, have no problem meeting their daily protein requirements.

Another question that seems to quickly concern you when you go vegetarian, vegan, or to the raw food diet is: "Where, oh, where am I going to get vitamin B-12?"   Well, let's talk about cows again, shall we? Do you know that cows have vitamin b-12 in their systems but yet they eat no meat or dairy? They don't eat the foods that provide us with vitamin B-12 yet they have vitamin B-12. How is that so?

We don't have to eat meat to get vitamin b-12 because bacteria of our intestines creates it and our bodies absorb it. Keep in mind that is the case in a healthy body. If your body is extremely enervated you may have a vitamin B-12 deficiency right now on your SAD diet.

There is almost no food that has vitamin B-12. Our bodies very wisely produce it for our needs. Create a healthy body so that it can continue on ever so wisely producing this vitamin for you and you will have no need to worry.

Chapter 8: The Conspiracy. Why The TRUTH About The Cure To Disease Is Kept Secret

How can a nation as technologically, scientifically, and medically advanced as the United States of America, not be able to develop cures for ailments, which continue to afflict millions, such as: Diabetes, cancer, heart disease, fibromyalgia and HIV? How can it be possible that we can send men to the moon and the Pathfinder to Mars yet still not have a cure for the common cold or the flu?

Is it at all possible that a CURE actually does exist but the information is being kept secret from you? Is there a slight chance that medical, pharmaceutical, and government agencies are so tightly intertwined that they have deliberately suppressed life-saving information from you so that they to continue to rake in the billions of dollars in profit that they take in from prescription drugs and surgical procedures. Could the answer to those questions be YES? You read this chapter and you decide.

WHY ISN'T THIS FRONT PAGE NEWS?

Millions of people have cured themselves from serious illnesses and disease, even such fatal diagnoses such as advanced cancer. Millions have cured themselves naturally, through Natural Hygiene principles, through fasting, through raw food diets, etc. So why isn't this information front-page news? Why don't we hear about these miraculous stories on the evening news, instead of being bombarded with program after program with information on yet another groundbreaking new surgical procedure or prescription drug that is taking the nation by storm?

The reason this information is kept secret is because if the TRUTH about the cause of and the CURE to disease gets out, a lot of people will lose a lot of money -- a whole LOT of money. Am I saying there is a conspiracy? Absolutely! It sounds a little dramatic I know, but it's the truth, and there may be a lot more people involved in this conspiracy than you would actually expect. You know the pharmaceutical industry doesn't want this information out for very obvious reasons. But who else doesn't want you to have this life saving information?

Before I knew that there was **ONE** cause and **ONE** cure to disease, even before I was on my road to recovery, I sent a package to the FDA with my story about what the birth control injections had done to me. In that same package I also send a print out of my web site **http://www.abcinternetmarketing.com/depo-provera**, so that they could see the growing complaint list from other women around the world who had also become desperately sick as a result of the birth control injections.

I sent all of this information to the FDA via USPS priority mail with delivery confirmation, so that it would have to be signed for. I sent it to their correct department at

FDA Med Watch
US Food & Drug Administration
5600 Fishers Lane
Rockville, MD 20857

This was sent out on May 31, 2001. I still have the receipt and stamped delivery confirmation tag. In that package, I provided the US Food & Drug Administration with all of my contact information so that someone could respond to me. No one from the FDA ever responded to me. On my web site, I encouraged other women to send in their stories to the FDA too. Many did. Yet nobody from the FDA ever responded to them either. I couldn't understand it, I contacted the government agency that is suppose to be responsible for monitoring the safety of drugs, gave them information on hundreds of women who had also experienced horribly adverse side affects from the birth control injections, yet nothing. I couldn't believe it.

The silence I received from the FDA was the SECOND time the thought of a conspiracy or a cover-up entered into my mind. The first time I thought there was some type of cover-up going on was when I saw the notation the osteopath/general practitioner had made in my medical records noting that my headaches were improving now that I was off the birth control injections, yet he never discussed that with me. He, at first, treated me for about 8 months with manipulations, traction and drugs, and I finally quit going because he wasn't helping me. I kept bouncing in and out of his office over the years, yet not once did he ever say, "Shelly, I've noticed that your headaches started to get better after you got off the birth control injections." So seeing that was the first time I thought there might be a conspiracy. I live in a very rural community so I thought the conspiracy was just doctors protecting other doctors.

It wasn't until I started doing further research to help myself reverse my disease naturally that I saw the enormous conspiracy that is really going on to keep this type of information -- information on how toxic drugs really are and information on how you can reverse most every disease through natural methods, in particular: Fasting, raw food diets and lifestyle changes to incorporate appropriate amounts of rest, relaxation, fresh air, sunshine and exercise – from the general public.

In my wildest dreams I would have never imagined that the roots of this conspiracy were so deep or so vast!   You might think this sounds crazy, and I'll tell you honestly had I not researched the information for myself, I too would have thought it implausible.

WHO IS INVOLVED IN THE COVER-UP?

- Drug companies are involved

- Medical schools are involved

- Some doctors are involved

- Some organizations that have set themselves up to "find a cure" for a particular disease.

- Some charitable organizations claiming, "we're fighting for a cure" are involved.

- Some government agencies, like the FDA are involved.

- The meat industry is involved.

- Even some in the alternative health care field are involved.

I'll go into a little more detail on some of the points below.

SOME DOCTOR'S HAVE BEEN DUPED TOO!

Doctor's know all drugs are toxic. They know this because they are taught this. But, in their defense, it is the medical schools themselves that are really to blame. Don't get me wrong, it is very true that there are **some** doctors that are not sharing the truth with you because they know that when **you** become informed you won't need them or their drugs, and when they have a smart patient, they will have one less patient. With that said however, I do believe the **majority** of doctors do go into medical school with the very best of intentions and do so out of a true desire to help save lives. The doctors themselves are unfortunately misled and misinformed by their **medical schools** that do not teach the truth to them.

Doctors try and treat you with drugs, chemotherapy and radiation or surgeries. Even though all drugs are toxic, chemotherapy and radiation actually CAUSE cancer, and surgeries are always risky. That is how doctors treat you because that is all they know. In fact, doctors can lose their jobs with the medical establishment if you have cancer and they don't treat you with chemotherapy and radiation!   Many doctors are nothing other than victims of the medical sand pharmaceutical cartel. I'm not overly sympathetic with most doctors however because nobody is holding a gun to their head to keep them in that profession. They can quit at anytime.

The reason the medical schools and the pharmaceutical companies don't want you to know the truth -- that there is one cause and one cure for disease -- is quite negative and very sobering. And, it can be summed up in one word -- **GREED**. If you were told the truth about symptoms, the truth about the cause of disease, the truth about detoxification and nutrition, the truth about curing disease naturally, THEY would be **out of business**. Period. It is as simple as that. There are billions of dollars to be lost if we as a society learn this information and apply it to our lives.

THE MEDICAL COMMUNITY'S REASON TO
KEEP THIS INFORMATION SECRET

The medical community, the community responsible for training your doctors, is funded in large part by the pharmaceutical companies. If the medical schools were to start teaching their doctors to treat you with drug-free methods, why on God's green earth do you think the pharmaceutical companies would give them any further backing? They wouldn't. And what do you do when someone does you a favor? You know the old saying, "You scratch my back and I'll scratch yours". Well, sorry to over simplify it, but that is what is happening and you need to know about it. The pharmaceutical companies support the medical schools. And, in turn, the medical schools support the pharmaceutical companies by teaching the doctors to treat with the pharmaceutical companies' drugs. They go hand in hand. You can't have one without the other.

Yes, it really is that simple. Don't worry, though, you won't just have to take my word for it. There are doctors, professors, scientists, and authors who have researched this subject extensively and can provide you with information that will absolutely blow your mind! I can't go into it all in detail here as it is far too extensive, but I will provide you with the resources so that YOU can take charge of your life and learn the information that they don't want you to know. Don't remain ignorant to this information. It's very real. If you remain ignorant you are doing exactly what they want you to do. Look at your state of health now. You've followed doctor's orders, you've taken their drugs and where has that gotten you so far? I'll tell you where it's gotten you. It has gotten you here, to this book, because what you are doing now isn't working.

THE PHARMACEUTICAL INDUSTRY'S REASON
TO KEEP THIS INFORMATION SECRET

Uhhhhhhh, hello? Do I even need to explain this one to you?
Pharmaceutical companies would simply go bust if the truth about
the cause and natural cure of disease became common knowledge.

Pharmaceutical companies aren't searching for a cure. Are you out
of your mind?
The word **CURE** is the dirtiest four-letter word to anyone working
in the pharmaceutical industry. No matter how brainwashed you
may be by the allopathic medical community and pharmaceutical
industry, you are smart enough to realize that the pharmaceutical
company is a profit-driven organization.

If everyone in the U.S. that was sick right now, did nothing other
than make a change to a plant-based or raw food diet for an
extended period of time, do you know what a major blow that
would be to the pharmaceutical industry? People would be coming
off their medications right and left. If that happened, the drug
companies would soon be trying to figure out how to give "raw-
food injections" for those who are too lazy or too unwilling to
change their diet on their own.

THE MEDIA'S REASON TO KEEP
THIS INFORMATION SECRET

It should also be no surprise to you that pharmaceutical giants
take such advantage of the power of the media. The
pharmaceutical companies know what type of society we are.
They know that we are enormously influenced by what we see on
television, listen to on the radio,and see in the magazines. You
can hardly watch one set of commercials without seeing an
advertisement for a new drug. Often times you will see more than
one drug commercial in a two-minute set of commercials. If you
can do it, I suggest you devote one day of your life to doing
nothing other than watching television and documented how many
drug commercials you see. You can stay on one channel if you
like, or flip from channel to channel. You will be astounded at the
amount of commercials you see for prescription drugs. It's unreal.
We are a sick society. We are a drugged society.

The networks make billions of dollars in advertising from the
pharmaceutical companies. The drug companies have the money
to spend and the networks are taking it. The media doesn't

question the safety of the drug before they advertise it to you. They don't care about that; all they care about is how much money they are being paid to run the commercial. They protect themselves of course from any legal implications by saying, "the drug is FDA-approved," and "How were we to know it was unsafe? We're just the media."

THE CHARITABLE ORGANIZATIONS' REASONS
TO KEEP THIS INFORMATION SECRET

There are many charity organizations that are "pretending" to look for a cure for one disease or another. The American Cancer Society has it written in their rules that they **must** disband the day a cure is found. They bring in $400 million dollars a year. Do you think they really want to give up that $400 million dollars a year? Less than 5% of the money they bring in actually goes to assisting the patient -- **LESS than 5%**!

The American Cancer Society is just one on a very long list of charitable organizations created to find a cure. Are any of these organizations really looking for a cure? I don't see how they could be when so many individuals have successfully cured themselves from disease by following Natural Hygiene principles, yet not one of the organizations has made this information public. How could that be? I believe it all comes down to the tremendous amount of money these organizations are bringing in. When they are bringing in millions of dollars a year, do they really want to give that up? No, they don't.

HOW MANY PEOPLE LOSE THEIR
JOBS IF YOU LEARN THE TRUTH?

Once a cure is found, forget about it, a lot of people are out of jobs. Think about it. Look at who could be out of a job if society learned the truth about the one cause of and the one cure to disease....

- Pharmaceutical companies and all their millions of employees, this includes everyone from secretaries to research scientists to CEO's!
- Pharmacists
- Medical School employees
- Many Doctors
- Many Nurses

- People employed by Charity Organizations that are trying to find a cure
- Many FDA employees
- Even many in the alternative health care fields who are selling natural, herbal and vitamin supplementation & other alternative therapies.
- Farmers who refuse to grow organically

We are talking about millions of people who will have to find a new line of work once society starts informing themselves about the real cause of and cure to disease. As you can see there are many people who do not want you to know the truth about the cause of and the cure to disease.

MORE AND MORE MD's ARE SPEAKING OUT AGAINST THE DANGERS OF DRUGS AND CONVENTIONAL MEDICINE

Dr. Rath, who founded a research and development firm in Nutritional and Cellular Medicine in 1992, is just one of the large growing numbers of physicians who is coming forward to speak out against the pharmaceutical companies. Below are his six points that I agree accurately outline the nature of the pharmaceutical industry.

The following points were taken from Dr. Rath's web page:

http://eu.dr-rath.com/mr-publishing-internet/network/health_system/uk/medical_breakthrough.htm

The Nature of the Pharmaceutical Industry

1. The **natural purpose and driving force** of the pharmaceutical industry is to increase sales of pharmaceutical drugs for ongoing diseases and to find new diseases to market existing drugs.

2. By this very nature, the pharmaceutical industry has **no interest in curing diseases**. The eradication of any disease inevitably destroys a multi-billion dollar market of prescription drugs as a source of revenues. Therefore, pharmaceutical drugs are primarily developed to relieve symptoms, but not to cure.

3. If eradication therapies for diseases are discovered and developed, the pharmaceutical industry has an inherent interest to suppress, discredit and obstruct these medical breakthroughs in order to **make sure that diseases continue** as the very basis for a lucrative prescription drug market.

4. The economic interest of the **pharmaceutical industry itself is the main reason why no medical breakthrough has been made** for the control of the most common diseases such as cardiovascular disease, high blood pressure, heart failure, diabetes, cancer, and osteoporosis, and why these diseases continue like epidemics on a worldwide scale.

5. For the same economic reasons, the pharmaceutical industry has now formed an international cartel by the code name "Codex Alimentarius" with the aim to **outlaw any health information in connection with vitamins** and to limit free access to natural therapies on a worldwide scale.

6. At the same time, the pharmaceutical companies withhold public information about the effects and risks of prescription drugs and life-threatening side effects are omitted or openly denied.

There are many other MD's (trained by the allopathic medical community) that are speaking out. Most of who are doing so, are doing so because they, themselves, had to overcome disease, and conventional medicine -- the medicine they were trained in -- would not cure them. These MD's set the proper conditions for their bodies to heal themselves naturally and it worked! They are now spreading the word and so are more and more others.

Dr. Lorraine Day in her VHS tape Cancer Doesn't Scare Me Anymore goes into great detail about this conspiracy between the drug companies, the AMA (American Medical Association), the FDA (Food and Drug Administration), and even the American Cancer Society. I feel Dr. Day's VHS tape is a must watch for anyone who is frustrated at the lack of results they've received from conventional medicine. Her information comes to you as a medical professional who was on the inside of conventional medicine and saw with her own eyes how conventional medicine worked and DIDN'T work. Her tapes and books give you an insider's standpoint of the cover-up that is really taking place with our health. www.drday.com

YOUR HEALTH ... YOUR CHOICE!
YOU NEED TO TAKE RESPONSIBILITY FOR YOUR HEALTH.

We need to become responsible for our own lives and stop leaving the most important aspect of our lives, **our health**, in the hands of others, no matter what degrees may be hanging on the walls! We need to stop drugging our problems -- that's only suppressing our problems and possibly causing more problems to erupt in the future. We need to start allowing our bodies to do what God created them to do, repair themselves naturally.

The answer to why we are ill is simple. The truth about symptoms and disease is also equally as simple. Once learned and experienced for yourself, nobody can silence you. Knowledge really is power! Give yourself the knowledge and stop letting the medical community and pharmaceutical companies, who **make money off you being SICK**, control your life. If you are tired of going from doctor to doctor to no avail, if you are sick of taking harmful medications, if you are sick and tired of being **SICK AND TIRED**, then understand YOU must take control of your life! By drugging your problems you really are just "DYING TO GET WELL." These drugs are killing you. If you've been told you need chemotherapy or radiation PLEASE, PLEASE research this thoroughly before subjecting yourself from such a disease causing treatment! Chemotherapy can cause secondary, rare cancers, and radiation will cause cancer, too, by radiation exposure. These treatments are almost always deadly.

You need to be responsible for you. I realize it is hard when you don't realize that what you are doing is wrong or bad for you! You trust the trained professionals. Believe me, I understand. I've been there, done that! I didn't know prescription drugs were bad for me. That may sound like a cop-out, but it's not. I didn't know. I had no idea that I was causing further damage to my system by taking the drugs the doctors told me would help me. None of them ever did, by the way.

It is very easy for us to place the blame on others. I spent many months saying, "poor me, look what these doctors and what their drugs they have put me on has done to my body." I've also moaned and groaned about the additional harm I caused to my body by following the ever-popular, high-protein diets. But, I finally got over it. If you are also saying, "poor me", then you too need to get over it and the quicker the better. What is done is done. Dwelling on it will not do you any good. It will only cause you unneeded stress that is also bad for your health.

It is now time for you to take responsibility for your own health. You can't buy your health. Good health will not come to you in the form of a prescription drug or even alternative medicines for that matter.   You must earn your good health! You will earn good health through a proper diet (some will find their diet will have to be much stricter than others, i.e., raw food). But, it is not diet alone however that will bring you good health. You must also earn your good health through daily exercise, fresh air, sunshine, relaxation, and adequate rest.

I am, in heart, with you every single step of the way. You can reverse disease. It is possible. I am living proof. But it is not just me; there are literally millions who have reversed disease naturally. Knowing the truth will give you the power to take control of your life.

If you want more information on the widespread conspiracy that is going on between the drug companies, the fund-raising communities, the medical schools, and even some of the allopathic doctors, please see my resources list below for further information.

BOOKS:

- **AIDS What The Government Isn't Telling You: CENSORED**. - Lorraine Day MD

- **MAD COWBOY: Plain Truth From The Cattle Rancher Who Won't Eat Meat** - Howard Lyman.

- **Immunizations: The Terrible Risks Your Children Face That Your Doctor Won't Reveal** - by Robert S. Mendelsohn

- **The Medical Mafia: How to Get Out Alive and Take Back Our Health and Wealth -** Dr. Guylaine Lanctot

- **Murder by Injection: The Story of the Medical Conspiracy Against America** - by Eustace Mullins

- **The Cancer Industry** - Ralph W. Moss

- **Betrayers Of The Truth: Fraud and Deceit in the Halls of Science** - William Broad and Nicholas Wade

- **Racketeering in Medicine: The Suppression of Alternatives** - James P. Carter MD

Please note: I, myself, believe that you do not need any special drug or naturopathic or homeopathic treatment (with the exception of colonics) to cure the majority of diseases. Some of the information in a few of the books above talks about particular alternative therapies that were suppressed, for example: Chelation therapy. The reason I reference these books to you is that they will show you how strongly the government, the medical community, and the pharmaceutical companies will work to keep any information about alternative healing out of your hands. However, I don't believe that any alternative pills or treatments are required for disease to be reversed because there is only one cure to disease, and that is the healing ability of your own body.

WEB SITES:

- http://drugconspiracy.netfirms.com

- http://www.senet.com.au/~brains/cancer.htm

- http://neuro-www.mgh.harvard.edu/forum2/HeadacheF/6.10.998.27AM Whythehostil.html

- http://www.tetrahedron.org/articles.html

- http://www.cancer-coverup.com

VHS TAPES:

- Cancer Doesn't Scare Me Anymore - Dr. Lorraine Day

- Everything You Want To Know About AIDS But Haven't Been Told - Dr. Lorraine Day

ARE YOU BEING SCARED INTO ACCEPTING CONVENTIONAL MEDICINE?

There are a lot of people who are going to try and scare you into believing that only conventional medicine can heal the sick, but conventional medicine is NOT healing the sick. Even the Journal of the American Medical Association acknowledges that about 85% of conventional medical treatments have NOT been proven both safe and effective in double-blind placebo, controlled studies.

When you are trying to find the treatment to cure your disease CONSIDER THE SOURCE. Does this person make money off your ill health? The next time you go into your doctor's office ask them if they will help put you on a plant-based diet and specific exercise regimen. Ask him/her if they will work with you to start weaning off your medications. See if they are willing to help you do these things. If not, question why they are not willing to help you.

Chapter 9: FASTING

As I stated several times already in this book, we are sick because we are toxic. The quickest, most efficient way to detoxify almost diseases is through fasting. Some less serious illnesses/diseases may be able to be cured via dietary change alone. Let me reiterate the fact that Dr. Fuhrman, in his book Fasting and Eating For Health, states he has successfully helped people get rid of diabetes and migraines with simple dietary change alone. Others who are *able*, however, may need to combine some form of fasting with their dietary change in order to cure their disease.

We live in an "I WANT IT NOW!" society. Most people demand immediate relief to their pain and disease, without ever stopping to consider how long it took for their body to actually get in the horrible condition that it is now in. For some it took literally decades, and they want a cure to happen overnight. They love the immediate relief they receive when they pop a pill. It does exactly what they want it to. It takes their pain away, NOW! However, the majority are either not taking into consideration or not realizing the further damage they are causing to their system by doing this.

I believe there are three types of sick people:

1   TYPE 1. The first type is the type I already mentioned above. The type of person that only wants an immediate suppression of their pain. These are the types of people that will take whatever drug or undergo whatever surgery is presented to them as long as they know they will get relief from pain. These are the people who either don't KNOW or don't CARE about the severe consequences of taking the drugs and/or having the surgery.

1   TYPE 2. The second type of sick person is the type of person who KNOWS that drugs and surgery are only SUPRESSING their problems, and they desperately want a safe and natural alternative that will CURE them. They are willing to

do whatever it takes to make the necessary dietary and lifestyle changes that are required no matter how long it takes or how difficult it may be for them for them to reverse their disease. These people understand that their disease was caused by the wrong foods, Rx drugs and or other chemicals, or toxins.

1   TYPE 3. The third type of sick person is a mix between the 1st and 2nd type of sick person. This person KNOWS that wrong foods and drugs have put them in the state they are now, but they are impatient. They don't want to take the 8 months, 9 months or 2 years to completely cure their disease. They want to be well NOW!

This 3rd type of sick person will be the one that is most thrilled with the benefits and powers of fasting. While fasting is not a **cure**, it inarguably sets the most perfect healing conditions for your body to heal itself quicker than any other detoxification method has the ability to. Fasting is not for everyone however. Some diseases will respond favorably or even require a fast for the reversal of disease. Others, however, may not need to fast to reverse their disease. They may be able to reverse their disease through dietary change alone. Others may find that they are physically unable to fast. (I will give you a list of people who it is said should not fast later in this chapter.)

WHAT IS FASTING?

Fasting in its truest sense of the word is total abstinence from food. Fasting is not new; it has been around since biblical times. The bible makes many mentions of fasting; however, most of them refer to fasting for spiritual reasons. Keep in mind too that in biblical times people were not dying from the 10,000+ diseases that we now have today. I think the lack of reference in the bible of fasting for healing purposes was simply because there was not the great need for healing then as there is now. Back then people didn't gorge themselves with junk foods and prescription drugs because they didn't exist. And because they didn't exist, disease as we know it today did not exist. People were much closer to God back then. They were obeying his rules much more diligently and in much larger numbers than we do today. Disease and illness were not as rampant then as today.

Even our three fathers of western medicine -- Hippocrates, Galen and Paracelsus -- **all** used fasting as a remedy to cure disease. Somewhere along the line, the Hippocratic Oath that all doctors take to "First Do No Harm" has been dreadfully lost! Physicians today no longer practice the basic information that was laid out for them by the forefathers of medicine. I've already explained that it is not our doctors we need to blame so much for this ignorance, as it is the medical schools that are teaching them.

When we fast, our body goes into a state of rest that allows it to focus all of its energy on the elimination of superfluous (unneeded) tissue and waste that is locked inside it. This toxic waste for most people is unable to be broken down because of the constant state of feeding and/or drugging that is taking place. Once we stop this intake of food and/or drugging, vital repair work can begin.

When you fast, all of the systems inside your body get a rest. Your digestive system of course gets a rest because you are no longer eating. But all other systems inside your body get a much-needed rest too. Your respiratory, circulatory, glandular, and nervous systems get a rest; your heart and your arteries get a rest, etc. When this rest takes place, the energy that was once used to digest, assimilate, and eliminate the intake of food and/or drugs you were taking in on a daily basis can now be used repair your body. Fasting gives your body the power and energy it needs to remove the toxins from within. When fasting, your body can use all the excess energy it has acquired to get to work and start cleaning house! Your body will use that unspent energy to start removing the toxins that has stored themselves in the cells and tissues in your body. When you fast, you give your body the rest it needs to cure itself.

My own personal experiences with fasting have given me the irrefutable proof I need to know that the body has miraculous healing powers, if we set for it the perfect condition for healing to take place. I have also, through my research for this book, seen documented reports where countless people with numerous illnesses and diseases, such as, but NOT limited to: Acne, autoimmune diseases, arthritis, asthma, atherosclerosis, benign tumors, Bright's disease, cardiac conditions, Crohn's disease, cervical dysplasia, colitis, chronic neck and back pain, diabetes, depression, eczema, fibroids, fibromyalgia, glaucoma, hypothyroidism, hypertension, migraines, polymyalgia rheumatica, rheumatoid vasculitis, schizophrenia, sinusitis, systemic lupus erythematosus (SLE), tinnitus, and vertigo, *just to name a few,*

have had their diseases either completely cured or dramatically
improved through fasting.

For almost all who will fast, especially those who undergo a
prolonged, supervised fast, their diet will have to change even
before they undergo the fast. This dietary change is needed to
better prepare the body for the cleaning process that takes place
during the fast.   Proper diet must be maintained after the fast,
too, if one wants to retain his new-found, good health.

**NOTE: FASTS DO NOT CURE! Fasts give your body the
necessary rest it needs so that it can cure itself. It is only
the miraculous healing power of your body itself that can
cure you.**

Animals, when ill, fast. Most domesticated animals would fast, if
we weren't rushing them to the vet the moment they refused food.
It is instinct for animals to fast. They are smart enough to know
that by fasting their body will heal itself. Those who are around
undomesticated animals know those animals innately fast and rest
when they are ill or injured. We could all learn a priceless lesson
from these gorgeous, **fascinating** creatures! They are indeed far
more intelligent than we will ever be!

Below are some quotes from doctors, philosophers, and others on
the subject of fasting that might be of interest to you.

"Man lives on one quarter of what he eats. On the other three
quarters lives his doctor." - Translated Inscription from an Egyptian
Pyramid 3800 B.C.

"Everyone has a doctor in him or her; we just have to help it in its
work. The natural healing force within each one of us is the
greatest force in getting well. Our food should be our medicine.
Our medicine should be our food. But to eat when you are sick, is
to feed your sickness."-- Hippocrates, MD, 460-377 B.C.

"Fasting is the greatest remedy, the physician within." --
Paracelsus, 15th century physician

"Instead of medicine, fast for a day." -- Plutarch, Greek
Philosopher

"Nature, alone, is the teacher of standard science of truth. She
heals thru one thing - FASTING - every disease that it is possible

to heal. This, alone, is proof that Nature recognizes but one disease, and that in every body the largest factors are always, waste, foreign matter and mucus (besides uric acid and other toxemias, and, very often, pus - if tissues are decomposed)." -- Arnold Ehret (The Mucusless Diet Healing System)

"The fast cure method is not limited to our dumb fellow creatures. It is a common experience that pain, fever, gastric congestion and even mental afflictions take away appetite and only unwise nurses will try to thwart the purposes of Nature in this respect." -- Dr. Felix Oswald

"Fasting is, without any doubt, the most effective biological method of treatment. It is the 'operation without surgery' ... it is a cure involving exudation, reattunement, redirection, loosening up and purified relaxation. While fasting, the patient improves her or his physical health and gains much. But he or she will have neglected the most important thing if the hunger for spiritual nourishment that manifests itself during fasting is not satisfied."-- Otto Buchinger, Sr., MD

"No process of therapy ever fulfilled so many indications for restoration of vigorous health as does fasting. It is Mother Nature's very own prime process and
Her first requirement in nearly all cases. After a fast the circulation is better, food can be assimilated better, while endurance, stamina and strength are increased. After a fast the mind becomes more receptive to logic and a sensible, natural way of living." -- Paul Bragg, ND (The Miracle of Fasting)

"Fasting helps the body help itself." -- Paul Bragg, ND (The Miracle of Fasting)

"The time to fast is when it is needed. I am of the decided opinion that delays pay no dividends; that, due to the fact that the progressive development of pathological changes in the structures of the body with the consequent impairment of its functions does not cease until its cause has been completely and thoroughly removed. Putting off the time for a fast only invites added troubles and makes a longer fast necessary, if indeed it does not make it futile. I do not believe that any condition of impaired health should be tolerated and permitted to become greater. Now is the time to begin the work of restoring good health; not next week, next summer, or next year." -- Dr. Herbert Shelton

"Vitamins are not generally required (during the fast) because within the body's cells are adequate reserves of protein, fast, minerals, and vitamins that can be called upon during periods of famine, food scarcity, or fasting. Even in prolonged fasts (those lasting from 20 to 40 days) no deficiency diseases develop, illustrating that the body has the innate ability to utilize its stored reserves in a highly exacting and balanced manner." -- Joel Fuhrman, MD (Fasting & Eating For Health)

"There are millions of 'closet' fasters. I am constantly amazed - and pleased - to discover in my travels just how many people throughout the world are 'into' fasting. At a dinner party I learned my host and three other guests - all professional people - fast one or two days every week to maintain the weight losses they achieved from longer fasts." -- Alan Cott, MD (Fasting the Ultimate Diet)

"When I lecture I am often asked, 'Is fasting safe?' It is certainly safe for almost everybody. Each person is adaptable to fasting in a different manner and degree."
 -- Alan Cott, MD (Fasting the Ultimate Diet)

"The fast does not merely detoxify; it also breaks down superfluous tissue--fat, abnormal cells, atheromatous plaque, and tumors--and releases diseased tissues and their cellular products into the circulation for elimination. Toxic or unwanted materials circulate in our bloodstream and lymphatic tissues, and are deposited in and released from our fat stores and other tissues. An important element of fasting detoxification is mobilizing the toxins from their storage areas. This process occurs best and most efficiently during total fasting." -- Joel Fuhrman, MD (Fasting & Eating For Health)

"Fasting and natural diet, though essentially unknown as a therapy, should be the first treatment when someone discovers that she or he has a medical problem. It should not be applied only to the most advanced cases, as is present practice. Whether the patient has a cardiac condition, hypertension, autoimmune disease, fibroids, or asthma, he or she must be informed that fasting and natural, plant-based diets are a viable alternative to conventional therapy, and an effective one. The time may come when *not* offering this substantially more effective nutritional approach will be considered malpractice." -- Joel Fuhrman, MD (Fasting & Eating For Health)

"If disparaging doctors would take the time to examine the evidence [referring to fasting] dispassionately, they would finally stop warning of "dangers" that simply do not exist for most people. They owe it to their patients to become more knowledgeable because this remarkable discipline has stood the test of time - at least five thousand years. It apparently needs to be said over and over again: Fasting is *not* starving, fasting is *not* starving, fasting is *not* starving.." -- Alan Cott, MD (Fasting As A Way Of Life)

"At the end of any fast you should feel much better than you did before you began it - and probably better than you have for a long, long time." -- Alan Cott, MD (Fasting The Ultimate Diet)

"In my opinion, regular fasts are far more conducive to rejuvenation that monkey- or goat-gland transplantations, hormone injections, face lifts, massive vitamin intakes, or any of the other extreme and expensive measures used "to turn back the clock." -- Alan Cott, MD (Fasting The Ultimate Diet)

"Fasting is the great system renovator. Three fast-days a year will purify the blood and eradicate the poison-diathesis more effectively than a hundred bottles of expurgative bitters." -- Felix L. Oswald, MD

"Fasting regularly gives your organs a rest and helps reverse the aging process for a longer and healthier life." -- James Balch, MD (Prescription for Nutritional Healing)

"Sensible fasting gives the body an opportunity to return to its natural state of homeostasis, or balance. During a fast, toxins are drawn out of the cells and tissues throughout the whole body." -- Jacqueline Krohn, MD with France Taylor, MA (Natural Detoxification 2nd Edition Revised and Expanded)

"The reason many people are so afraid of fasting and find the mere thought of it so unpleasant is that when they skip even one meal they feel awful. They assume fasting would be very uncomfortable. These individuals - who exhibit uncomfortable signs early in the fast - are in the greatest need of a fast. Headaches and other discomforts brought on by not eating are signs that the body has begun to withdraw and detoxify waste products retained in body tissues. When we delay eating or fast, these tissue stores of toxic waste are mobilized for removal. Thus fasting is "cleansing" of the internal system." -- Joel Fuhrman, MD (Fasting & Eating For Health)

"Fasting is a valid experience. It can benefit any otherwise healthy person whose calories now have the upper hand in his/her life." -- The New England Journal of Medicine

"After fifty-five years of sojourning in the wilderness of medical therapeutics, I am forced to declare, without fear of successful contradiction, that fasting is the only reliable, specific, therapeutic eliminate known to man." (J.H. Tilden, MD - 1851-1940)

"Undertaking a fast when you're seriously ill often brings amazing results. When a person turns to fasting in the earlier stages of illness, the results come easier." -- Lee Bueno Aquer (Fast Your Way To Health)

"Therapeutic fasting is most beneficial to those who are sick and want to get well without drugs and doctors. Therapeutic fasting, however, should also be viewed as a modern form of disease prevention and health maintenance. For the sick person, fasting should become the favored means to restore health. For the healthy person, fasting should become the favored form of health insurance." -- Lee Bueno Aquer (Fast Your Way To Health)

"In a fast we can observe the body gleefully going about getting rid of the toxins and wastes accumulated for years with the greatest capability and intelligence, all on its own." -- Dr. William Esser

Even Benjamin Franklin had good things to say about fasting. While he never used the word 'fast' I believe that is exactly what he refers to when he says..

- "Eat to live, not live to eat." -- Ben Franklin
- "Many dishes, many diseases." -- Ben Franklin
- "To lengthen thy life, lessen thy meals." -- Ben Franklin
- "Dine with little, sup with less: do better still, sleep supperless." -- Ben Franklin

CAN I FAST WITHOUT SUPERVISION?

Some books I have read on the subject of fasting say that almost any adult, regardless of their illness, can undergo shorter duration fasts of 1 to 3-days without supervision. Some books say that **nobody** should ever undergo even a 1-day, water-only fast **without** doctor supervision or approval. Every book seems to have its own rules on this subject, so I am not going to confuse you. Personally, I underwent an unsupervised, 4-day, water-only fast. I, however, do **not** recommend that **anyone** follow in my footsteps! I was detoxing very heavily because of my high toxicity level, and I had a lot of pain and dizziness that I had a lot of questions about. Eventually I became unnecessarily scared and quit. Had I been under professional supervision, I could have set my mind at ease by being able to ask questions and know confidently that my vitals were being monitored. **I urge everyone to seek a doctor's permission to even undergo a short 1- to 3-day, water-only fast, and to seek professional supervision for any prolonged water-only fasting you do.**

At the end of this chapter I will list for you clinics that help in supervising fasts. Remember, even if you just want to try a 24 hour water-only fast it is best to have a trained professional first speak with you and give you the go ahead to do it on your own. I don't want to scare you. Fasting is not dangerous when done properly! Fasting is NOT starving. Those are myths. But seek the professional guidance of a doctor who is trained in supervising fasts to assist you.

Keep in mind that your current doctor, the one who, to put it bluntly, makes money off you remaining sick, may tell you that fasting is dangerous or can kill you. That simply is not true. Don't expect that your doctor is going to be the one who is going to help you through a supervised fast. His ignorance isn't really all his fault; it is the medical schools that trained him that are to blame. There are doctors out there to help you, just see my **Resources** chapter.

WHO SHOULD NOT FAST?

The answer to this question also appears to depend on what book you are reading at the time. It seems everyone has his or her own opinion on the topic. From the many books I have read on the subject of fasting I have come up with the following list of people who it is said **cannot** fast.

Before I get to the list I want to say that if you are fearful of fasting, DON'T fast. Your fear will be your downfall. If you are fearful when you begin your fast, you might freak out when you experience the **good** pain of a healing crisis that, more likely than not, will take place when you fast. Reading up thoroughly on the subject of fasting can usually alleviate any fears you may have.

Below is a list of people who cannot fast. It may or may not be all inclusive.

- People who have inactive kidneys accompanied with obesity
- People on almost every Rx drug has to be weaned off it before fasting
- Pregnant women
- People with severe anemia
- People with severe nutritional deficiencies
- People with porphyria
- People severely malnourished due to advanced stages of cancer or AIDS
- Pregnant women
- Children

Remember you will be seeking out professional supervision so they will let you know if you can or cannot fast.

PREPARING FOR AND BREAKING YOUR FAST

Properly preparing for and breaking your fast is as important as the fast itself. If you follow my advice and seek out a professional to help you through your first or even all of the fasts that you undergo, they will give you all of the information you need to help you prepare for and end your fast. The professional who assists you will help set the standards for preparation and ending your fast based on your specific condition. It is important to have professional assistance and not just pick up a book because, if you have a blood-related disorder like diabetes, drinking fruit juices before a long fast and after the fast, like I do, might not be what you should do. Some of the books I have read on fasting sort of lump everyone into one category, and say this is how you should break your fast and this is how you should prepare for it. While it is true that many people might be able to follow the exact same plans for preparing for and breaking a fast, there will still be others who cannot follow those plans. That is why I say professional guidance, at least in the beginning so you know what to do for **your** body and **your** condition, is very important.

On **my** first three- and four-day fasts, I prepared for and broke them only with juice, never solid food, for the entire day before and after. On my weekly, 24 to 36-hour water-only fast, I usually always prepare for it and break it the same way. My last meal before my 24 to 36-hour fast begins is usually only a juice meal -- fruit or vegetable juice. The meal that breaks my fast is always just a fruit juice meal. The other two meals of the day before and after the fast consist of just raw food or raw food and/or freshly squeezed or juiced juice.

HOW LONG SHOULD I FAST?

The answer to this question depends on many factors. If you are seeking out professional, supervised assistance in a fasting clinic, the doctors there will be the ones who will determine this for you. It really depends on your particular situation and whether or not you can or even need to be fasted.

I've never fasted more than 4 days on water-only fast. I've also undergone a series of properly spaced 2 to 3-day water-only fasts, and I continue to do weekly 24 hour to 36-hour water-only fasts. I can tell you that I have received many benefits from these shorter-duration fasts.

Dr. Shelton, who fasted more than 30,000+ patients, routinely fasted people for 21 to 40 days and he reported his longest supervised fast was 90 days. One of Dr. Shelton's patients, now doctor, Dr. Fuhrman, says he considers a fast of 90 days risky. Dr. Fuhrman had himself undergone a 46-day fast under the supervision of Dr. Shelton's health clinic. Dr. Fuhrman, who now supervises prolonged fasts in his clinic in New Jersey, says, "Most individuals who are fasting for an existing medical condition should fast between 14 and 28 days to get a significant benefit from the fast. I usually recommend at least two weeks, because I have seen from experience that it is after the first week that the large health benefits begin to reveal themselves. Depending on the nutritional reserves of the individual, I prefer to fast a person with a chronic ailment close to three weeks." He goes on to say, "Occasionally, individuals fast under my supervision for longer than 21 days. I have conducted numerous 30-day fasts and a few even longer, but those were the exceptions."

Two famous healers from the past, Paul Bragg and Arnold Ehret, each also supervised the water-only fasts of thousands of patients. They've both stated that they believe shorter duration fasts are the way to go the majority of the time. Paul Bragg states in the book The Miracle of Fasting, "I personally don't believe in the longer fasts unless it is really an emergency - and then it is imperative that it be supervised by a health expert."
Arnold Ehret, in the Mucusless Diet Healing System stated, "The most exact unerring diagnosis we have is a short fast."

SHORTER FASTS NEED TO BE PROPERLY SPACEDAND PROPER
NUTRITION MUST BE TAKEN IN BETWEEN YOUR SHORTER FASTS

If you go for the shorter unsupervised fasts like I do, and you get PERMISSION by a doctor trained in supervising fasts, you need to know that you have to have them nicely spaced out. Don't ever do anything like fast 2 to 3-days every week! *Anything* in excess is harmful.

I did one 4-day water-only fast one month; the next month I did one 3-day water-only fast; the next month I did another 3-day water-only fast, the following three months I did 2-day water-only fasts. Every week in those months that were not weeks in which my 2- to 4- day water-only fast took place, I fasted 24 to 36 hours once a week. From this point on, I do a 24- to 36-hour water-only fast every week, and at the beginning of every new season, I will do a 3-day water-only fast. Spring, summer, winter and fall.

You have hopefully already learned that you have to be eating the right foods. The **right** foods are plenty of fresh -- especially raw -- fruits and vegetables, also legumes, nuts, seeds and some whole grains. Don't even bother with fasting if you are going to continue eating hamburgers, french fries, potato chips, soda, candy, etc. This is a new lifestyle, a life-long commitment to your good health. You shouldn't fast as a means just to purge one meal or a few bad meals. People who do this end up with serious eating disorders! Fasting in that method is nothing other than an endless circle. Fasting and continuing to eat "crap" will never cure your disease, and it will also cause you to end up with a new one: An eating disorder! If you are going to continue the diet and lifestyle you are living that is of course a choice you will make. I want to encourage you however to reach out for that new healthy life. It is within your grasp. I was very ill, as most of you reading my book will be, and I grabbed on to good health, and I am holding on to with a death grip. Once you experience what it is like to feel good again, I am confident you will be smart enough to keep up the proper maintenance.

WHAT SHOULD I EXPECT WHEN I FAST?

How sick you are is usually an indication of how you are going to feel when you fast. In The Mucusless Diet Healing System, Arnold

Ehret states, "The more rapidly the patient feels 'worse' thru a short fast, the greater and the more poisonous is his encumbrance. Should he become dizzy, suffer severe headaches, etc., he is greatly clogged up with mucus and toxemias. If palpitation of the heart occurs *it is a sign that pus is somewhere in the system*, or that drugs, even though taken many years ago, are in the circulation for elimination."

YOU CAN EXPECT TO FEEL SICK WHEN YOU FAST: Every book I have read on fasting has stated in its own way that the worse you feel when fasting, the more your body is in need of a fast. Now, from EXPERIENCE, let me tell you that I found this to be very true. My first four-day fast was grueling. In fact, my first few 1-to 3-day fasts were pretty icky. BUT NOTHING IN COMPARISON TO THE PAIN I LIVED WITH DAILY FOR 5+ YEARS! I can also tell you, from my own personal experiences, each fast that I undergo gets easier and easier. Now, almost all of my 24-to 36-hour weekly fasts are a breeze. The only time I find I get a headache when doing these is if I have slipped up here or there in my diet and have eaten something I should not have eaten. Once again proving to me that it is indeed what we put into our bodies that make us sick.

The **reason you will feel sick when you fast** is because toxins are being picked up, circulated through your body and eliminated. It is in this circulation and elimination of the toxins that you will feel sick. You will have periods of feeling okay, maybe even great, and then feeling miserable. This is often referred to as a healing crisis. The healing crises come as the toxins are in circulation in route to being eliminated. I have found that by increasing my water in take to about 12 to 14, 8oz glasses a day helps ease the pain of the healing crises. The reason this happens is because by drinking plenty of water you dilute the toxins that are in circulation.

In my first, four-day, water-only fast I had many side affects. Even though I was having pain, I can't tell you how amazing it was. I could actually feel particularly areas of my body being worked on. I could feel a vein or blood vessel or something on the side of neck that ran down into my chest and down my arm, being worked on for literally hours. I had many strange sensations like this.

It is very common to have "good" pain when you fast. Remember the pain you will experience when fasting is almost always a sign that your body is detoxifying. It is not uncommon to experience headaches, or heart palpitations. These are all signs your body is cleaning house. But because you will be detoxifying at such a high rate, it is imperative you are under professional supervision.

YOU CAN EXPECT TO BE COLD, STINKY, AND TIRED WHEN YOU FAST: It is not uncommon to become very cold while you fast. It is not uncommon to become very "stinky" when you fast, and, it is not uncommon to become tired when you fast. Again, to the degree that you experience these things will depend directly on how toxic you are.

You will notice body odor and bad breath that can be quite fierce. I was so constipated with mucus and disease that in the previous 3 years to my finding this cure, I didn't sweat nor have body odor. That is a bad sign! I was not doing these normal things that our bodies need to do to rid ourselves of toxins. I remember the day my armpits started to sweat again. I hadn't experienced it in so long that I had really forgotten what a gross feeling it was. I put my hand in my armpit, looked at my hand and it had a large amount of water on it. NOW DON'T PANIC! Getting detoxed doesn't mean you are going to walk around all sweaty and stinky for the rest of your life! This is something that will only happen while you are detoxing. Once your body is cleansed of toxins this will go away. Some people claim that once their body is perfectly cleansed and maintained through proper diet, they never need deodorant again!

You can expect to become very tired in your first few fasts (if you are doing several series of shorter ones) or in your one longer fast. You will want to rest, and by all means get plenty of rest. More than likely, for those of you who will undergo prolonged, supervised fasts, you will be in a clinic that will require you to rest. This is the best place for you.

After having undergone several shorter fasts, I now have many fasts where I actually feel ENERGIZED when I fast. I still am detoxing however, so it is not uncommon for me to have a day where I fast and still have a healing crisis.

You may even experience unpleasant smells and or tastes of chemicals that you have come in contact with. You will experience these while they leave your body.

I experienced bad dreams with my fasts. These nightmares and bad dreams are said to be what happens when prescription drugs are leaving your body.

It is very common to experience headaches and hunger at the very beginning of your fast. Your hunger will pass really quickly. Some say by the end of the 2nd and others say by the end of the 3rd day, that your hunger is gone. Headaches are generally experienced as the result of drugs or chemicals leaving your body.

YOU CAN EXPECT TO LOSE WEIGHT WHEN YOU FAST! I have never lost weight easier in my life through any other method as I have with fasting. I believe the maintenance of my weight loss is maintained not only through my vegan diet, but also in my weekly 24 to 36 hour fast. I laugh when I think of people spending money on that Hollywood Miracle Juice Diet. PEOPLE, YOU CAN DO THIS ON YOUR OWN! SAVE YOURSELF THE MONEY. Juice your own juice; you don't need to buy this stuff. The reason this "juice diet" works is because you are abstaining from food.

Many doctors, who supervise fasts, do so with the sheer purpose of helping the patient lose weight. If you are struggling with obesity, I encourage you to consider learning more about professionally-supervised, prolonged water-only fasts. I shutter when I hear of people undergoing such life-threatening procedures such as stomach stapling and liposuction. There IS a safer alternative, and that is fasting. What damage are you causing to your body by having these surgical procedures? Are you willing to trust what the doctors tell you? I did some research on gastric bypass surgeries and read that 1 in 200 people die from this surgery! 1 in 200??? Are you willing to take that chance? Just one of the web sites I found covering the pros and cons of this procedure was

http://www.thecarolinachannel.com/health/1220432/detail.html

I was horrified to see the comments, "I was going to die anyway" and "having it *[referring to the surgery]* can have fatal complications; not having it almost always does." Why aren't these people suffering from obesity given information on fasting? Well, actually we know why, that has already been covered in my last chapter. In the case of gastric bypass surgery, people are taking a 1 in 200 chance of **dying** to lose weight! This is unbelievable to me! These safer alternatives have to be made common knowledge so these people stop killing themselves. When an obese person thinks the only option to surviving is having a surgery that they have a 1 in 200 chance of surviving, it is clear that our society needs to wake up and learn about other safer alternatives, such as fasting.

I can guarantee you that 1 in 200 people do **not** die from **_professionally_ supervised** fastings. In fact, I have only read of a few deaths from people fasting, and none of the deaths occurred when a **properly-**supervised fast was being conducted. Dr. Joel Fuhrman's book Fasting and Eating for Health mentions a case in which an obese man was fasted for **seven months**. Seven months is clearly an unnecessary and unsafe amount of time for the duration of a fast. In the two other reported deaths that Dr. Fuhrman mentions in his book, he clearly states that these individuals were also fasted improperly. These were not total fasts, but the patients were given unrestricted amounts of coffee, tea, and fruit juice as well as drugs! In Lee Bueno Aquer's book she makes mention of a man named Bobby Sands who was fasting for political reasons. He lost his life on the **66th day** of his unsupervised fast. Bobby Sands was having no fasting supervision whatsoever. In just looking at the two noted cases, look at the length of time it took for death to occur. The duration of these fasts, 66 days and 7 months, actually proves that people don't die from abstaining from food for one day, or even for one month for that matter. If people were to starve immediately from missing a few meals, how could these two men have lived for 66 days and approximately 210 days without food?

Do the research on your own. The numbers don't lie. Millions of people have fasted to reverse their disease, and very few cases of deaths have been recorded, and those that were recorded were not professionally supervised. I do not know of one case where a death occurred when the fast was being properly supervised by a professional trained in supervising fasts! Compare the number of yearly deaths from properly conducted supervised fasts to the 100,000+ **REPORTED** deaths who die from Rx drugs every year. Drugs are killing people; properly conducted supervised fasts are not.

In The Miracle of Fasting, Paul Bragg stated, "Fasting works by self-digestion. During a fast your body intuitively will decompose and burn only the substances and tissues that are damaged, diseased, or unneeded, such as: Abscesses, tumors, excess fat deposits, excess water, and congestive wastes. Even a short fast (1 to 3 days) will accelerate elimination from your liver, kidneys, lungs, bloodstream, and skin. Sometimes you will experience dramatic changes (cleansing and healing crises) as accumulated wastes are expelled. With your first fasts you may temporarily have cleansing headaches, fatigue, body odor, bad breath, coated tongue, mouth sores, and even diarrhea as your body is cleaning house. Please be patient with your body!"

TIPS FOR A SUCCESSFUL FAST

* Drink **PLENTY OF PURE WATER** during your fast!
* Never fast if you are afraid to fast!
* Learn the truths and the myths about fasting before you fast!
* Stay warm.
* Stay stress-free and relaxed. Listen to soothing music or read.
* Read material on the subject of fasting during the duration of your fast.
* Prepare for your fast properly, with knowledge and the correct diet.
* Have your fast professionally supervised.

I've read many books on the subject of water-only and juice fasting. Below is a list of my personal favorites on the subject of fasting:

* The Miracle of Fasting - Paul Bragg, ND
* Rational Fasting - Arnold Ehret
* Fasting Can Save Your Life - Dr. Herbert Shelton
* Fast Your Way To Health - Lee Bueno Aquer

WHAT IS THE DIFFERENCE BETWEEN FASTING & STARVING?

This question was covered in every book I read on fasting. I would assume that the reason this question is answered in every book I read on fasting is because it is the most frequently asked question: "Won't I starve to death if I fast?"

Let me share the answers to this question from some of the many books I have read on fasting.

"Fasting and starving are entirely different entities. But it is a distinction that eludes many people even in the medical profession; the words can not be used interchangeably. Fasting is a self-rewarding act. Starving is a disaster inflicted upon the hungry by fate or occasionally self-inflicted by the mentally disturbed. During the fast the body is well nourished from its stored-up reserves. Starvation begins when the body is deprived of food after the return of appetite. The average overweight person must fast about four weeks before there is return of appetite, which is the signal to break the fast and start eating again. In starvation the body craves food and, being deprived, must consume itself." (Alan Cott, MD - Fasting The Ultimate Diet: Lose 5 lbs. On A One-Day Fast)

"Those who think fasting is equivalent to starvation are entirely wrong. There are basically two periods in the process of abstaining from food that should concern us here - the fasting period proper and the period of starvation.   As we study the phenomena of abstinence in greater detail, the distinction between these two phases will become clear. From the outset however, it is essential to understand that the fasting stage continues so long as the body supports itself on the stored reserves within its tissues. Starvation begins when abstinence is carried beyond the time when these stored reserves are used up or have dropped to a dangerously low level." He further stated, "Starvation is a process of dying, in effect. You cannot starve yourself into good health. You can fast for proper and reasonable periods and thereby improve your physical condition and often restore yourself to good health. It is impossible to abstain from food for long periods of time with beneficial effects. At the point where the experienced advisor who conducts the fast realizes that the second phase of abstention from food is imminent, the fast is broken." -- (Dr. Herbert Shelton: Fasting Can Save Your Life). Dr. Herbert Shelton conducted thousands of fasts ranging from a few days duration, to ninety days duration, for both weight reduction and in assisting the body to recover from physical illness.

"Contrary to what many people believe, fasting is not starvation. Starvation begins when abstinence is continued beyond the time when the body's stored reserves are used up or have dropped to a dangerously low level. During the fasting stage the body supports itself from the stored reserves within its tissues. When food is eaten at normal intervals, the body stores sufficient amounts of nutritive matter to last for a rather lengthy time during later periods of abstinence. Even thin people carry a reserve of nutrients in their tissues to tide them safely over a period of fasting." -- (Dr. Joel Fuhrman - Fasting and Eating For Health)

"We must not confuse fasting with starvation. Unfortunately, the two words are used interchangeably in virtually all medical circles. All but one in a thousand doctors react negatively to the subject of fasting. They have never fasted, know little about the subject, and respond only to bizarre stories they've heard. Lack of understanding creates unnecessary fear and results in unfounded, imaginary dangers and the use of scare tactics by doctors to avoid fasting. Remember fasting is not starving. Fasting begins with the omission of food, and it ends with the return of natural hunger. In contrast, starvation begins with the return of natural hunger and ends in death." -- (Lee Bueno Aquer - The Miracle of Fasting)

What everyone is saying in their own way is that starvation begins when our reserves are used up. People with anorexia for example could NEVER fast to cure their disease. The reason people with anorexia can't fast is because they have not eaten for extended periods of time and they would not have any reserves to be used up during the fast as a normal person would. This is why I urge everyone to have professional supervision for your first fast, be it prolonged or even a one-day, water-only fast. Many may find they are given permission to undergo a 1- to 3-day, water-only fast on their own, but permission needs to be obtained by a professional who is experienced in water-only fasts.

WHERE CAN I GET PROFESSIONAL SUPERVISION FOR A PROLONGED WATER-ONLY FAST?

Below I have listed for you the clinics that I have found in the United States that help in the supervision of water-only fasts. There are not many of them, I know. But DON'T let that discourage you. This might be the crucial part of your recovery. Some diseases will completely be reversed by simply going on a raw food diet for an extended period (example: 30 to 90 days) alone. Some diseases can be reversed by a simple modification to a mostly vegetarian diet. And, there will be other diseases that **will** require fasting in addition to the dietary change that has to be made. Two such diseases that most times require fasting according to Dr. Fuhrman are lupus and arthritis. Cancers usually do not respond favorably to fasting. If you have cancer PLEASE find out more info on Dr. Lorraine Day's web site. I gave you her information earlier in the book, but have provided it for you, too, at the end of this chapter.

PROFESSIONAL SUPERVISION OF WATER-ONLY FASTS

Dr. D.J. Scott D.M., N.D., D.C.
Scott's Natural Health Institute
P.O. Box 361095
Strongsville, OH 44126
Phone: 440-238-6930

http://www.fastingbydesign.com

* This is the fasting clinic that was recommended to me by my nutritionist Paula DuVall.

===

Dr. Alan Glodhamer
True North Health Center
6010 Commerce Blvd. #152
Rohnert Park, CA 94928
Phone: (707) 586-5555

http://www.healthpromoting.com

* This one also came recommended to me by my nutritionist.

===

Regency House Natural Health Spa
2000 South Ocean Drive
Hallandale, Florida 33009
phone: (800)-454-0003

http://www.regencyhealthspa.com/fasting.htm

===

Loren Lockman
Tanglewood Wellness Center
6135 Mountaindale Road
Thurmont, MD 21788
(301) 898-8901

www.tanglewoodwellenesscenter.com

==

Preventative Medical Center of Marin
25 Mitchell Blvd. #8
San Rafael, CA 94903
(415) 472-2343

This is the center of Elson Haas, MD author of The Detox Diet. He guides clients on both fasting and diet detoxification programs.

http://www.elsonhaas.com

ADDITIONAL RESOURCES

If you would like to try and find a fasting clinic that may be closer to you, you can go online to the IAHP's list. IAHP stands for International Association of Hygienic Physicians.

Therapeutic fasting is sometimes called "water fasting". IAHP-certified members have completed an internship in this specialty. They also are specialized in juice fasting, juice diets, raw vegan diets, and other detoxifying diets and programs.

Additionally I will try to keep compiling a list, and as I do I will put it up on my message boards at
http://www.rawandjuicy.com/messageboard.html

If you are not going to try a water-only fast and want information on institutions and clinics that help you with juice fasting and or raw food detoxification diets, please see Chapter 11.

Chapter 10: Why The One Cure Sometimes Fails

THERE ARE THREE REASONS THE 1 CURE TO ALL DISEASE WILL FAIL YOU...

1) Your body is too far gone for a reversal of disease to take place. (see below)
2) You're too lazy to make the necessary permanent dietary & lifestyle changes.
3) You're ignorance scares you into falling back to your old SAD diet.

My book is not about giving false hope. Not every single person that is diseased can reverse their disease even if they adopt a permanent plant-based diet, get exercise, sunshine, fresh air, etc. There may be certain cases where a person has been too sick for way too long and the body is simply too far gone for recovery. It is my opinion that these are limited cases. I have read of many accounts of even advanced cancers being completely reversed.

However, no matter what state your body is in, if you have something that is too far gone to be completely reversed, an improvement can still be made no matter how far gone you are. For the majority, a complete reversal of disease is completely within your grasps.

With the exception of being too far-gone for complete recovery, there is only two other ways the one cure to disease - **YOUR BODY'S MIRACULOUS HEALING ABILITY** - will fail you. That failure will come if you do not *make* and *maintain* the necessary dietary and lifestyle changes that are required for you to *achieve* and *hold on to* optimum health. The failure will come from you simply being too lazy to want to make the necessary changes, or from your fear of the unknown.

In Fasting and Eating for Health, Dr. Fuhrman made the statement, "Whether the patient has a cardiac condition, hypertension, autoimmune disease, fibroids, or asthma, he or she must be informed that fasting and natural plant-based diets are a viable alternative to conventional therapy and an effective one. The time may come when not offering this substantially more effective nutritional approach will be considered malpractice." When I interviewed him for this book, one of the questions I asked Dr. Furhman was:

Q. My last questions to you are, do you believe the time you speak of above, a time where not offering a viable alternative to conventional therapy will be considered malpractice, will come about in your lifetime?   If No, Why?

A. "No. The knowledge in 'Eat to Live' and 'Fasting and Eating For Health' is a opportunity to be healthier and happier in our lives. Many may take advantage of this life-saving information. However, the masses will continue to seek instant gratification via dangerous nutritional habits and drug-seeking."

This seems to be the consensus of many of the authors' books I have read in my research for this book. Many feel the majority will remain eating the wrong foods and consuming prescription and non-prescription drugs to ease their suffering. Dr. Fuhrman didn't state **why** he felt the masses would continue to seek instant gratification via dangerous nutritional habits and drug seeking, just that they would. Some believe the majority will remain drugged because of sheer lack of research on their own part. Some believe the majority will remain drugged because conventional medicine will never teach the truth. And other people believe the majority will remain on the wrong diet and drugged out of sheer laziness, for it is no doubt that making the proper dietary and lifestyle changes requires quite a bit of effort.

I am a little more optimistic, however, than most. I do believe in my lifetime I will see a world where the majority will learn the truth, and intelligently make the proper changes to their diet and lifestyles to ensure for them good health and longevity. I, for one, am going to do everything in my power to make sure this information - the truth about the cause of and cure to disease - continues to be brought to the forefront. For those of you who have the same success in reversing your disease through dietary and lifestyle change either coupled with fasting or not, please share this life saving information with others.

Had someone told me one year ago that I could feel the way I do today, without drugs, without surgery, I would have called them a liar. I am now trying to convince people of what I would not have believed. This is a large task, but one I am committed to. I can only tell you from my own personal experience, that once you feel GOOD again, you will never want to go back to feeling BAD.

THE 3 QUALITIES YOU MUST POSSESS TO HAVE SUCCESS WITH THIS METHOD OF NATURAL HEALING

- **Patience**
- **Knowledge**
- **Commitment**

You must have patience: Optimum health will not return to you overnight. It took you years to get in the much declined state of health that you are in today. Many of us have been poisoning ourselves since childhood! You can't expect for **all of those many years of damage** to be miraculously undone overnight! I know you are probably used to the instant relief that comes through the swallowing of a pain pill, but you are going to have to forego that and give yourself the proper amount of time for your body to heal. I had such huge improvements in just my first 30-day, raw-food-only diet and my two-week juice fast that I gained great encouragement to continue on full speed ahead!

You must have knowledge, you must know what to expect: Know that during the detoxification process you are more than likely going to experience moments of sickness and weakness. This is NORMAL. If you do not know what to expect you can easily give up on this unerring, disease-reversing process.

If you stay ignorant to the facts, you may get scared when you experience a healing crisis and fall back into your old ways. Many make this **huge** mistake. We don't like feeling bad. It sucks, I know. But you must know that by taking in drugs or the wrong foods only suppress the problem, it does not cure it. By suppressing the problem you are only prolonging the inevitable. Disaster will eventually strike when you continue with the wrong diet and drugging away of your symptoms. You might as well take these steps now, instead of waiting until it is too late.

My healing crises were never worse than the worst pain I experienced during my 5+ years of illness and suffering. Just tell yourself, this will pass. Some may never even experience healing crises through the detoxification process, but many do. This is why I URGE you to read, read, read!! When you know what to expect you are not fearful. When you have no fear you will continue through, even if a healing crisis arises, for you will know what it is and you will know how to handle it.

You must be committed to succeed: The honest truth is there will be people that are going to try and pull you down. It my surprise you and even sadden you that some of these people that will try to drag you down are your best friends or family members. Don't expect your doctor to be standing behind you on this path to recovery either -- I've already explained why. This will take 100% -- NO, this takes 110% commitment on your part. You must be committed!!

You must be willing to stick to this no matter what. You must be willing to give it your all, more than your all. You must be willing to get rid of your old ways, for some this may be very difficult to do. You may find that you have to stop going out with friends and or family if all they want to do is "go out to eat." For at least the first couple of months you shouldn't go to a restaurant at all. We go to restaurants, very, very, very, rarely; and if we do, I try to only eat things that are permissible to a raw vegan diet.

This is a new life for you; you are soon going to see how very addicted to food we are as a society. When you start this you are going to see how so much of our lives actually revolves around eating. It is actually quite disgusting.

You have to be committed because if you are not you will be looking for any excuse out. It will be very easy for you to blame others: "But I had to eat that piece of cake, it was my best friend's birthday," "but I had to take that Excedrin because I couldn't have made it through the work day without it." -- excuses, excuses, excuses. A committed person will make **NO** excuses.

A committed person, unless their body has been to completely ravaged by disease, will be able to completely reverse their disease or at least greatly improve their condition by using the methods described in this book. A non-committed person will fail. It is really that cut and dry. Which type of person are you?

I hope you are one who can make the commitment. You can live a better life. I'm living proof.

Attack your disease! Come at this as you would any other goal you would want to achieve! Does someone who continually comes into work late or leaves early with every excuse in the book get promoted? Does an Olympic athlete make it into the Olympics by practicing an hour or two here or there? The answer is no, of course not! If you want to achieve this goal, if you want to obtain optimum health, you have to work at it. Is it easy? It is for me now. In fact I can't see me living my life any other way, but the first few months took a lot of determination and a lot of will power.

You are human; you will make a mistake here or there. What makes the difference between you succeeding or failing however is how you handle that slip up. If you say, "screw it, I went out for a steak last night and already blew it, I might as well eat whatever I want tonight too and start again next week", you are going to fail. If you screw up once say, "okay, I made a mistake." Then, get right back on that horse and don't allow yourself to make that mistake again. You can succeed.

Stay patient, don't expect a miracle overnight. Stay informed. Knowledge is power! Stay committed!

Chapter 11: Knowledge is POWER!

HIGHLY RECOMMENDED READING LIST

Knowledge is POWER!! I've done extensive research to heal myself naturally from the debilitating pain I lived in on a daily basis. I did yet further research in the writing of this book. I have read countless books, numerous magazine and newspaper articles, and surfed thousands of web sites to gather information for my book. I witnessed a few authors claim that their way was the only way to cure disease. I wasn't a bit surprised to see that their information was nothing other than regurgitated information of those past who were successfully curing disease many, many years ago. I think those people do their readers a great disservice by not giving credit where credit is due. I do not wish to do this same injustice. I don't want you to just buy **my** book. In fact, if you purchase just my book then I feel I have failed. I tried to explain to you in my book that your good health is now in your hands! I've tried to stress to you that it is now up to you to take up where conventional medicine had failed you. I've tried to make it crystal clear to you that knowledge will give you power! The meat industry, the junk-food industry, the medical schools, and the drug companies WANT you to stay ignorant to the truth. **Never stop learning.** Put your health in YOUR hands and God's hands, not anyone else's.

My collection of books on the subject of natural healing, fasting, and eating to cure disease is gargantuan and ever growing. No matter how large my collection seems to grow I always go back to the same books when I have questions or when a friend asks me their advice on which book they should read. I have put together the following Recommended Reading List for you as a list of the books and tapes that I have found made the **biggest impact** on my newfound good health. **KNOWLEDGE IS POWER!!**

* Dr. Robert Sniadach's: **Essential Natural Hygiene Course**
* Professor Arnold Ehret: **The Mucusless Diet Healing System.**
* Professor Arnold Ehret: **Rational Fasting**
* Paul Bragg, ND: **The Miracle of Fasting**

- Dr. Herbert Shelton MD: **Fasting Can Save Your Life**
- Howard Lyman: **Mad Cowboy: Plain Truth from the Cattle Rancher Who Won't Eat Meat** (this should be a mandatory read for **all** who eat meat)

Knowledge is power! If money is an issue for you, I encourage you to check your local library and see if they carry any of the books that you are interested in. If they don't carry them and you don't want to pay retail, go online to places like amazon.com where you can get discounts off retail prices, and half.com where you can buy used books for some really good prices. (I buy a lot of my books from half.com)

http://www.amazon.com
http://www.half.com

I can honestly tell you that the used books I have purchased from half.com were all in great to excellent condition. Half.com is a great site because it lets the seller of the book tell you what condition the book is in, as well as allows you to see how many items the person has sold. You can also read reviews from customers about the sellers. You can get some real rock-bottom prices if you don't mind a few pages that have been dog-earred or have highlighted text.

I know that Dr. Sniadach's course is only available through the web site **http://www.transformationinst.com** so you can't get it discounted, however he does offer payment plans on his Natural Hygiene course. I can't recommend it highly enough. Hands down it is the best purchase I've made so far in my life.

Chapter 12: Homeopathy vs. Naturopathy vs. Natural Hygiene

THE INVENTION OF NATURAL HYGIENE, NATUROPATHY, AND HOMEOPATHY

Isaac Jennings, MD (1788-1874): According to "Hygienic" literature, the first "Hygienic doctor" was Isaac Jennings, MD. He is referred to as **"The Father of Orthopathy"** and he is also often referred to **"The Father of Natural Hygiene"**.

Dr. Isaac Jennings taught that obedience to "physical law" facilitates obedience to "moral law." The basis of his teaching was that healing was a process of "purification" and repair via natural methods.

Isaac Jennings, MD of Fairfield, Connecticut, having practiced medicine for 20 years and being thoroughly discouraged with the results, begins to administer placebos of bread pills, starch powders, and colored water tonics to patients, while instructing them in healthful living. He soon observed that his patients that were taking these placebos and following his instructions or "right living and eating" were getting well. This was a complete change from the results he was seeing with the drugging and bleeding practices that were used at the time.

In 1802 Dr. Jennings and physiologist/minister Sylvester Graham (originator of Graham Bread and the Graham Cracker) started a healing system called "Orthopathy."

For more info on Orthopathy please go to the web site:

http://members.austarmetro.com.au/~hubbca/orthopathy. htm

The Orthopaths (Natural Hygienists) were drugless doctors. Orthopaths very rarely prescribed medicine, and if they did it was only as temporary assistance if there was an urgent need for a drug to be used. They did not use drugs as the allopaths of today do, using it on a continuing basis to suppress pain.

Many who write on the principles of Natural Hygiene today does so as a result of the groundwork that was laid by Dr. Isaac Jennings and the "orthopathy principles." Two others that helped blaze the trail of Natural Hygiene were the already-mentioned Sylvester Graham and Trall.

Dr. Samuel Hahnemann: Known as the founder of Homeopathy. In 1810 Dr. Samuel Hahnemann developed homeopathy. More than likely you have heard the term "homeopathic remedy" before. This is where that term comes from.

In homeopathy people are treated with small amounts of the substances that are similar to those that are believed to have caused the disease. The basis of homeopathy is *like cures like*.

During Hahnemann's time, medicine was at a very primitive stage with frequent use of bleeding and leeches for most conditions. One of the few medicines that was very effective was quinine in treatment of malaria. Hahnemann decided to experiment by taking some quinine himself. He found himself developing the typical relapsing fever of malaria. Thus he had discovered the central principle of homeopathy - of likes being able to treat likes, or that medicines capable of treating symptoms are also able to produce those same symptoms in a healthy person. Homeopathy means "like disease."

Benedict Lust, MD: The founder of Naturopathy. The origins of naturopathy in North America are traced back to 1896 the year Benedict Lust, a German immigrant, founded the first school of naturopathic medicine in New York City. His first graduates from his school graduated in 1902.

The naturopathy treatment uses diet, herbs, homeopathic treatments, fasting, exercise, hydrotherapy, manipulations, and more to treat disease.

Herbert M. Shelton, D.C., N.D. (1895-1985): In 1928 Dr. Shelton released his first book, "Human Life: Its Philosophy and Laws." Shelton's book caused great controversy. He stirred things up by proving the concepts of health and disease as were held by schools of healing, were **incorrect**.

You may see Dr. Herbert Shelton, just like Dr. Isaac Jennings, referred to as the **Father of Natural Hygiene**. I think this is because when Dr. Isaac Jennings was teaching via what we **now** call Natural Hygiene methods, he was doing so under what he called "'Orthopathy."   I guess it would be safe to say that Natural Hygiene was created from the principles of Orthopathy.

From 1928 through 1968, Shelton wrote more than 35 books. In 1939, he began publishing a monthly journal, *Dr. Shelton's Hygienic Review.* He continued to publish that journal for over 40 years. Many who write about fasting today often quote his words and works. The main purpose of his teachings was to educate and stress the simplicity of obtaining and maintaining optimum health, without the dependence of costly drugs and therapies, but on the correct diet combined with natural detoxification methods, if necessary.

Dr. Shelton faulted both the doctors and the patients for their disregard of the simple laws of cause and effect. He made it well known that "cures" would not come from a laboratory, but from within our own bodies. His books stressed the simplicity of obtaining and maintaining good health with proper nutrition and not dependence on costly and dangerous prescription drugs and surgeries.

I've listed for you below just some of the great books that Dr. Shelton wrote.

- Fasting Can Save Your Life
- Natural Hygiene The Pristine Way of Life
- Fasting For Renewal of Life
- Health For The Millions
- Superior Nutrition
- Food Combining Made Easy

Dr. Shelton did much more than just write books, however. He also started a health school, Dr. Shelton's Health School, in San Antonio, Texas. There he helped restore the health of more than 30,000 people through his fasting and natural food diet methods.

THE DIFFERENCES BETWEEN HOMEOPATHY NATUROPATHY & NATURAL HYGIENE

I have given you a brief look at how and when the different alternative medicine practices of homeopathy, naturopathy, and Natural Hygiene were developed. I would also like to give you a brief rundown on the major differences between homeopathy, naturopathy, and Natural Hygiene, as well as my personal opinion on the healing abilities of all three methods.

Homeopathy uses tinctures or homeopathic drops and other concoctions to treat disease believing that like cures like.

Naturopathy uses a combination of things like homeopathic remedies (from the practice of homeopathy), as well as other things such as manipulations, hydrotherapy, herbs, vitamins, diet, exercise, etc. to treat disease.

Natural Hygiene principles are based on the body's ability to cure itself when the proper conditions are set for it. Natural Hygiene focuses on dietary and lifestyle changes such as plant-based diet, exercise, rest, etc. Natural Hygiene makes no mention of having to take supplementation or manipulations for you to be cured.

I do not believe in using naturopathy or homeopathy to cure disease, because I know that the **cure** to disease **cannot** be found in manipulations, homeopathic drops, or herbal concoctions. To treat via naturopathic or homeopathic remedies alone, with no strict dietary and lifestyle changes being made to rid the body of all toxins and detoxifying the body, is a waste of time and money. I do believe that many things, such as deep tissue massage, are extremely beneficial, and if you enjoy these treatments as I do, continue to have them. But don't rely on them to cure disease. No amount of homeopathic drops, no amount of massage or acupuncture sessions is going to completely reverse your disease if you continue to eat an unhealthy diet, live an unhealthy lifestyle, or never detoxify the toxins from your body.

Yes, I do believe that some degrees of relief can be brought on via some of these types of methods used in homeopathy and naturopathy but a **cure** will never come from these two methods. Alternative medicine's herbal, vitamin, or homeopathic supplementations work just like Rx drugs, in the sense that they are almost always only a band-aid. They cover the problem. Not cure it. If your diet and lifestyle is not changed, a cure will not come to you from homeopathic or naturopathic treatment alone. Then, there are other alternative therapies such as deep tissue massage, that I believe, *once you have cured your disease or have gotten it under control*, are **extremely beneficial** for your body. I would highly recommend massage to anyone. I just know that deep tissue massage alone did not cure me. If you continue to eat the wrong foods, drink the wrong beverages, expose yourself to chemicals or stress, etc., you will not reverse your disease no matter how many homeopathic drops or naturopathic treatments you are receiving.

RX DRUGS ARE BIG BUSINESS, BUT SO ARE SAFE, ALTERNATIVE HERBAL AND VITAMIN REMEDIES!!

In my 5+ years of illness, I was bounced back and forth from doctor to doctor to no avail. Throughout those years I would try different vitamin and herbal supplementations promising to end my fatigue and weakness, but they never did. It was just hard-earned money down the drain. I also underwent months of weekly deep muscle massage treatments and several cranio-sacral treatments, but those too proved to be useless. While I would feel better for a few hours after my massage or cranio-sacral treatment, the pain would always come rushing back and once again I would be in tears. Thankfully the wonderful massage therapist who was trying to help me with massage did what doctors never would do. She told me there was something else that was wrong with me; something that massages alone could not cure. She urged me to find the cause of what was making me sick and told me she didn't want to continue taking my money because she just couldn't explain why I was so ill. It is very rare however to find someone as caring as she was who will admit "Look, I'm not doing you any good; you have to find the source of the problem." Others would not be so honest.

I also underwent months of treatment of something called the "Whole Body Health Scan." It did not work either. I took numerous homeopathic drops and herbal concoctions in conjunction with the Whole Body Health Scan system. Some didn't bring any relief at all. Other drops that did bring relief stopped working as soon as I stopped taking them. I tried tapping on the temples of my head; something called E.F.T., emotional freedom technique, that also failed me.

I lost thousands of dollars to the allopathic medical community because their Rx drugs and surgeries failed me. But, I also lost thousands of dollars to the health food stores and their "miracle" pills, the massage therapy, and the chiropractic and homeopathic treatments.

My book will undoubtedly piss off a lot of people in the fields of allopathic, naturopathy, and homeopathy. So be it. I'm not trying to make any new friends. My book has one sole purpose, to share the information that I used to get me well with others who are in that same black hole that I once was. You are already sick; you don't need to be broke too. For years all of the money that I earned went to trying to get me well.

It took me over 5 years to find out that getting well wasn't going to have to cost me any money. Well, that's not entirely true; I did have to see a nutritionist for a couple of months to get colonics. I believe all of my treatments together didn't total $400.00. But the rest of the healing for me was free. That's the great thing about letting your body heal itself: It will save you tons of money! Some may have to go away to a fasting clinic and you will incur some cost there, but it will be nothing like what you will spend in healthcare for the years to come if you don't start reversing your disease right now.

It was the principles of Natural Hygiene, (even though I didn't know at the time that that those were the principles I was following), that WORKED for me! There is but one cause and one cure to all disease -- this I found to be the truth. This is the truth that is taught in Natural Hygiene.

I've said this before in my book, but I'll say it again here. When trying to cure what ails you, consider the source of the information. Most diseases can be reversed through dietary and lifestyle changes alone. If you are told you need special treatments or homeopathic drops or herbal remedies, to cure you, consider the source of the information. Does this person make money off of you when you purchase these things? More than likely they do. Be careful and know this, there is but one cure to disease, and it is free. It comes from within! Only your body can reverse your illness/disease, and it will only do so if you set for it the proper conditions for that self-repair to take place!

TWO OTHER MEN YOU SHOULD KNOW

Arnold Ehret (1834-1922): Arnold Ehret received his degrees at 21 and taught college until drafted for military service. Released after nine months because of "neurasthenic heart trouble," Ehret resumed his teaching career at 31 despite chronic ill health, suffering from kidney trouble with consumptive tendency.

Under the care of 24 different physicians at one time or another, Ehret finally turned to natural methods, vegetarianism, and mental health but still without completely satisfactory results. A sojourn to Nice, living on a radical milk-and-fruit diet proved helpful but only partially beneficial.

The following winter, Ehret traveled to Algiers, living almost exclusively on the plentiful native fruits. His condition rapidly improved, and he was emboldened to try short fasts, hopefully desiring to assist Nature in the cleansing properties of the fruit and climate. Success crowned his efforts, for not only did he regain good health, but unbelievable energy, strength, and joy of living. He and a companion undertook an 800-mile bicycle trip from Algiers to Tunis returning completely exhilarated by their feat!

Through years of continuous experimentation on himself and others, studying diets in Central and Southern Europe and the Middle East, Ehret successfully developed his MUCUSLESS DIET HEALING SYSTEM. Thousands of patients were taught these methods of regaining health in what he called Fruit Fasting Sanitarium in Switzerland.

Coming to the United States just before World War I (which conflict later necessitated his stay here) Ehret embarked upon an **immensely** popular lecture tour teaching the basic principles of rational fasting and a mucusless diet to cure disease.

Professor Ehret's teachings are not a fad or a cult. His teachings are simply a way of eating natural foods to cure disease and to maintain optimum health. Health seekers have followed his teachings for over 100 years, proving that his information stands the test of time. **Many** diet plans you see today that center on plant-based diets that teach you to limit your intake of starchy vegetables or mucus-forming foods use Ehret's work as the basis for their plan.   Some give Ehret the proper credit, others do not. I feel that Arnold Ehret is someone you will definitely want to learn more about if you are trying to free yourself from disease.

At fifty-six, while enjoying a superior state of health, Professor Ehret died as the result of a very unfortunate accident. On October 8 1922, the night Ehret died, he had just finished giving one of his most successful lectures. It was said that at least 100 people had to be turned away because it was a full house. After leaving the lecture hall Prof. Arnold Ehret was hastily making his way to the railroad station when he lost his balance stepping off the curb on a poorly lit street. He fell backwards striking his head on the stone curb, and suffered a basal fracture to his skull, which caused almost instant death.

I have Ehret's books Rational Fasting and The Mucusless Diet Healing System, which I have highly recommended in the previous chapter. He was truly a fascinating man.   While alive, he helped countless others regain their health, and even in death his word is still helping many learn how to reverse their diseases.

****

Paul C. Bragg, ND, Ph.D.: Crippled by TB as a teenager, Paul Bragg developed his own eating, breathing and exercising program to rebuild his body into an ageless, tireless, pain-free citadel of glowing, super health. He excelled in running, swimming, biking, progressive weight training and mountain climbing. He made an early pledge to God that in return for his renewed health, he would spend the rest of his life showing others the road to health. He honored his pledge! Paul Bragg's health pioneering made a difference worldwide.

Dr. Paul C. Bragg graduated from Dr. Lust's first School of Naturopathy in the U.S.

A legend and beloved counselor to millions, Bragg was the inspiration and personal health and fitness advisor to top Olympic Stars from 4-time swimming Gold Medalist Murray Rose to 3-time track Gold Medalist Betty Cuthbert of Australia, his relative and pole-vaulting Gold Medalist, Don Bragg and countless others. Jack LaLanne, the original TV Fitness King, says, "Bragg saved my life at age 15 when I attended the Bragg Crusade in Oakland, California. From the earliest days, Bragg advised the greatest Hollywood Stars and giants of American business. J.C. Penney, Del. E Webb, Dr. Scholl, and Conrad Hilton are just a few who he inspired to long, successful, healthy, active lives! Paul was also the inspiration for today's Mega Companies such as Schiff, Thompson, Twin Labs, Shaklee, Herbal Life, Gardenburger, and even the Good Earth Restaurant chain was inspired by Paul to start restaurants to serve health foods instead of fast foods.

Paul Bragg, ND has authored over 20 books. I've listed a few of them for you below. For all the books available please go to http//www.bragg.com

- The Miracle of Fasting
- Water The Shocking Truth That Can Save Your Life
- Bragg Healthy Lifestyle Vital Living to 120
- Build Powerful Nerve Force
- Super Power Breathing For Super Energy

When reading Paul Bragg's book The Miracle of Fasting, and by learning the Bragg Healthy Lifestyle, you can see that his system is similar to the Natural Hygiene principle, even though he graduated from Benedict Lust's school of Naturopathy.

Paul Bragg lived to be 97 years old! What is more phenomenal than his very long life however, is the fact that he was still physical fit and active at age 97!
Like Ehret, Paul Bragg also met with an unfortunate end. Paul died

tragically, still in excellent health, after drowning in a surfing accident in Hawaii at the age of 97; the date was Dec. 7th 1976. Do you know of any 97-year-olds that are surfing? Heck do you even know any 97-year-olds? Forget whether or not they are SURFING!

If you only purchase one of his books, I recommend his book, The Miracle of Fasting.

CHAPTER 13: Additional Info, Tips, & Resources

In this chapter I wanted to share with you some tips on transitioning to a raw diet, vegetarianism, veganism, juicing, skin brushing and some additional resources that were helpful to me on my road to recovery.

TRANSITIONING TO A RAW FOOD DIET

I hope that my book has shown to you the urgency of increasing your raw food intake. For those of you who just want to increase your raw food intake by say 25% to 75% you should have no problems doing so. Simply replace your breakfast with abundant amounts of fresh fruits, and your lunches with fresh salads filled with mixed greens and veggies. (NO STORE BOUGHT DRESSING THOUGH!) Go to my message boards at **http://www.rawandjuicy.com/messageboard.html** for some excellent raw salad dressing recipes.

Others are going to feel the want or the need to go to a 100% raw food, or the Natural Hygiene raw food diet as I myself did. Some will be able to do this cold turkey, others will not. I highly suggest you seek out the assistance of a professional to guide you with this task. Two natural Hygienists that I highly recommend are Dr. Douglas Graham, DC or Dr. Robert Sniadach, DC. Their web sites are:

http://www.douglasgraham.cc
http://www.transformationinst.com
http://www.transformationinst.org

And if you need the support of others who are on this same path, or want to journal your progress online as others are doing go to the message boards I have set up and interact with the others there also on this journey to raw foodism.

Those of you who are big meat-eaters or junk-food junkies may find the task of going raw cold turkey impossible, and you will need to transition slowly. One way of doing this may be going from your high-protein, meat-eating diet to a vegetarian diet for a couple of months. Then transition from a vegetarian diet to a vegan diet. Then you can transition from a vegan diet to a high-raw vegan diet, and from that point a 100% raw diet. There are huge differences in a typical raw food diet however and a Natural Hygiene raw food diet, and I will explain those in detail later in this chapter. It is important for me to explain these to you because I, and many others have problems on a typical raw diet. For those of you who are not armed with the proper information, you may go raw doing a typical raw diet and have problems and wrongfully blame it on the raw diet. In actuality it is just that there are components of the raw diet that are causing the problems. I ran into this myself so I can discuss this with you in great detail. For now, however, let me cover the topics of vegetarianism and veganism.

WHAT IS THE DIFFERENCE BETWEEN A VEGETARIAN AND A VEGAN?

The one thing vegans and vegetarians have in common is that neither of them eat meat, fish or poultry.

The basic difference between a vegetarian and a vegan is that a vegan does not consume any animal products at all, as opposed to a vegetarian who can consume dairy and/or eggs.

There are also two types of vegetarians: Ovo-lacto vegetarian and lacto vegetarian. See the following bullet points for more info.

- An ovo-lacto vegetarian eats eggs and dairy products.

- A lacto vegetarian eats dairy products but does not eat eggs.

- A vegan diet does not eat dairy or egg products.

VEGETARIAN AND VEGAN ONLINE RESOURCES

If you want more information on vegetarianism and veganism please check out the web sites below.

VEGAN RELATED SITES

http://www.veganstreet.com (I love this site!)
http://www.vegansociety.com
http://www.vegan.org
http://www.veganoutreach.org
http://www.veganchef.com
http://www.govegan.net/indexx.html
http://www.veganrecipes.com
http://www.veganmercantile.com
http://www.veganmania.com
http://www.coolvegan.com
http://www.veganforlife.org
http://www.vegan-food.net
http://www.vegweb.com/food

VEGETARIAN RELATED SITES

http://www.vrg.com
http://www.vegetariantimes.com
http://www.vegkitchen.com
http://www.vegdining.com
http://vegetarian.lifetips.com/OurGurus.asp
http://www.pbs.org/regina/
http://www.vegetarianstuff.com
http://www.vegetarian-meals.com/become_a_vegetarian.html
http://www.jtcwd.com/vegie/index.html

There are literally millions of web pages on vegetarianism and veganism. I found more information on veganism however. If that information isn't enough just surf the net some more; you will find all information you could want.

One thing I want to stress with you however, if you choose to transition your way to raw via way of a vegetarian diet or a vegan diet, is that you may not feel any improvement. I did not, and many others do not fare well on these diets either. One of the reasons for this is that both of these diets, vegetarian and vegan, contain not only foods that are processed, but they contain cooked foods too and cooked foods simply do not give us the nutrients we need as I have already proven to you in earlier chapters. Additionally, there are alterations that do take place in some cooked foods that actually make it toxic and the body will react when you put toxin in it. For some, however, going vegetarian or vegan is the easiest way for them to transition. Just keep that in mind if you do choose to transition this way.

If you aren't going raw cold turkey, my grocery list below that my husband and I used to go vegan might be of help to you. Again, keep in mind, I did not get well on a cooked vegan diet, but it is how I transitioned.

SHOPPING LIST FOR THOSE WISHING
TO TRANSITION TO A VEGAN DIET

When leaving your SAD (Standard American Diet) behind for a healthier vegan diet, your grocery lists should mainly consist of fruits and vegetables if you are trying to detoxify your body or even if you are just trying to maintain good health. Other food items you may add to your grocery list are things like whole grains, RAW nuts and seeds (without roasting or salt), legumes, sprouts and some soy products (if you are not allergic to soy).

Like I said earlier, hardly anything I buy comes in a bag, box or a can. Currently I am on 100% raw food diet so I don't use any of the items on the list below, but my husband does and I want to share this information because these things will help you transition to the vegan diet or the 100% raw food diet. I have made a list for you below of some of the canned, bagged,and/or boxed food we do purchase.

1   Rice Dream rice milk (occasionally) if we need milk for a recipe. My husband eats much more cooked foods than I do, so if a recipe requires milk he uses rice milk. If you don't have a problem with soy products you may want to get soy milk instead of rice milk. I recommend rice milk however.

1   Organic brown rice or organic wild rice.

1   Purity Foods Vita Spelt pasta or Ancient Quinoa Harvest pasta (pronounced "keen-wa") instead of white flour or wheat pasta.

1   Organic Spelt Flour instead of white flour. (You can find organic spelt and quinoa flour in your local health food stores)

1   Soy Garden Soy butter. I never used this in the transition but my husband does on his toast and steamed veggies and he loves it. He uses it in place of butter and says it tastes just as good.

1   Fantastic Taco and Chili mix. ("Fantastic" is actually the name). If you are dying for a taco or chili my husband and I recommend these products highly! I used these in the transition, and my hubby still uses them. Currently I am on 100% raw and do not know if I will ever add cooked food back into my diet, but this did help in the transition stage. http://www.fantasticfoods.com

1   Vegan Boca Burgers. These are soy but I don't seem to have problems with them. I don't eat them very often either, just because I don't eat that much cooked food. My husband has found these very helpful in his transition from the SAD (Standard American Diet) to a vegan diet. Boca Burgers make different types so be sure to read the package. I believe only one of their Boca burgers are vegan. It will say "vegan" on the package.

1   Muir Glen organic salsa and Muir Glen organic pasta sauce. These are really delicious. http://www.muirglen.com

1   Ezekial bread. This is the only type of bread I ate during the transition. It comes in plain, sesame, and cinnamon raisin. I did enjoy all three during the transition. I do not recommend you eat grains, but while you are transitioning and trying to get off bread this is a replacement that is better for you than the majority of bread on the market. The company name is Food for Life.

1   Bragg Olive Oil. http://www.bragg.com

1   Imagine Organic Soups. During the transition I did eat canned soups occasionally,but the majority of the time I made my own. WATCH THE SODIUM CONTENT IN THESE SOUPS THOUGH. Even though they are preserved with sea salt, salt is salt and it is not good for you.

1   ShariAnn's Organic Refried Beans. http://www.shariannsorganic.com

NOTE: I stay away from ALL canned, boxed, and bagged products. I only give you that shopping list if you cannot go raw cold turkey on your own or with the help of a professional. If you want to transition to a vegan diet, those products will be of help to you. Don't get discouraged if you go vegetarian or vegan and feel like crap, most people do because those diets still contain chemicals or other toxic substances that our bodies are not designed to digest, assimilate, and eliminate. Also, know that I feel so much better when I am eating a 100% raw diet.

But we are all different, so the choice will, of course, be up to you and what is best for YOUR body and what you are capable of. Let how your body reacts to the food be the determining factor of whether or not you add a particular food back into your diet or not. Many who have used raw food to detox themselves have ended up turning into 100% vegan raw foodists permanently because that diet brings them such optimum health they do not want to go back to any other way. Learn to listen to your body and let it tell you what works and what doesn't. It is a process, and you should feel comfortable with it, not pressured. Good health will not come to you over night. For most of you who will read my book it has taken decades for it to get in the state it is in now. This takes awhile to reverse.

Once you transition to raw, *if you don't do it cold turkey with a 30-day limited raw food diet as I did*, remember: If you start feeling bad again after the reintroduction of cooked foods, **ELIMINATE** them! One of the best tips I can share with you is to make sure when you get off your 30-day raw food detox diet and your two-week juice-fast, only enter mono-meals back into your diet. A mono meal means one food at a time. This will help you determine exactly how your body reacts to each food.

The shopping list I have provided for you should not be used as a crutch that allows you to eat large amounts of cooked or preserved food. It is just a list I wanted to provide you with so that you know what cooked foods I ate as I transitioned to a 100% raw food diet.

Listen to your body. If you find cooked foods bother you, as I have and many others have, stick with a higher percentage of raw foods. If your health problems start to subside on a vegan diet or a vegetarian diet alone with cooked foods, stick to that plan. As you become well you will start to hear your body. Let it guide you. If you are feeling perky and energetic, don't mess with success. If you feel yourself slipping into a downward spiral, eliminate anything new that you may have added from your diet. In the beginning it will seem like a daunting task, but the huge reward of OPTIMUM HEALTH will make your hard work all worthwhile! Remember if you feel like you need support turn to the internet and visit my online message boards at **http://www.rawandjuicy.com/messageboard.html.** Sometimes, just being able to interact with others who are going through similar situations is all you need to help you push through the hard times.   Now for a more detailed discussion of the differences between a basic raw food diet and a Natural Hygiene raw food diet:

GOING RAW!
BASIC RAW FOOD DIET VS. NATURAL HYGIENE RAW FOOD DIET

Raw food is raw food right? Wrong! You can have an unhealthy raw food diet. Many people that say the raw'diet doesn't work say this because they did the typical high-fat, raw diet, consisting of too many avocados, nuts, and seeds, or they did a raw food diet with improper food combinations, or the use of such foods that while they are technically "raw" they are proven to be toxic in the body and hence cause stomach bloating, gas, etc. I know this because I have experienced it firsthand to be true.

There are many fabulous raw food recipe books on the market, which I am thrilled about. However there will be two different types of people who will go raw. There will be the crowd who goes raw because it is suddenly the "in" thing to do (however I believe is still quite a ways down the road) and then there will be the crowd that goes raw to reverse their disease. I, of course, went raw to reverse my illness. When Paula had me go raw, I didn't have any idea that there were actually people that called themselves raw foodists.

So what's the problem with all of the raw food recipe books? Isn't that a good thing? It depends. There may be individuals, like myself, who can't tolerate a lot of the ingredients used in raw food recipes such as sea salt, nama shoyu, vinegar, garlic, etc.   I, thankfully, did a lot of studying and researching into the subject. Others may not do this and go raw by following a basic, raw food diet and not get well. They may have bad results on the basic, raw food diet, not improve health-wise, and get the very wrong

impression that raw didn't work. While the reality may very well
be that it wasn't raw that failed them, but that particular raw food
diet. Again, that is why I suggest everyone get to a point where
they can do at least a 30-day, limited raw food diet (Natural
Hygiene raw diet) and eat only fresh fruits and vegetables and
avoid the nuts and avocados for just a short period. See how you
feel. Track the results. From that point add foods back into your
diet one food at a time and again, track the results. This worked
wonders for me! This allowed me the clarity to be able to truly see
and feel how my body truly reacts to each and every food I put in
it.

If you have an internet connection and you look up "raw food
diets," I am quite positive you will come across message boards or
other discussion groups online that have heated debates on which
raw food diet is the best. Personally I believe this is something
you will be able to tell for yourself. Just know, if you go raw with
no strict plan to follow and the majority of your meals are meals
that you are making from raw food recipe books and you don't feel
well, there is an alternative.

Natural Hygienist raw foodists say that the ideal diet is the
80/10/10 diet. This means a raw diet that consists of 80%
carbohydrates, 10% proteins, and 10% fats. Having lived this diet
myself I can tell you with 100% honesty that when I do eat this
way I feel my best. It can be a hard diet to stick to, I won't lie,
but that is because it is new to me, and old habits die-hard.
Others who have done it for years say it is second nature to them.
It isn't hard work at all is what they tell me. "It's simple." When I
ask them what makes it so simple the reply is always very similar:
"Because it makes me feel good!"

Do I stress out and feel I have to eat a Natural Hygiene 80/10/10
diet every day? Absolutely not. There is no stress involved in it. I
know some days I will fall off my little raw wagon, and I'm okay
with that. In fact, I've learned a lot about my health from falling
off my raw wagon. For example when I fall off my wagon and eat
pizza I suffer the consequences. My nose stuffs up; I can't
breathe; I get sinus pressure, and I learn "'WOW! This is how my
body reacts to dairy."   Mucous forms as a means of eliminating
the toxins from my body. If I fall of my raw wagon and I eat
something like organic corn chips, and I retain water and I bloat
and I learn, "WOW! This is how my body reacts to salt."

It is a learning experience. It is a day-by-day process. Often times we learn more from our mistakes than we do anything else. The truth is, the information I have shared with you in this book IS the exact information that has helped me learn how to help my body heal itself. As I learned all of this information I felt completely overwhelmed. I had to take it all one day at a time. I didn't find all of this information in one place either like you are finding here in this book, so I know that you must probably feel quite overwhelmed yourself. It is a lot to take in. I know. I've lived it. Take it one day at a time. Turn to the internet, go to my message boards and meet with myself and others who are also on this same path. It is a very supportive board filled with tons of free information and resources to help you.

http://www.rawandjuicy.com/messageboard.html

JUICING

I've already discussed with you how I used a two-week juice fast at the beginning of my detoxification process. For many, their bodies are so enervated that the benefits of juicing in the first few months of detoxification are immeasurable.

Freshly squeezed or freshly juiced juice is simply bursting with loads of vitamins, minerals, enzymes and phytochemicals that give your body optimum health! For example: One cup of carrot juice contains the equivalent nutrition of four cups of raw chopped carrots. More than likely you won't sit down and eat four cups of raw chopped carrots, but you could easily drink one cup of carrot juice.

Juicing can be used to enormous benefit in bodies that are so enervated that they are lacking nutrients because fresh juice has such highly concentrated nutrients. One thing you have to keep in mind about juicing is that our bodies are not designed to handle such high concentrations of nutrients; so, when you juice you should sip your juice, not chug-a-lug it. For really sick individuals that need to build their strength up as quickly as possible and who cannot undergo a water-only, fast juicing is ideal.

Juicing, unless being used for a prolonged, supervised fast, should not be used for an extended period because when we fill our body with an overload of such concentrated nutrients our bodies will have to work overtime to expel the excess that they cannot use. We should not work against the body, but with the body. So to reiterate, juicing should be used by very enervated bodies in the beginning of a detox program or in replacement of a water-only fast in cases where water-only fasts can not be performed (supervised of course) but not for extended periods of time because they will cause imbalances in the body.

Don't Juice With Bottle Juices: Juicing with bottled juices that you purchase from the supermarket or even health food store may be tempting, but DON'T give into that temptation. Most bottled juices lack any nutrients and are preserved with dangerous chemicals. Juices that are not made fresh and sold in the store in bottles or cans have been heated to kill all the enzymes. The enzymes are one of the key reasons why making fresh juice with your juicer is so beneficial to your health. Do not try to substitute store-bought juice for homemade juiced or squeezed juice!

Tips On Buying A Juicer: There are cheap juices and expensive juicers. Prices range anywhere from around $79 to $2,000. You are not going to need it for long, so my opinion is go with the Juiceman or Jack Lalanne's juicer; both sell for under $100.

Two books that I highly recommend you read if you want more information on juicing are:

- **The Juiceman's Power of Juicing - Jay Kordich**
- **Juice Fasting & Detoxification - Steve Meyerowitz**

Jay Kordich, author of The Juiceman's Power of Juicing said that freshly juiced fruits and vegetables cured his bladder cancer. Dr. Lorraine Day, in her video You Can't Improve On God, stresses that juicing was an essential part of her curing herself from advanced breast cancer.   I've read countless stories of individuals who have cured their diseases with juicing and juice fasts.

SKIN BRUSHING

What is skin brushing? Skin brushing is exactly what it sounds like; you brush your skin. Every morning when I get out of bed before I take a shower, or do anything else for that matter, I go into the bathroom, take off all of my clothes, get out my dry loofah sponge and brush my skin.

Why Do I Want To Brush My Skin?: The skin is the largest organ of the body, and it is responsible for 1/4 of the detoxification that takes place from your body each day. By brushing your skin, you open your skin's pores, and this help your lymph system cleanse itself of toxins that collect in the lymph glands. Because skin brushing stimulates circulation, increases cell renewal, and helps clean the lymphatic system, it also helps to reduce cellulite.

How Do I Brush My Skin?:

- You want to make sure you brush your skin dry, not wet. Brushing wet skin can defeat the purpose of why you skin brush in the first place. You brush your skin to remove dead skin. Brushing wet skin can also cause the skin to stretch and pull.

- Use a dry loofah sponge, or a natural (not synthetic) bristle brush. Brush your skin in long sweeping motions always towards your heart.

- Be sure to cover every area of your body. Start with the soles of your feet and work your way up. Brush the ankles, calves, and thighs; then brush across your stomach and buttocks, your chest (do not brush your nipples) and your breasts (do lighter strokes over your breasts); brush your hands to the arms; brush your neck, and very lightly brush the skin on your face. When skin brushing your face, be sure to only use a loofah face sponge or special soft brush designed for your face. You can get these face brushes or loofah sponges at most health food stores and even cosmetic stores.

- Brush each part of your body several times completely. Spend at least five minutes daily brushing your skin. I like to do it in the morning and at night.

<h2 style="text-align:center">FLETCHERIZING</h2>

What Is Fletcherizing?:   Fletcherizing was a term coined by **Horace Fletcher** (1849-1919) in 1898. Horace Fletcher of Lawrence, Massachusetts evolved a system of chewing food called "*Fletcherism*." Fletcher, at 40, considered himself an old man. He was overweight, contracted the flu every six months, and constantly complained of indigestion and feeling constantly tired. After a deep study, he made some important discoveries and created the rules for Fletcherism which are as follows:

1 Chew your food to a pulp or milky liquid until it practically swallows itself.

1 Never eat until hungry.

1. Enjoy every bite or morsel, savoring the flavor until it is swallowed.

1. Do not eat when tired, angry, worried, and at mealtime refuse to think or
   talk about unpleasant subjects.

Horace Fletcher followed these rules himself for five months. As a result, he lost more than 60 pounds and felt better than he had for 20 years.

Fletcherism is the slow mastication (chewing) of food. He believed each bite of food should be chewed 50 times so that it becomes liquefied before swallowing it.   If you follow Fletcherism, you will chew each bite of food until it becomes a watery mass in your mouth before swallowing.

Horace Fletcher ran an experiment on a military population in Canada. He required half his experimental group to chew thoroughly and the other half to gulp things down as usual. His study reported significant improvement in the overall health and performance of the group that persistently chewed their food thoroughly. Fletcher's report recommended that every mouthful be chewed 50 times for half a minute before being swallowed.

Fletcherizing your food has two effects. First, if you chew a bite of food that long, you will be consuming your meal at a slower rate. Secondly, the reduction of this food to a watery mass means that it will be less difficult to extract nutrients from the food and much easier to digest and assimilate. By Fletcherizing your food, you take a great deal of energy out of the digestive and assimilating processes your body has to go through when eating.

Some of the books he wrote are ***Glutton or Epicure*** (1899), **The ABC of Nutrition**, published in 1903, and ***Fletcherism: What It Is*** (1913).

While I cannot honestly tell you that I chew each bite of food 50 times, I can tell you honestly that I do try and chew each bite very thoroughly. I did have a very serious problem with digestion, and Fletcherizing my food did help me tremendously with my digestion problems.

NOTE: Fletcherizing your food and continuing to eat junk food should not even be considered. I am sure someone with some glimmer of hope that they can continue to eat Ding-Dongs as long as they chew each bite 50 times is reading this book. NO! It doesn't matter how thoroughly you chew junk food, because your body gains no vitamins or nutrients from junk food. Use Fletcherizing only in combination with a healthy, preferably plant-based diet.

WHERE CAN I GET PROFESSIONAL SUPERVISION OF A JUICE FAST OR RAW FOOD DETOXIFICATION DIET?

If you do not have the willpower or determination to make the necessary dietary changes you will need to reverse your disease, you can seek professional assistance in this department too, just like you can water-only fasts. Below I have put together a list for you of institutes, retreats, clinics and spas you may find very helpful to you.

Creative Health Institute, *"The Wheatgrass Place"*, is a natural health learning center which provides two- and three-week programs of body purification, nutrition and rejuvenation through the use of fresh, raw fruits, vegetables, juices, nuts, sprouted seeds, grains, beans, chlorophyll-rich greens and wheatgrass juice.

Creative Health Institute
112 West Union City Road
Union City, MI 49094
(517) 278-6260

* This is a facility that my nutritionist recommended to me.

Eden Retreats
Nature's First Law
PO Box 900202
San Diego, CA 92190 USA
888-729-3663
E-mail: nature@rawfood.com
Web-site: www.rawfood.com

Nature's First Law conducts several raw-food retreats each year.

Hippocrates Health Institute
1443 Palmdale Court
West Palm Beach, FL 33411
800-842-2125
Fax 561-471-9464

Hippocrates is a healing retreat run by Brian Clement emphasizing the use of raw plant foods. For more information write or call.

Optimum Health Institute (OHI)
6970 Central Ave.
Lemon Grove, CA 91945
(619) 464-3346
Fax 619-589-4098

OHI is one of the best detoxification institutes in the United States. They have 1-, 2-, 3-, and 4-week programs. 100% raw plant-foods are served on the premises. OHI offers affordable rates. Write or call for a free brochure.

Optimum Health Institute (OHI)
Rural Route 1
Box 339-J
Cedar Creek, TX 98612
(512) 303-4817
Fax 512-303-1239

The new OHI in Texas operates a similar program to that found at OHI in San Diego. Write or call for a free brochure.

Rhio's Raw Energy Hotline
(212) 343-1152
http://www.rawfoodinfo.com

Rhio's Raw energy hotline is a raw foods help line and also a resource directory of events and classes related to the raw food diet.

Hallelujah Acres
PO Box 2388
Shelby, NC 28151
http://www.hacres.com
(704) 481-1700

Hallelujah Acres is a religious, spiritual, raw foods and fasting retreat center founded by Rev. Paul Malkmus.

5 TIPS TO MAKE YOUR RAW FOOD DIET EASIER

Once you transition to a 100% raw diet, whether you plan on just doing it for a short period or whether you plan on making it a permanent dietary change, the following tips may be of help to you:

1) Eat a variety of fruits and vegetables so you don't get bored. Go online and gather some free raw food recipes. I will be compiling some recipes and sources for free, raw food recipes, and I will be listing them on my raw food resources board at the web page **http://www.rawandjuicy.com/messageboard.html**

Keep in mind you may very well find that you don't do well on raw food recipes, AND you may just have to stick with a more Hygienic raw food diet. You can get plenty of information on this subject too at my message boards.

2) Stay full. At your meals eat as much as you want, pile those veggies up a mile high if you want to! Try to stick to three to five main meals a day instead of eating all day long. For example, if you find yourself eating every ½ an hour you are not giving your digestive system a rest and that is not good.

3) Listen to your thirst. When you body goes through heavy detoxification it may request large amounts of water to dilute the toxins in your system. This is normal.
Be sure to eat adequate amounts of fresh raw fruits and vegetables, but if you have a thirst be sure to quench it by drinking only pure (distilled or reverse osmosis) water. Your body tells you when you are thirsty. Listen to it, and give it what it needs.

4) Never stop learning. Surround yourself with information on raw foodism. I've already discussed it earlier, but one thing you should prepare yourself for when winding your way through the world of raw food is that there are two very different raw food viewpoints. One is that you can eat whatever you want as long as it is raw -- raw food gourmet recipes, a high-fat raw food diet (lots of avocados and nuts), and the viewpoint that the ideal diet is a Hygienic raw food diet. Where do I stand on this issue? Safely in the middle J! No, in all seriousness and in all honesty, when I am on a Hygienic raw food diet I absolutely, hands down, feel the best. There are no arguments there. What I hope my book helps and encourages you do to is read ALL of the information, experiment with both of the different raw food diets yourself, and track your results. How do you feel best? That is the key. Do what makes you feel best. You are smart; you will know when you feel good and when you don't feel good. I don't have to tell you that.

Don't take anyone's word and run with it. Not even mine. Apply the information. Spend a few weeks on a loose raw food diet and see how you feel. Spend a few weeks on a Hygienic raw food diet and see how you feel. Learn by experiment and experience how your body reacts to different foods, spices, herbs, etc.

But I strongly urge you to not only study raw foodism but Natural Hygiene too for the sole purpose of learning how *your* body works. This is how you really grab control of your health -- by understanding it. It is never too late to learn.

For reading material on Natural Hygiene, I give my highest recommendation to Dr. Sniadach's Essential Natural Hygiene Course. I truly believe that the information in his course should be taught throughout high schools worldwide. No, I do not receive any monetary compensation for giving this recommendation. It truly has been, to date, the best purchase I have made for the betterment of my health. His course information is at http://www.transformationinst.com

5) Seek out support. Believe it or not you are not in this alone. Thousands are turning to raw food and Natural Hygiene to reverse their diseases. These concepts of raw food and Natural Hygiene are foreign to most. Don't be surprised to feel extremely alone when you make the wise and bold decision to travel this route for optimum health. But you are not alone. You can find support on my message boards themselves, but you can also find links to other raw food message boards and support groups from my raw food resources message board at http://www.rawandjuicy.com/messageboard.html

There are no fees to visit any of the message boards or support groups that I provide links to. It is important to feel a connection with others who are also in the same situation that you are. On my boards you can even read through journals of individuals who are tracking their progress as they transition to or carry out life on a raw food diet.

Another online raw food group I belong to is Ruth Shivani's Harmonious Living group. It is filled with the nicest bunch of guys

and gals you could ever want to meet. All of them are in different
stages of the raw food life; so no matter if you are a newbie or you
have been living a raw food lifestyle for decades, you will feel right
at home there.
To subscribe to Ruth's Harmonious-Living group send a blank email
to Harmonious-Living-subscribe@yahoogroups.com Or you can go
to Ruth's web site directly at http://www.harmonious-living.com.
If you need the support of a Hygienic doctor, I can't say enough
good things about Dr. Douglas Graham and Dr. Robert Sniadach.
They are both wonderfully kind and caring men who do take the
Hippocratic Oath's "First Do No Harm" to heart. They can be
contacted through their web sites at:

http://www.doctorgraham.cc
http://www.transformationinst.com

CAN I EVER EAT COOKED FOOD AGAIN?

Many people who have come to me advice about getting well
through a raw food diet ask me, "Can I ever eat cooked food
again?" My answer is always the same: "It is entirely up to you.
It is your health. It is YOUR decision."   Almost inevitably their
next question is usually, "Shelly, will you ever eat cooked food
again?" My answer is almost always, "I'm certain I will." One
should never say never. Even if I live the rest of my life with only
taking one bite of cooked food, one bite is exactly that one bite,
and it is cooked. This is a learning and growing process. While I
am certain I will eat cooked food again, I know that my diet will
always be one that, for the majority of the time, is the one that
gives me the best health. I've lived the alternative, and trust me
when I tell you I am not going back.

While my diet is currently a 100% raw Hygienic diet, I know that I
will always remain on, at the **very least,** a high raw diet all of my
life. The results are inarguable. I went from be so sick that I
wanted to die to feeling physically better at 32 years old than I did
even at 19 years old. This miraculous transformation took place in
a little over a year's time, as opposed to the five+ years of poking,
prodding, x-raying, and drugging that I went through with
conventional medicine to no avail! I owe this awesome, HEALTHY
life to raw foods and Natural Hygiene and they will be a part of my
life for the rest of my life. Nobody can achieve this state of health
and let it go. I don't see how that could even be a possibility.

Will I eat cooked food again? Perhaps, but if I do, I can say with 100% certainty that it will be vegetarian if I do. I think my comfort zone is with the Hygienic diet for the majority of my days (as that is what keeps my body in top shape), occasional raw food gourmet recipes or higher fat recipes from time to time and, yes, even the possibility of a periodic cooked food vegan meals, such as a bowl of homemade vegetable stew once in awhile.

But just to reiterate, it is without a doubt a Hygienic raw food diet that will be my main diet because it simply brings me the best results.

Chapter 14: To The Critics:

There will unquestionably be critics to my book. To the critics I ask the question, **"What can trying a natural method, such as dietary change, increasing your pure water intake, getting ample fresh air, sunshine and exercise, etc., hurt?"**

How can something that doesn't cause harm, **NOT** be worth a try? If it fails, it fails, so what! No irreparable damage will be done.

To the critics who oppose this type of method I also want to ask, are you only opposing this natural method because its success means your failure?

To any doctor who is pushing their drugs and not giving their patients the information on these natural alternatives I ask you: **WHY**? If the reason you continue to push your drugs and not offer up this information to your patients is because you know with certainty, through proven research studies that you have conducted with your own patients that this will **not** work, I say show me the proof. If the reason you continue to push your drugs and not offer up this information to your patients is because you were not taught this information, I tell you: Do some research -- the information isn't hard to find. Just go to the internet and type in Natural Hygiene, fasting, juicing, or raw food, and you will find thousands of web pages on Natural Hygiene and other natural cures that have been proven to cure disease.

To the MD's: If you really entered into the medical profession to save lives, and I truly believe the majority of you do, then I ask you as a patient, "Why don't you feel you owe it to your patients to try and help them without harming them?" You are taught that all drugs are toxic. You were smart enough to become a doctor, so how in the world can you honestly feel that treating people with something that is toxic is the answer?

I am telling you I cured myself from daily debilitating pain of which none of the doctors or specialists I saw could cure me. I am telling you millions of people have used these same methods I have used and they too have cured their so-called incurable diseases. The information is out there. If you really want to save lives, if you really want a cure as you claim you do, why don't you do the research on your own and stop relying on what the medical schools and the drug companies tell you. You were smart enough to make it through medical school; aren't you smart enough to form your own opinions?

To the Charitable Organizations Struggling To Find A Cure:
Would you be willing to give this natural Hygienic method of treatment a try? Would you be willing to take 100 of the people that are suffering from the disease you are trying to find a cure for and have them try this method? If yes, GREAT - CALL ME! If no, why not?

If you work for one of these charitable organizations that are walking to fight breast cancer, jumping rope to fight heart disease, auctioning off dates to find a cure for MS, etc., etc., and you read this book, take this to the head of the organization and get their opinion. Will they be willing to try this or won't they? If they are not willing to try or research the subject further, you have to ask yourself if they are really trying to find a cure, or are they really just trying to bring in more money?

I saw Sharon Stone and Richard Gere on television last night on some news entertainment program, and they were speaking out about how there was no cure for AIDS, and they felt it was their duty to help out. I just wanted to say, *"Give me Richard's phone number! There are cases of people being cured from AIDS."* Are these celebrities just like I was, uninformed?

I just want to round all of these celebrities up in one great big auditorium and say, "Look, there **is** a cure to the disease you are donating your time and money to.   If you really want to 'find the cure'... look everywhere and anywhere for it - NOT just in the world of conventional medicine. There is one cause to all disease: Auto-intoxication! There is a cure for disease: Remove the toxins from the life of the individual that is sick, and detox the body."

Do these celebrities get paid to give these appearances with the charitable organizations? I would certainly hope not for, if they do, the conspiracy may reach even deeper than the profit-hungry charitable organizations themselves. Maybe I am naive, but I don't think these celebrities are making any money from helping these charities.

I believe that the celebrities that are pitching in really do have the best interest at heart. The only problem is they are terribly misinformed. They are being given information from the medical communities and the pharmaceutical industries. They then spread the misinformation and, instead of making the problem better, they make it worse. The celebrities have only half the story. The celebrities have the story the doctors, the pharmaceutical companies, and the FDA want them to have. This is very DANGEROUS! They are trying to create awareness to help out, but all they are really doing is spreading misinformation. All that does is multiply the problem.

To The Celebrities Trying To Find A Cure For Disease: With your celebrity, you have the power to move mountains, there is no doubt. So here it is, my personal plea to you: If you are working for a charitable organization to try and find a cure for a particular disease, PLEASE research for yourself the subject of Natural Hygiene. If you just devote a **little** of your time, you will see for yourself that millions of people with just about every disease you can imagine are **CURING** themselves from these so-called incurable diseases.

If you really care about these people you are trying to help, doesn't it make sense to try and help them get well via natural methods that do not cause further damage to their already weak and enervated systems?

Perhaps you are working with an organization that is trying to find a cure for disease that has struck someone in your family. If this is the case, and this person is still with us and not passed on, why not help them try these natural methods and see for yourself what our bodies are capable of when we set the proper conditions for our bodies to heal themselves? One thing that can't be argued: The principles I used to cure myself, the principles that millions of others have used to cure themselves, the principles of Natural Hygiene, will not cause any further damage to the body. **So, isn't it worth a try?**

To The Drug Companies: There is really nothing I have to say. God himself could come down and tell you to stop making these unnecessary drugs, but you won't. You make money because people are dependent on the drugs you make. Many of the drugs you make do nothing other than cause more problems, and you've already got a back up drug waiting on the shelves to fix the new problem the last drug created.

THE CRITICS WILL FALL INTO 1 OF 3 CATEGORIES...

To anyone who wants to criticize my book for the writing style or content -- go ahead; please feel free to do so. To anyone who wants to criticize the underlying message of my book -- the fact that our bodies have the capability of healing themselves when we set for them the proper conditions to do so -- I say you must be greedy, addicted, or uninformed.

- Greedy - making money off of Rx drugs, non-Rx drugs, homeopathic remedies, surgeries, herbal and vitamin supplementation.

- Addicted - addicted to food, alcohol, cigarettes, sweets, and they don't want to fathom these things are responsible for their illness because, quite simply, they do not want to give them up.

- Uninformed - truly have never heard information like the information I am sharing in my book. They've never heard of Natural Hygiene before or any accounts of people curing themselves from cancer, diabetes, arthritis, or any other disease without drugs.

If you fall into one of the top two categories it will be pretty difficult, if not impossible to change your mind. If you fall into the last category, as I did, you may be more willing to do further research and find out the truth to the cause and the cure to disease. I encourage you to do so! This information may just one day save your own life or the life of a loved one.

Chapter 15: Closing

A cure does not come in a bottle or from lying on an operating table. A cure comes from within. In fact, in Natural Hygiene, the disease is said to be the CURE, as it is the body's way of fighting off the toxins that have invaded it. There is no miracle pill, nor is there any ground-breaking, new, surgical procedure that will give you good health. Good health cannot be purchased; it must be earned!

There is but one cause and one cure to all disease. People who have set the proper conditions for their bodies to reverse their doctor-diagnosed, **in-curable** diseases, even **advanced stages of cancer**, will not dispute this information. Most doctors practicing conventional medicine and pharmaceutical companies on the other hand **will** dispute this information. From whom do you want to get your information?   Just remember: Always consider the source.

As I've said in my book, this is not new information. It is just hard-to-find information that has been, in a way, kept secret from you for numerous reasons. Most of these reasons are either centering around ignorance and/or greed.

Reversing disease completely, or in worst-case scenarios greatly, is not complicated. Don't make it so. A whole new life is waiting for you. Better yet, this brand new, fit, trim, **HEALTHY** life that is waiting for you will come to you from drugless healing! No more suppressing your pain with dangerous, even deadly, drugs or surgery. That chapter of your life will happily be over. You've learned that only your body can heal itself and it will only do so if you set forth the proper conditions for this miraculous self-healing to take place.

It was my goal to help you understand not only WHY you are sick, but to show you how to now reverse your illness or disease without drugs, without surgery. With conventional medicine today, the cure is often worse than the disease itself! I am hoping, with all of my heart, that we will soon see a future in which the doctor's practice revolves primarily around drugless healing and Natural Hygiene.

Getting well is not half as hard as being sick! Don't just blindly accept an incurable diagnosis. Make yourself knowledgeable. Knowledge is your power. By passing on this valuable information to you, you are now free to take control of your own life. You are free to free yourself from the drugs, incurable diagnosis, or even death sentence that your doctor may have given you. You are free to choose the healthy diet and lifestyle choices that God intended for you. There is still a lot of information for you to learn. I can't recommend Dr. Sniadach's Essential Natural Hygiene Course highly enough and, no, I don't get paid for telling you about it. Reading his course, *and I'm not even finished with it yet*, is by far the best purchase I have ever made.

It is my sincerest hope that you will have the same great success that I have had. I wish you all the highest achievements in your road to recovery. It's YOUR health. It's YOUR decision!

If we all work together, we can help ourselves and each other live healthier, happier lives that are free from pain and disease. On my road to recovery, I have meet so many phenomenal individuals who have also cured their so-called incurable diseases.

If my story is not enough to inspire you, I encourage you to find out about the many others who have gotten well with these same steps. I am currently working on a second book that is a compilation of the real-life stories of others who have used a high-raw vegan diet or a 100%-raw vegan diet and Natural Hygiene principles to set the proper condition for their bodies to heal themselves. The book I am working on currently can be found at my web site http://www.rawandjuicy.com.

Please do not just read the information I have provided you. Apply it! DO it! Change your life. When you do, please contact me. I would love to hear your testimonials. I have a guest book set up for testimonials at my web site http://www.dyingtogetwell.com. Once there, simply click on the "Sign Guest Book" link to leave your comments.

Best Wishes!
Shelly Keck-Borsits

Bibliography

1   Airola, Paavo, Dr., How to Keep Slim, Healthy and Young With Juice Fasting, (Health Plus Publishers 1984)
2   Boutenko,Victoria, 12 Steps To Raw Food, (Raw Family Publishing 2002)
3   Batmanghelidj, Fereydoon, Your Body's Many Cries For Water, (Global Health Solutions, 2nd edition, 1995)
4   Bragg, Paul C., MD Ph.D, Apple Cider Vinegar, (Health Science)
5   Bragg, Paul C., MD Ph.D, The Miracle of Fasting, (Health Science)
6   Broad, William, Wade, Nicholas, Betrayers of Truth and

Deceit in the Halls of Science, (Simon & Schuster 1982)

7   Bueno-Aquer, Lee, Fast Your Way To Health, (Whitaker House, 1991)

8   Carter, James, MD, Racketeering in Medicine: The Suppression of Alternatives, (Hampton Roads Publishing Company 1992, 1993)

9   Cott, Alan, MD, Fasting The Ultimate Diet Lose Up To 5 Pounds On A One Day Fast, (Hastings House, 1997)

10   Day, Lorraine, MD, AIDS What The Government Isn't Telling You CENSORED, (Rockford Press 1991)

11   DeVries, Arnold, Therapeutic Fasting, (Chandler Book Co., 1963)

12   DuVall, Paula, The New World of Eating (Nutritional Services Publishing, 1994)

13   Ehret, Professor Arnold, Rational Fasting, (Ehret Literature Publishing, 1971)

14   Ehret, Professor Arnold, The Mucusless Diet Healing System, (Ehret Literature Publishing)

15   Eisnitz, Gail, Slaughterhouse: The Shocking Story of Greed, Neglect, and Inhumane Treatment Inside The U.S. Meat Industry (Prometheus Books 1997)

16   Epstein, Samuel S., Steinman, David, The Safe Shopper's Bible: A Consumer's Guide to Non-Toxic Household Products (John Wiley & Sons, 1995)

17   Esser, William, Dictionary of Natural Foods, (Natural Hygiene Press, 1972,1983)

18   Fox, Michael W., Eating With Conscience: The Bioethics of Food(New Sage Press 1997)

19   Fuhrman, Joel, MD, Eat to Live, (Little Brown and Company, 2003)

20   Fuhrman, Joel, MD, Fasting and Eating for Health, (St. Martin's Griffin, 1995)

21   Kelly, William, D.D.S., M.S., Cancer Curing The Incurable Without Surgery, Chemotherapy, or Radiation, (New Century Promotions, 2000)

22   Kordich, Jay, The Juiceman's Power of Juicing, (Warner Books, 1993)

23   Krohn, Jacqueline, MD, Taylor, Frances MA, Natural Detoxification A Practical Encyclopedia (Hartley & Marks Publishers, 2000, 2nd edition revised & expanded)

24   Lanctot, Guylaine, The Medical Mafia: How to Get Out of It Alive and Take Back Our Health and Wealth (Here's The Key Inc., 1995)

25   Lapchick, J. Michael, The Label Reader's Pocket Dictionary of Food Additives: A Comprehensive Quick Reference Guide

to More Than 250 of Today's Most Common Food Additives (John Wiley & Sons, 1993)

26   Lyman, Howard F., Mad Cowboy: Plain Truth From The Cattle Rancher Who Won't Eat Meat, (Simon & Schuster 1998)

27   McGregor, Tom, Eating in Freedom, (Freedomyou Publications, 2000)

28   Meining, George E., Root Canal Cover-Up (Price Pottenger Nutrition, 2nd edition 1994)

29   Mendelsohn, Robert S., Immunizations: The Terrible Risks Your Children Face That Your Doctor Won't Reveal (Second Opinion Pub. Inc., 1993)

30   Meyerowitz, Steve, Juice Fasting & Detoxification (Book Publishing Company, sixth edition 2002)

31   Moss, Ralph, PhD., The Cancer Industry (Equinox Press 1999, 2002)

32   Nestle, Marion, Food Politics: How The Food Industry Influences Nutrition and Health (University of California Press, 2002)

33   Oswald, Jean A., and Herbert M. Shelton, Fasting for the Health of It, (Nationwide Press Ltd.)

34   Prince, Derek, How to Fast Successfully (Whitaker House, 1995)

35   Robbins, John, Diet For A New America (HJ Kramer reprint edition)

36   Shelton, Herbert M., Fasting Can Save Your Life, (Natural Hygiene Press, 1964, 1978)

37   Sniadach, Robert, D.C., Essential Natural Hygiene Course http://www.transformationinst.com

38   Tilden, John H., MD, Toxemia, (Natural Hygiene Press)

39   Towns, Elmer, The Beginner's Guide to Fasting, (Servant Publications, 1979, 1980,1982)

40   Williams, Dave, The Miracle Results of Fasting, (Decapolis Publishing, 1997,1998)